500

Urban Renegades

Urban Renegades

The Cultural Strategy of American Indians

Jeanne Guillemin

1975
Columbia University Press
New York and London

The Andrew W. Mellon Foundation, through a special grant, has assisted the Press in publishing this volume.

Library of Congress Cataloging in Publication Data

Guillemin, Jeanne, 1943–
  Urban renegades.
  Includes bibliographical references and index.
  1. Micmac Indians—Urban residence. 2. Indians
of North America—Urban residence. 3. Micmac Indians
—Social conditions. 4. Indians of North America—
Social conditions. I. Title.
E99.McG54   301.45'19'7074461   74-30434
ISBN 0-231-03884-4

Acknowledgments

WHEN I FIRST BEGAN to write up my research on American Indians in Boston, many people I talked to about my fieldwork were surprised to find out that the city supported an Indian population. Some I talked to lived only a few miles from where the Micmac were carrying on a most important part of their community life. It seemed to me then as it does now that the most important thing I could do would be to increase the general awareness of the fact that this group of Eastern Indians, far from having disappeared into the past, is as reliant on the urban economy and as familiar with its demands as any other contemporary people. The prior work of Wilson D. and Ruth S. Wallis (*The Micmac Indians of Eastern Canada*, Minneapolis, University of Minnesota Press, 1955) and Philip Bock's "The Social Structure of A Canadian Indian Reserve" (unpublished Ph.D. thesis, Harvard University, 1962) greatly facilitated my own work.

Many people have helped me with this task. The support and encouragement of George W. Goethals and Richard Sennett was crucial to its completion. Those who served on my doctoral committee—Kurt Wolff, Everett Hughes, E. V. Walter, and Rosabeth Kanter— were excellent guides to good thinking and organization, although the responsibility for *Urban Renegades* and the sentiments expressed in it is mine alone. Two wonderful secretaries, Alice Close and Shirley Urban, patiently assisted in the typing and retyping of revisions. Their efforts were a much appreciated contribution from the Department of Sociology at Boston College. A generous friend and impeccable role-model, Professor Miriam Kallen, gave me the kind of understanding of which only the very wisest and most humane of educators is capable.

Within my family, my sincerest thanks go to my mother, Mrs. Eileen D. Garrigan, for practical assistance motivated by an unquestioning belief in the value of my work, to my husband, Bob, for being personally unconventional enough to tolerate a serious woman, and to my two sons, Robert and John.

My thanks also go to the Ford Foundation and the Radcliffe Institute for financial support which permitted me the time to write.

The Micmac people were the most generous of all. By fictionalizing the names of all the Indians described in this volume, I have tried to protect the privacy of my informants while giving an accurate account of their lives. I dedicate this book to them, the urban renegades who survive a hostile environment with courage and grace.

J. G.

Contents

Urban Renegades

Introduction

ON THANKSGIVING DAY in 1970, several hundred American Indians converged on the town of Plymouth, Massachusetts, to stage a political demonstration at the historical site of the Pilgrims' landing. While many Americans celebrate the enterprise of the first Pilgrims, these Native Americans assembled to communicate what little reason for gratitude or celebration their people have found in the successful colonization of America. The Indians' immediate audience, aside from the media people on the scene, was made up of White tourists, most of them in apparently mild and conventional family groups. Yet their sympathy for and identification with the demonstrators was almost instantaneous and almost impassioned. After witnessing the demonstrators' ceremonial burial of Plymouth Rock, they eagerly flocked to the landing where the Mayflower replica was docked and applauded the Indian take-over of the vessel. As the leaders of the demonstration began their orations on injustices done to American Indians, the references to forced migrations, to bloody massacres, and to the theft of Indian land drew sighs and some tears from this White audience. Jokes about General Custer and his "arrow" shirt and a mock effort to send the Mayflower with its costumed dummies back to England elicited laughter and scattered cheers. In fact, when the local police moved in to reclaim the Mayflower, it was the White people who refused to disperse and who stood their ground to obstruct the passage of the police. When the Indians they were trying to protect filed submissively down the gangplank and away from the landing, the White audience seemed surprised and not a little disappointed. Having lost the oppressed they would have championed, they lost their entertainment and the brief moment of political unity to which they had been moved. The Indians reassembled on a knoll overlooking the harbor and began a circular dance of unity around a statue of that first, friendly native, Massasoit. There was no room in the shuffling, chanting circle for White people and so most of the visitors to Plymouth that day left, driving home with their families to eat turkey and pie, and give thanks.

From the organizers' point of view, this first Plymouth demonstration was a success. No one had been arrested or hurt and, very importantly, the event had been covered by national press and television. The Boston Indian Council and the leaders of the American Indian Movement who had jointly arranged the affair wanted little more than public communication. It seems, however, that such demonstrations are by nature simply one-shot dramatic intrusions into the public consciousness; they inevitably fail to convey the complex coexistence of social groups involved in the same economic and political state and instead are consumed themselves by the media for the brief distraction of a mass audience. The rhetoric of this Indian demonstration, in addition to emphasizing the history of Indian-White relationships, dwelt on relatively abstract contemporary issues which many Americans feel are as much beyond their province of responsibility as the dead past—for example, the continued White encroachment on Indian lands and natural resources, the organization of the Bureau of Indian Affairs, and the indifference of the federal government to the Indian situation. A spectator at Plymouth might catch a glimpse of himself on the evening news and hear once again an Indian voice recite the list of injustices done to Native Americans. But neither he nor any other non-Indian viewer can reasonably go beyond empathy for a traditional victim, an updated and mildly politicized version of the stereotype described by Vine Deloria: the "food-gathering, berry-picking, semi-nomadic, fire-worshipping, high-plains-and-mountain-dwelling, horse-riding, canoe-toting, bead-using, pottery-making, ribbon-coveting, wickiup-sheltered people".[1]

The places and lives to which the Indians demonstrating at Plymouth returned have nothing to do with this primitive image. Most, if not all, went home to cities—to Minneapolis, Milwaukee, Cleveland, Los Angeles, and San Francisco—or to reservations whose

[1] *Custer Died for Your Sins*, New York, Macmillan, 1969.

economic viability cannot in any way be divorced from urban industry. More than half the demonstrators returned home to Boston, traveling north from the marshes of the South Shore until they reached their own turf, the city streets, factories, bars, rooming houses, and apartments which make up the scene of their very present-tense, very urban way of living.

For an American Indian to live in a city is hardly a rarity today. At least a third of United States Indians and probably a similar proportion of Canadian Indians have taken up residence in high-density urban areas. If methods of acquiring census data could handle a high rate of geographic mobility, it is also probable that an even greater percentage of Indians could be considered urban, not simply by residence category but on the basis of job experience, contact with corporate structures, and a particular organization of tribal and kinship networks. Despite the fact that Indians are found in cities and the reasonable assumption that the lives of most American Indians are affected by urban industrialism, a conglomerate stereotype of the Native American persists. It includes elements that are sometimes noble, sometimes comic or grotesque, and it includes traces of a romantic proximity to nature, all of which are located in another dimension of time—the past. The persistence of this traditional stereotype is comprehensible only if one understands the long history of Indian exclusion from the dominant society and the corporate system that has developed to maintain racial segregation. The roots of that corporate system go back to the earliest days of American colonization and the first assessments which European traders, missionaries, and farmers made of the aborigines. Whatever the exact point of contact between a specific Indian tribe and the intruding Whites, it is generally true that the natives were considered a poor source of agrarian labor, a poor or only temporary source of trade goods, a good but again only temporary and potentially treacherous source of militia. How Indians could be used was a very important question for early colonizers and when they ran out of answers they began to find the Indian presence intolerable because it could not be justified in their economic terms.

With the late eighteenth- and nineteenth-century increases in European migration, it became apparent that the Indians had, if not a service to render, a possession to give up, land, and that their absence, rather than their submissive presence, was functional. Either retreat from White expansion or legislated isolation was the price colonial expansion exacted from all tribes still extant during the last century. The reservation, eventually the only legal place for Indians, began as a practical means of clearing from a territory one of the natural obstacles to civilized settlement, in the same way that trees might be felled and stones carted away by oxen. Finally, the maintenance of Indians in isolation was fully incorporated in the Bureau of Indian Affairs as a way of unburdening the dominant population and the federal government proper of the responsibility of dealing with the continuing reality of Native Americans. It is in written works published just at the turn of the century, when that institutionalized unburdening was complete, that one finds the most frequent references to

American Indians in the past tense, as if their legal isolation and consignment to bureaucratic management excluded them from the ongoing narrative of history. The control which any post-colonial bureaucracy can have over native people varies with the strength of racist sentiment and the extent to which its overt expression is nationally sanctioned. In its management, the United States Bureau of Indian Affairs has wavered between neglect and coercion—neglect in the lack of aggressive protection of Indian rights, and coercion in occasional programs to turn Indians into Whites, as in the detribalization and urban relocation efforts of the 1950s. The Canadian Bureau of Indian Affairs and Northern Development appears more paternalistic and less manipulative than its American counterpart but it performs the same task of managing native groups. Even a quick look at the administration of natives in other countries clarifies the situation of American Indians and helps us to begin to understand how it is that they survive as legislated people. In South Africa, for example, the full intensity of bureaucratic organization is visited on the native so that travel from reservation to urban shantytown is thoroughly supervised and, with that, the details of personal and family associations are brought, to use a Heideggerian image, into that terrible public light that makes all darkness. Bureaucratically accounted for, the native is a social cipher whose presence on the street or in a factory is ignored because it is not understood as the presence of a human being. In Australia, on the other hand, native political movements have formed in protest of the fact that legal definition of aboriginal civil rights barely exists and that it is needed to protect them against non-institutionalized forms of racism. The invisibility of the Australian aborigine lies in the unwillingness of the legitimate government to admit responsibility; the invisibility of the South African tribesman lies in the efficient bureaucratization of racism.

For the American Indian, there exists a plurality of experiences between these two extremes and more than a single cause for the fact of his invisibility. The Canadian and American Bureaus of Indian Affairs are both organizations which jurisdictionally control reservations. The indirection of their rule is such that being governed often means getting around and getting away from the Bureau personnel who are the last link in the chain of command from the national capital to the reservation. The more an Indian agent is a stranger to the reservation community, one with ambitions to better his position in the Bureau and/or with little respect for contemporary Indian social organization, the more strategies of evasion and counter-manipulation become necessary for those Indians who depend upon the support which is channeled down from a federal level. There are other institutions which, like the Bureau, have their loci of power in the dominant society and send their representatives to Indian reservations. Religious, educational, and medical institutions as well as local police forces have long included Indians within the province of their responsibility and their agents, with greater or lesser formality, have officiated over native well-being. To gain whatever material or abstract benefits can be gained or to avoid being victimized, many Indians have had to develop ways of presenting themselves publicly without sacrificing their cultural integrity. If this were a better world and American Indians could have both tribal autonomy and national government responsive to their situation, the defensive ingenuity developed under oppression would cease to be necessary. Despite brighter political eras, as during John Collier's term as U.S. Commissioner of Indian Affairs, and despite some small progress today towards Indian self-management, the means to political action remains within White-controlled bureaucracies at a level generally beyond the control of tribal groups and often seemingly beyond the control of even the Indian offices, which receive low priority when national policy is being formed and the national budget meted out.

Theoretically, or perhaps optimally, a Bureau of Indian Affairs is a service organization which represents and defends native interests. This is a particularly important role for a Bureau to play in contemporary times because the principal enemies of Indians now appear in corporate form—private industry seeking access to natural resources and, upon occasion, other departments of the government itself seeking to draw upon Indian land to enlarge the public domain. It is only logical to conclude that the less a Bureau of Indian Affairs represents Indians, the more it rules Indians, whether the failure to represent comes from decisions inside the organization based on its self-perpetuating motives, or from obstacles imposed by the national government, or from some combination of both. Not unlike colonial administrations, both United States and Canadian Bureaus of Indian Affairs do govern the natives and, in fulfilling that responsibility, render them invisible—people of no concern to the dominant population, people bureaucratically accounted for.

The second reason for the invisibility or museumizing of American Indians has to do with their passage into another bureaucratically controlled area, the city, where the poor in general are governed by municipal institutions. To circulate between an Indian reservation and the kind of low-income urban areas to which migrant wage-earners gravitate amounts to changing the physical context of what is basically administered by the same political machinery. Every urban slum is administered by service agencies equivalent to the welfare, religious, educational, medical, and policing organizations found on reservations and in reservation areas. The isolation of American Indians from a wider society is surely not different from the segregation of a variety of ethnic groups and poor Whites in cities; it is the demographic scale, rather than differences of racist motivation or economic or political means, which distinguishes one environment from another. Both environments have literally become reserves of cheap, expendable labor whose inhabitants are statistically more likely to look and act like minority people than not. When an Indian goes to an urban industrial area, he has to adjust his strategies for dealing with White institutions to suit the scale of the city; he does not necessarily have to develop new strategies. The urban people he encounters, however, commonly understand the creation of a

Bureau of Indian Affairs to have been a successful solution to the preservation of Indian culture as that culture was a hundred years ago. The more committed the non-Indian is to the idea that bureaucracies can successfully supervise anyone, the more likely he or she will be to consider the city Indian "out of place" and a curious, if not annoying, anachronism. It is difficult to think of another minority group so burdened with the belief that they belong in a mythic world of beads and barter. American Indians arrive in cities like unexpected guests, even though their numbers in some Western cities are considerable and many have a history of urban migration which goes back for generations. The governing arm of a Bureau of Indian Affairs barely extends to the city and yet the urban institutions that deal with the always problematical poor resist including American Indians in that category and often refuse the responsibility to overcome cultural and linguistic barriers.

Reacting to the grand scale of city life, many Indians are likely to resist contact with service institutions and to be even more wary of municipal personnel than of reservation bureaucrats. The notable exception to this lies in the public drinking and fighting of Indian men, which invariably brings them to the special attention of the police, "the keepers of the peace." But this behavior is, I believe, a whole risk-taking venture that explores not only what is appropriate action for a man but the legal boundaries of civic behavior. Otherwise, urban Indians develop their cultural strategies in an area beyond the comprehension of the wider society, namely, in the domain of family and tribal organization.

The Micmac Indians of the Canadian Maritime Provinces represent a kind of urban tribal community which can develop out of a history of legal and social segregation from the dominant society. Being among the first aboriginal groups to feel the effects of European expansion, their isolation from White settlements began as early as the eighteenth century and continued until, by the end of the nineteenth century, they occupied only the most remote forest and coastal areas. The Micmac seem to be eliminated from historical record at this point, getting little attention from the Canadian Bureau or from appointed or self-appointed documenters of the Maritimes.[2] Nonetheless the tribe has endured and not entirely without having broken out of its geographic isolation to participate in the cash economy. There are older Micmac living today who remember their grandfathers leaving the Maritimes to work laying railroads, harvesting grain, and doing factory work in Canada and New England. Involvement of the Micmac in urban industrialism has increased over generations, so that with the growth of urban areas and improvements in transportation, this group relies fully on wage labor to survive. The economically depressed Maritimes offer little economic incentive to the Micmac or to any other group, yet the Indians have a land base there and the necessary migration to cities is tempered by this fact. There is security in the human resources available on the reservations and there is a minimal material security available through government channels if times get

[2] The two exceptions to this, of course, are the work of Wilson and Ruth Wallis, and that of Philip Bock.

hard. For this reason, because times do get hard frequently enough, Micmac men and women circulate between the Maritimes and industrial centers, particularly Boston, rather than settle down in the city. Even without a legal reservation to return to, the Micmac, like many other minority people, would be on the move in search of jobs simply because of their economic marginality, a relationship to the larger economy which requires making oneself available over space and time to unskilled labor opportunities.

Once a Micmac Indian is off the reservation and across the American border, the Canadian Bureau of Indian Affairs adopts an out-of-sight, out-of-mind attitude, making no inquiry into his financial situation and offering little or no service. Nor is the United States Bureau interested in Canadian charges, having enough difficulty accounting for its own urban wards. When the vulnerable members of the Indian community—the young people who have just arrived in Boston, the sick and the old, and sometimes women with children— come into contact with municipal institutions, past policy has been to send them back to Canada, busfare paid, as if the solution to the Indian problem is the restoration of legal order effected by putting the Indians in their place, that is, back on the reservation. In disposing of the people, the municipality only temporarily avoids the problem, for the Micmac, like many other Indians, are an urban people who must participate in the kind of job market Boston affords and who will return again and again. Given the fact that some two-and-one-half to three thousand or more Indians are located or, more accurately, are locatable in the greater Boston area, with the Boston Indian Council now organized to represent them, shipping transient Indians outside civic boundaries has become an inappropriate and less frequent response.

In coming to the city, the Micmac and other Indians have had to create for themselves a place within the diversity of other groups in the general category of urban poor. In doing so, they have continued to participate in a structure which replicates on a much larger scale the specific neo-colonialism of the reservation. In a very real sense, urban Indians have joined other economically marginal people on the megareservations of core cities which are administered by a dominant population which is sequestered away from the poor. Because the business of governing urban groups has been delegated to bureaucratic service institutions, just as the "Indian problem" was delegated to a Bureau of Indian Affairs, the real responsibilities of rich to poor are buried in bureaucratic indirection. In medieval Europe, the coexistence of rich and poor was symbolized by the image of a tree, which represented the wealthy, upon which grew a vine, which represented the indigent. In our society, the notion of a social reality continuously shared by people of wealth and people of poverty is seldom entertained and never experienced. Instead the civil servant manages the poor, handling them according to the divide and rule principle. As William Ryan has pointed out, the only way bureaucracies seem to have of handling the poor is to define each individual or family unit as a pathological case.[3] Each civil servant, himself individuated within the context of the institu-

[3] *Blaming the Victim*, New York, Pantheon Books, 1971.

tion, fails to perceive the larger structure which determines the material poverty of some, the material wealth of others, and his own stewardship to the rulers of society. In addition, he fails to see the vitality of poor communities, unless like a George Orwell in Burma, he one day senses the cultural strength of the natives. The truly affluent and powerful can disclaim any immediate responsibility for the poor who, like Indians, are out of place when they threaten to jump the boundaries of the ghetto or demonstrate in bureaucratic buildings. And although the natives may occasionally be restless, corporate rule commands a speedy restoration of the apathy fostered by indirection. The good civil servant extinguishes his sense of responsibility as he extinguishes the light in his office and retreats to the private life earned by public performance.

For many people, it is difficult to break out of individuation and ally oneself to one camp or another, to the governors or the governed. A good percentage of men with corporate power and personal wealth assign themselves to the politically and economically neutral category of "middle-class" as a means of avoiding acknowledgement of the responsibility for ruling. What the label middle-class implies is the existence of a higher authority, a locus of power and decision-making which is somewhere else, with other people or in the corporate body. Every chairman of the board has the prerogative to act like a *petit fonctionnaire*. There are also many people who assign themselves to the category of middle-class for status reasons, in order to dissociate themselves from the onus of poverty. In debt for every material possession of importance, and subsisting on an income which is insufficient to protect them from the disasters of accident or sickness or unemployment, they choose the label middle-class in denial of their social vulnerability. They fear and hate the category of public poverty and those who are publicly poor because they themselves are precariously close to proverty.

The function of class labels and perhaps the whole idea of stratification is only an interpretive veneer for the single, large fact that the enormous populations concentrated around cities today are living in separate camps, one of rulers and their managers in residential suburbs, and one of the ruled in the abandoned inner city. As these camps become more socially isolated from one another, and as bureaucratic management tends more to rule than to intermediate, our society begins to resemble the colonizing empires of the last century, with the distance between a wealthy suburb and a city slum politically, socially, and economically the same as the distance between the Crown and Calcutta a hundred years ago. The older hierarchical relationships between elites and civil servants and between civil servants and natives have been duplicated within national and state limits and the latter group is now transformed into a conglomerate of minorities with the basis of their homogeneity in economic deprivation. Whatever cultural variety exists among the urban poor has yet to be fully understood. What is understood, and what bureaucratic labeling has helped us to understand, is the way in which all the urban poor fail to meet the value standards of the dominant society. Just as being a native was

a condition of wrong color and a lack of the greatest
good, Western Civilization, being one of the urban poor
is a condition, often enough, of the same wrong color
and a similar lack of values and attitudes held dear by
the governors. Those involved in the corporate rule of
this society believe, and expect everyone else to believe, that man is an independent social atom personally
responsible for his fate, free within the scope of written
law with no restraint greater than his conscience. Ideally,
each individual within the law is entitled to privacy and
to a personal control over and limiting of social interaction. Yet to operate as a social atom requires at least one
of two things, great personal wealth or the supportive
context of a corporate institution. Given either or both,
such individualism is, within reason, a possible and
even an efficient response. Failing either of these requi-
sites, social atomism is social regression and ultimately
means the death of the individual and the destruction of
the group. For those without wealth and outside the corporate system, the only proper context of the individual
is other people and it is in the group that one finds a
supportive structure. To give credit to the moral resources of outsiders, we must consider that the variety
of custom which is possible among groups ruled by bureaucracies could be as great as the cultural diversity
which seemed to wither before Western expansion.

Anyone committed to the goals of corporate rule
will have difficulty in accurately perceiving the integrity of outsiders and the nonpathological nature of their
behavior. To be committed to an institution, if we can
resist the slight distraction of the pun, is to be single-

minded, to prize above all the one efficient system, and to assume that effective bureaucratic management accounts for and comprehends all human reality. From this vantage point, other systems can be understood only as they lack the attributes of the corporation or as they aggress upon it and threaten its efficiency. Ruling corporate bureaucracies would prefer to manage only victims and to have communications always proceed down from the powerful to the powerless who are supposed to remain voiceless and without a conflicting perspective. Labels, definitions, categories, standards, forms, programs—all the subtle indictments of alternative systems flow down through a maze of departments and offices to the oppressed who are expected only to receive these messages and reform their behavior. This one-way direction of information and the demand for conventional behavior was as characteristic of western imperialism as of the present order. When colonial missionaries sought to convince natives that their customs were insufficient to the demands of civilization, they also argued that a change of behavior on the part of each individual would ensure his inclusion in, rather than his rejection from, the expansion of civilization. Yet the behavior of the governed, as long as the power of verbal definition and description is out of their hands, will always be termed inappropriate because it comes as a response to the realities of living outside the corporate context, not divorced from its impact but faced with a different set of problems. Strategies for survival can be expected to respond not to the abstractions of missionizing, but only to structural changes in the total society.

Nor can they be understood as efficient systems in themselves unless some reversal in the flow of information begins and the single-mindedness of the bureaucrat is shaken.

Urban ethnographic ventures, such as the fieldwork which resulted in this book, are part of a redirection of information, the academics' share which is at best only a rough translation of other people's reality. At the time of my research, from late 1969 through 1971, most of the ten thousand or so members of the Micmac tribe were living in the relative obscurity allowed by the reservation system and city life. Since that time the Boston Indian Council has been active in its efforts to publicize the presence of a Native American community in the city and to foster support, institutional and private, for the improvement of medical, educational, and employment services for Indians. The Micmac, however, who make up about ninety percent of the Indians in Boston, generally continue to accommodate themselves as best they can to the realities of their situation, much as they have done in the past.

The initial chapter of this book begins with the earliest historical accounts of Micmac social organization as described by seventeenth-century missionaries and traders who were already witnessing Indian reaction to the intrusion of Western civilization. The rise and decline of the fur trade and increases in the population of European settlers made excessive demands on Micmac culture, demands which tribal organization was successful in meeting. The gradual isolation of the Micmac into the more remote areas of the Maritimes begins in the early nineteenth century; by the end of that century, the reservation system was legally in effect and a segregated Indian population had begun its close involvement with urban industrial life.

Chapter 2 is basically a description of Micmac tribal organization as a system which encompasses the reservation and the city, with the former functioning as an important subcommunity in which children are raised, the aged and the sick are cared for, and working adults are offered some respite from travel and urban living. It is on the reservations that the values and attitudes which guide the socialization of children are most clearly expressed and linked with mythic images of power both physical and spiritual.

Chapter 3 describes the kind of urban life many Micmac Indians lead from the time they are in their mid-teens until age or sickness forces them out of the job market. This life requires all the strength and fearlessness encouraged in childhood and it also requires the sharing of goods and services among kin which characterizes Micmac extended families.

In chapter 4, attention is given to relationships between men and women who live in and around the city and to other Micmac Indians less central to the tribal community and more accounted for by municipal institutions. These other Micmac include small families, and the ill and aged who prefer the city to the reservation.

What the Micmac Indians do in order to survive is a response to large historical forces which, in one way, made them another group among a host of minority and poor people and, in another way, gave them and other

Indians a legal niche which sets them apart from all others. As both wards of the nation and urban migrants, American Indians represent a particular cultural configuration which has, at the tribal level, a basis for political autonomy. The nature of this configuration and the question of the moral responsibility due Native Americans are discussed in chapter 5.

The last chapter of *Urban Renegades* deals with my personal reflections on field work. Never have I been made so aware of my own conventionality as by this group of Indians surviving at the margins of society. By knowing the Micmac community and the customs by which it maintains itself, I experienced an entirely different mode of interpersonal behavior. To live in a small, stable community, to be subject to it, known by it, and also to find room for one's individuality within it gives a balance to life, a human scale, that seems to be generally missing or unnoticed in the mainstream of American society.

The main purpose for writing *Urban Renegades* is to bear witness to the human vitality and capabilities of a group which, like many others, has yet to be perceived as a viable community. The benefits of this perception accrue perhaps less to people like the Micmac, who are visible to each other and who recognize their own humanity even if the larger society does not, than to observers like ourselves. The emphasis on individuality in our values and behavior and our belief in the adequacy of the corporate context has left us barren of an intermediate guide to moral existence on a human scale. To quote Georg Simmel on the nature of custom,

A group secures the suitable behavior of its members through custom, when legal coercion is not permissible and individual morality not reliable. Custom thus operates as a supplement to these other two orders, whereas at a time when these more differentiated kinds of norms did not yet exist, or existed only in a germinal form, it was the only regulation of life. This indicates the sociological locus of custom. Custom lies between the largest group, as a member of which the individual is rather subject to law, and absolute individuality, which is the safe vehicle of free morality. In other words, it belongs to smaller groups, intermediate between these two extremes.

Our flexibility is not such that we can acquire at will the means to a new morality; but an appreciation of the integrity of other, nonbureaucratic systems can only make us more attentive to the relative, not absolute, value of our own ways and more hesitant in our will to rule.

CHAPTER I

The Micmac Indians in North American History

> When there were no people in this country but the
> Indians, and before any others were known, a young
> woman had a singular dream. She dreamed that a
> small island came floating in towards the land, with
> tall trees on it and living beings. . . .
>
> Rand, *Legends of the Micmac*, p. 225

First Encounters Between the Micmac and Western Europeans

As an Algonquin people living on the shores of eastern Canada, the Micmac were among the first American
Indians to feel the effects of European expansion into
North America. As early as the end of the fifteenth century, fishing fleets financed by Spanish, Portuguese, and

French entrepreneurs were making seasonal excursions to the Grand Banks for the abundance of cod available there. Thus, the first Europeans to make contact with the Micmac, to trade with them, to learn Micmac words, and to report back to European map makers with Indian place-names for the coves and bays of the eastern coast were fishermen, whose only testimony to having journied to the New World lies in fragments of commercial records and journals.[1] Although not documented in detail, the fact that as early as the beginning of the sixteenth century Indians and Western Europeans were well known to each other can be surmised. For example, both fishermen and Micmac Indians used the coastal shores during the summer, the former for drying fish and the latter for offshore fishing and gathering of clams, mussels, and bird eggs. That there were a good many Indians occupying the coast is strongly implied by the maps of the period which, as in the case of the Homen maps of 1550–1588, have labeled the northern coast of Maritimes with the description "place of many people." As for White expansion, by the time of explorer

[1] The arrival of European fishing fleets to the coast of Eastern Canada is generally reported in histories of the Maritime Provinces. See W. S. Eccles, *The Canadian Frontier 1534–1760*, New York, Holt, Rinehart and Winston, 1969; Alfred G. Bailey, *The Conflict of European and Eastern Algonkian Cultures 1504–1700*, Publications of the New Brunswick Museum, St. John, N.B., 1937; Bernard G. Hoffman, *Cabot to Cartier, Sources for a Historical Ethnography of Northeastern North America, 1497–1550*, University of Toronto, 1961. Hoffman in particular makes the case that contact was earlier and more widespread than generally acknowledged and relies on the evidence of early maps of northeastern North America to support that case (pp. 172–73, 186–97, and 214–15).

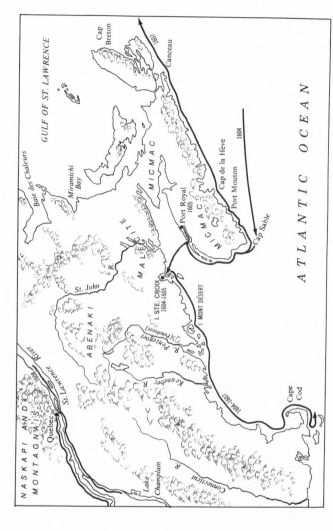

Map 1. *Champlain's Voyages to Micmac Country, 1604 and 1607*. The early written descriptions of the Micmac which come out of Champlain's explorations depict the appearance and customs of the Indians after they had been in contact for many years with European fishermen and traders.

Cartier's 1534 voyage, coastal fisheries for the processing of cod were established at fairly frequent intervals
from southern Nova Scotia to southeastern Labrador.
From Cartier's own description it is evident that the
Micmac that he and his crew encountered had had considerable previous experience in trading with White
men. It is also implied that trading might possibly have
included as an exchange item the sexual services of Indian women, a factor which could be indicative of an accommodation to White trade and some important reliance on it. On July 7, 1534, Cartier and his party had
their first encounter with the Micmac at Chaleur Bay:

And when we were half a league from the [Paspebiac] point,
we caught sight of two fleets of Indian canoes that were cross-
ing from one side [of Chaleur Bay] to another, which numbered in all some forty or fifty canoes. Upon one of the fleets
reaching this point, there sprang out and landed a large
number of Indians who set up a great clamour and made
frequent signs to us to come on shore, holding up to us some
furs on sticks. But as we were only one boat we did not care to
go, so we rowed towards the other fleets which were on the
water. And they [on shore], were seeing that we were rowing
away, made ready two of their largest canoes to follow us.
These were joined by five more of those that were coming in
from the sea, and all came after our long-boats, dancing and
showing many signs of joy, and of their desire to be friends.[2]

Suspicious of this ebullient reception, the French
dispersed the Micmac by shooting off a volley each from
two small cannons on board the boat and by igniting
two "fire-lances" of gunpowder to dramatize their mili-

[2] H. P. Biggar, *Voyages of Jacques Cartier*, Publications of the Public
Archives of Canada, Ottawa, 1924, pp. 49–50.

tary strength. The Indians did flee but returned none-theless the next day to where Cartier's ships were an-chored in the bay and proceeded to trade furs for European knives and other iron goods:

> The savages showed a marvelously great pleasure in possess-ing and obtaining these iron ware and other commodities, dancing and going through many ceremonies, and throwing salt water over their heads with their hands. They bartered all they had to such an extent that all went back naked without anything on them; and they made signs to us that they would return on the morrow with more furs.[3]

Two days later, in further exploration by longboat of Chaleur Bay, the French discovered another group of Micmac camped near the shore. The Indians made a present of cooked seal to the explorers who reciprocated with gifts of hatchets, knives, and beads, after which the Micmac brought out furs to barter for more European goods.

> They numbered, both men, women, and children, more than 300 persons. Some of their women, who did not come over, danced and sang, standing in the water up to their knees. The other women, who had come over to the side where we were, advanced freely towards us and rubbed our arms with their hands. Then they joined their hands together and raised them to heaven, exhibiting many signs of joy. And so much at ease did the savages feel in our presence, that at length we bar-tered with them, hand to hand, for everything they possessed, so that nothing was left to them but their naked bodies; for they offered us everything they owned, which was, all told, of little value.[4]

[3] *Ibid.*, p. 53.　　[4] *Ibid.*, pp. 55–56.

It was observed that the Indians "are people who would be easy to convert, who go from place to place maintaining themselves and catching fish in the fishing-season for food." [5]

Less than three weeks later, in the region of the Gaspé Peninsula, these same French explorers came upon a group of Huron-Iroquois Indians whose reactions to Cartier's party indicated a similar familiarity with and desire to trade, with perhaps a similar inclusion of women in the trade transactions. After having exchanged furs and iron goods, the explorers noticed the relative absence of Indian women:

But they had made all the young women retire into the woods, except two or three who remained, to whom we gave each a comb and a little tin bell, at which they showed great pleasure, thanking the captain by rubbing his arms and his breast with their hands. And the men, seeing we had given something to the women that remained, made those come back who had fled to the woods, in order to receive the same as the others. Those, who numbered some twenty, crowded around the captain and rubbed him with their hands, which is their way of showing welcome ["de faire chère"].[6]

The rest of the sixteenth century after Cartier's voyages was a time of intense development of the fishing areas off the coasts of western Nova Scotia and New Brunswick—then the country of Micmacs, Malecite, and Beothuk Indians. It was not, however, a time of the exploration and documentation either of traditional ways or of Indian-European relationships. Nonetheless, by

[5] *Ibid.*, p. 56.   [6] *Ibid.*, p. 62.

the late 1600's, a thousand fishing boats could be found each summer in eastern Canadian waters, and the size and number of coastal fisheries and, by implication, the frequency of Indian-White contacts proliferated accordingly. Although still seasonal in nature, the extent of European establishment in eastern Canada was in all likelihood sufficient to initiate the almost universal effects of Western expansion upon the American Indian population, namely, miscegenation, the reduction in native population through the spread of European diseases and the effects of alcohol, followed by the rapid accommodation of native social organization to both reduced numbers and the continued presence of Europeans.

The Initial Phase of Colonization (1600–1713)

By the beginning of the seventeenth century, when year-round French trading posts began to rise up next to coastal fisheries and documentation of life in the New World recommenced, the Micmac population was apparently already severely reduced. In 1610, at the settlement of Port Royal (now the town of Annapolis Royal in Nova Scotia), the Micmac *sagamore* Membertou told the Jesuit Pierre Biard that

in his youth he had seen *chimonitz*, that is to say, savages, as thickly planted there as the hairs upon his head. It is maintained that they have thus diminished since the French have begun to frequent their country.[7]

Among the first diseases affecting Indians in New France were syphilis and scurvy, the latter an affliction with which they were familiar but to which they became more susceptible as Indian reliance on European food and clothing (which was not as sanitary or protective as animal-skin clothing) increased during the sixteenth and seventeenth centuries. There are also indications that food which spoiled on the voyage from Europe and was subsequently traded to the Indians for furs also caused illness and death among them. Smallpox, typhus, dropsy, pleurisy, and consumption were other imports which caused a decrease in the Micmac population and other tribes of the Northeast.[8]

Documents dating from the beginning of the seventeenth century describe Micmac subsistence activity as

[7] Bailey, pp. 75–83, summarizes the diseases common among Northeast Algonkian tribes, including the Micmac, after contact with White missionaries and traders. The actual reduction in Micmac population is difficult to estimate. Biard in 1612 thought the Micmac numbered about 2,000 (*The Jesuit Relations and Allied Documents*, ed. Reuben G. Thwaites, Vol. II, p. 73) and later in 1616, changed his appraisal to 3,500 (*Jesuit Relations*, Vol. III, p. 111). A census taken in 1685 of the Nova Scotia area numbered the adult Micmac population at 858 people (Bailey, p. 111). At no time, however, were the Micmac a strictly sedentary people easily available to census-takers. It is reasonable, nonetheless, to assume that maximum decimation occurred from the end of the sixteenth through the seventeenth century, with a segregation and increase in Indian population beginning in the eighteenth and continuing through the nineteenth and into the twentieth century.

[8] *Jesuit Relations*, Vol. I, p. 177.

primarily fishing, on the sea coast in warmer months
and on inland rivers in colder months, with a secondary
reliance on hunting seal and big and small game at
various times throughout the year. In response to the
demands of the fur trade, Micmac forest hunting became as important as fishing, so that the traditional division of the year into coastal and inland settlements also
became an equal division into fishing and hunting activities, with an increase in the time spent inland.

Even with the establishment of such early colonies
as Port Royal, and before the profit to be made in
Europe on beaver skins had reached its height, Indians
were "courted" for the furs they could bring in. There
were, however, other influences which effected an increase in Micmac hunting and its alternation with a
more traditional reliance on fishing. For one, by the
time European cod fishing began its development the
Maritime seacoast was no longer exclusive Indian property. The fleets which arrived each year had to be flexible enough to accommodate themselves to shifts in the
best fishing grounds and practical enough to build
fisheries each year in close proximity to those grounds.
While in later times larger fishing outposts were set up
in one place, initial ventures required the convenience
of free access to coastal land. If the Micmac did not feel
hindered in their own activities by these first shifting
establishments, the later growth in the number of fishing fleets and increase in year-round settlements—for
example, on Cape Breton, in New Brunswick at the
mouth of the St. Lawrence, on the southern coast of
Novia Scotia, and in the western region of Nova Scotia

around Canseau—must certainly have brought home the message that rights to coastal lands were being assumed by the Europeans.

In addition, and especially in Nova Scotia, the interior riverways used by the Micmac in winter ran through what were the most fertile valley tracts, just the lands which were most desirable to settlers who came to New France to farm. Some forty families from the Laintonge district of Western France arrived in 1632 to cultivate the area around Port Royal and supply that colony with food. They became the basis of the large Acadian population which in less than a century had settled the Annapolis and Minas river basins.[9] Along with limiting Indian access to inland winter fishing spots, this must have also commenced the informal segregation of the Micmac to interior forests and more remote coastal settlements, a process which would be completed by the even more extensive immigrations from the British Isles and other parts of western Europe in the eighteenth and nineteenth centuries when Nova Scotia was under English rule.

Through the reports of early French missionaries and of seventeenth-century merchants and travelers in eastern Canada, we receive a description of the Micmac which has an interesting, historically significant bias. Trading posts and Catholic missions were the two earliest year-round kinds of European establishments and

[9] Brooke Cornwall, "A Land-use Reconnaissance of the Annapolis-Cornwallis Valley, Nova Scotia" in *Readings in Canadian Geography,* ed. Robert M. Irving, Toronto, Holt, Rinehart and Winston of Canada, 1968, pp. 245–65.

both attracted small aggregates of Indians. The trading posts naturally dealt directly with the most mobile Micmac, those who hunted forest game at a time when reliance on White supplies was increasingly important for survival and the simple relationship between Indians and a providential nature was forever disrupted. Because the goal of the missionaries was to civilize the Micmac by making them not only Christian but Christian farmers, they deplored the association of Indian and trader and were generally blind to the economic imperatives to which the native population was responding. The Indians they could gather around the mission, a group which was most certainly composed of older people, women, and children, received the support of some food and clothing. This group was praised for its docility even as it was pitied for a stubborn resistance to agrarian life. The missionaries contrasted their converts to the "forest nomads" who, after the fashion of the French traders, led "drunken, uncivilized lives" and who were further responsible for seducing young Indian girls to their evil ways. The belief that Indians should perform according to values at variance with the realities of their life situation only begins with missionaries who were, after all, fully conscious of the abstract nature of faith. The missionary mentality, which seeks to substitute its own order for less-valued, alien orders, which both lauds and pities the more vulnerable members of the native community who depend on the missionaries, and which sees a contaminating evil in native ways, will continue to be characteristic of the dominant society's assessment of the Micmac, as will be seen in later chapters, just as it typifies assessments of other tribes and other minorities. For the Micmac, it begins here in the seventeenth century with the descriptions written by men whose efforts to proselytize were truly remarkable and whose human concern for the Micmac as they suffered from disease, alcohol, and food shortages was genuine, if materially ineffectual. The failure of missionaries to make farmers out of the Micmac and the rapid involvement of the Micmac in the fur trade was causally linked to the traditional geographic mobility of the tribe. Their native familiarity with forest and waterways was one which the trade system capitalized upon and which even an occasional missionary could appreciate.

The savages of Port Royal can go to Kebec (Quebec) in ten or twelve days by means of the rivers, which they navigate almost up to their sources; and thence, carrying their little bark canoes for some distance through the woods, they reach another stream which flows into the river of Canada (the St. Lawrence), and thus greatly expedite their long voyages which we ourselves could not do in the present state of the country.[10]

Themselves strangers to survival in the forests of New France, missionaries were also generally appreciative of the ease with which the Micmac could move from one camp to another and rapidly reconstitute a comfortable dwelling—comfortable, that is, if one were a "savage." Biard, in 1610, offered the following description of how the Micmac arranged their campsites:

[10] *Jesuit Relations,* Vol. I, p. 101.

Arrived at a certain place, the first thing they do is to build a fire and arrange their camp, which they have finished in an hour or two, often in half an hour. The women go to the woods and bring back some poles which are stuck into the ground in a circle around the fire and at the top are interlaced in the form of a pyramid, so that they come together directly over the fire, for there is the chimney. Upon the poles they throw some skins, matting, or bark. At the foot of the poles, under the skins, they put their baggage. All the space around the fire is strewn with leaves of the fir tree, so that they will not feel the dampness of the ground; over these leaves are often thrown some mats or sealskins soft as velvet; upon this they stretch themselves around the fire with their heads resting upon their baggage; and, what no one would believe, they are very warm in there around that little fire, even in the greatest rigors of the winter. They do not camp except near some good water, and in an attractive location. In summer the shape of their houses changes; for then they nearly always cover them with bark, or mats of tender reeds, finer and more delicate than ours made of straw, and so skillfully woven, that when they are hung up the water runs along their surface without penetrating them.[11]

Involvement in the fur trade, and a greater emphasis on hunting from the autumn months through the winter, pushed that ease of mobility to its limits. With the help of muskets, the Micmac began to specialize in pursuing game when pelts were at their best, which was also at the same time when snow was deepest and forests least accessible. Hunting for the entire winter meant being adept enough to seek out many beaver houses over as wide a range as possible and mobile enough to follow larger game, such as bear and moose. While the Micmac could traditionally rely on a variety of river fish, turtle, fowl, and small game to survive the

[11] *Jesuit Relations,* Vol. III, p. 177.

winter, specialization in furs made Indian survival a "feast or famine" situation, as the following description illustrates:

If the weather is then favorable, they live in great abundance, and are as haughty as Princes and Kings, but if it is against them, they are greatly to be pitied and often die of starvation. The weather is against them if it rains a great deal and does not freeze; for then they can hunt neither deer nor beavers. Also, when it snows a great deal, and does not freeze over, for then they cannot put their dogs upon the chase, because they sink down; the savages themselves do not do this; for they wear snowshoes on their feet which help them to stay on top; yet they cannot run as fast as would be necessary, the snow being too soft. They have other misfortunes of this kind which it would be tedious to relate.[12]

The Micmac, nonetheless, did survive with hunting as an important economic activity and, during the seventeenth century, they evolved a hunter-warrior culture, patrilineal in emphasis, close to that of other Canadian tribes feeling the influence of the fur trade. As LeClercq describes:

They acquire no less glory and reputation from the number of Moose and Beavers which they capture, and which they kill in the chase, than from the number of scalps which they take from the heads of their enemies.[13]

The ritual feasting characteristic of summer months, when the Micmac were gathered in localized bands on the coast, celebrated the hunting ability of Micmac men

[12] *Jesuit Relations*, Vol. III, p. 77.

[13] Christien Le Clercq, *New Relations of Gaspesia* (first edition, Paris, 1691), trans. and ed. William F. Ganong, Toronto, The Champlain Society, 1910, p. 274.

and often gave priorities in eating and ceremonial participation to those who had just earned their status by killing a large game animal and to those who had not yet become too aged to hunt actively. Yet the summer gatherings were, in addition, a celebration of tribal unity, and the "festins à tout manger" (the ritual consumption of the settlement's total food supply) involved the hosting of other bands and the cementing of alliances between lineages. Long and detailed genealogies were recited during the feasts "in order to keep alive the memory, and preserve the tradition from father to son, the history of their ancestors, and the example of their fine actions and of their greatest qualities, something which would otherwise be lost to them and would deprive them of a knowledge of their relationships".[14]

New family alliances via marriage contracts were negotiated at this time and efforts were made to make sure that young people of marriageable age from different settlements met with each other. While a prospective son-in-law had to prove his abilities as a hunter during a year's residence with his future wife's family, the Micmac attitude towards the institution of marriage was apparently a relaxed one, with no forcing of an arrangement upon two partners by their families. A young woman might reject her suitor even at the last minute in the course of the wedding ceremony itself and have everyone concerned "as content and satisfied as if the mar-

[14] Nicolas Denys, *Natural History of the People, of the Animals, of the Trees and Plants of North America and of Its Diverse Climates* (first edition, Paris, 1672), trans. and ed. William F. Ganong, Toronto, The Champlain Society, 1908, p. 410.

riage had been accomplished, because, said they, one ought not to marry only to be unhappy the remainder of one's days." [15] Similarly, and to the distress of the missionaries, unhappiness in marriage for even a portion of one's days was not considered reasonable and where incompatibility and/or the lack of children presented themselves as problems, divorce was the custom.

If a young married woman has no children by her husband at the end of two or three years, he can divorce her, and turn her out to take another. He is not held to service as in the case of the first; he simply makes presents of robes, skins, or wampum. I shall tell in its proper place what this wampun is. He is obliged to make a feast for the father of the girl, but not so impressive a one as on the first occasion. If she becomes pregnant he gives a great feast to his relatives; otherwise he drives her out like the first and marries another. This wife being pregnant, he sees her no more. As to these matters, they take as many women as they please provided that they are good hunters, and not lazy. Otherwise the girls will not accept them. One sees Indians who have two or three wives pregnant at the same time; it is their greatest joy to have a large number of children.[16]

The inevitable depletion of game in the Maritimes made it increasingly difficult for even the most ambitious hunter to maintain a plurality of wives, although the value of children was a contribution not only to the stability of a marriage, as LeClercq observed,[17] but to the continuity of the larger extended family and of the tribe itself, especially as White intrusion maximized the threat of decimation. Women were invaluable for the

[15] LeClercq, p. 259.   [16] Denys, p. 410–11.

[17] LeClercq, pp. 262–63.

children they brought to the patrilineage, as well as for their supervision of the winter campsite, the preparation of game meat and skins after the kill, and the making of snowshoes, without which services the men of the family could not hunt. At least by the mid-seventeenth century, there were Micmac women at trading posts who were living as the "concubines" of French traders, receiving valuable food supplies and iron tools as payment, with the children from such unions being raised as Micmac tribal members.[18]

As for the organization of bands, each had its chief or sagamore, a position which at the time of early contact had been hereditary but which later went to the most competent hunter and warrior in the group.[19] The entourage which the chief gathered around him was undoubtedly duplicated in miniature in the other extended families in the band, although the demands of hunting and a reduced population acted to disperse extended families into smaller, more mobile units in the winter.[20] The following is an early description of a sagamore's household:

[18] As Bailey, p. 133, describes: "Miscegenation was general in settlement and hinterland, but, as far as the French were concerned, the movement was centrifugal"—with Indian women raising as Indians the children had by French fathers and Indian men not "mixing" with French women.

[19] *Jesuit Relations*, Vol. I, pp. 75–77; Vol. II, pp. 87–97; LeSieur de Dièreville, *Relation of the Voyage to Port Royal in Acadia or New France* (first edition, Paris, 1708), trans. Mrs. Clarence Webster, ed. John Clarence Webster, Toronto, The Champlain Society, 1933, p. 149.

[20] See Frank G. Speck and Loren C. Eiseley for a summary article on the Algonkian family group and the influence of the fur trade, "Signifi-

All the young people of the family are at his table and in his retinue; it is also his duty to provide dogs for the chase, canoes for transportation, provisions and reserves for bad weather and expeditions. The young people flatter him, hunt and serve their apprenticeship under him, not being allowed to have anything before they are married, for then only can they have a dog and a bag, that is, have something of their own, and for themselves. Nevertheless they continue to live under the authority of the Sagamore, and very often in his company; as also do several others who have no relations, or those who of their own free will place themselves under his protection and guidance, being themselves weak and without a following. Now all that the young men capture belongs to the Sagamore; but the married ones give him only a part, and if these leave him, as they often do for the sake of the chase and supplies, returning afterwards, they pay their dues and homage in skins and like gifts. From this cause there are some quarrels and jealousies among them as among us, but not so serious. When, for example, some one begins to assert himself and to act the Sagamore, when he does not render the tribute, when his people leave him or when others get them away from him; then as among us, also among them, there are reproaches and accusations. . . .[21]

A chief, then, had to contend with shifting alliances and, rather than having great authority, his responsibility was to advise band members and to respect the will and decisions of the group. As LeClercq described the sagamore, "all his power and authority are based only on the good will of those of his nation just in so far as it pleases them." [22] The occasional combination of the role of *jongleur* or shaman with that of the chief, as

---

cance of Hunting Territory Systems of the Algonkian in Social Theory," *American Anthropologist*, n.s. 41, 1939, pp. 269–80.

[21] *Jesuit Relations*, Vol. III, pp. 88–92.   [22] LeClercq, p. 234.

in the case of Membertou, increased the influence of the individual, but it was the band membership which had final authority.

The sagamore did, however, have the important responsibility of assigning hunting territories to families within the band. This assignment took place twice yearly during the seventeenth century, in what was probably a necessary accommodation to changes in family sizes and alliances and the decreasing area of land which was exclusively Indian.

There were other important factors involved in the apportionment of hunting territories. The widespread use of the gun in lieu of the bow and arrow was common among the Micmac at the midpoint of the seventeenth century. This made hunting an overly efficient enterprise which effected a general depletion of game and the necessity of covering ever more area to avoid starvation in winter-time. As LeClercq once again observed:

The musket is used by them more than all the other weapons, in their hunting in spring, summer, and autumn, both for animals and birds. With an arrow, they killed only one Wild Goose; but with the shot of a gun they kill five or six of them. With the arrow it was necessary to approach the animal closely; with the gun they kill the animal from a distance with a bullet or two.[23]

Thus, with the introduction of the musket by the trade system, the Micmac and other Northeastern Indians became increasingly dependent on the European foodstuffs and clothing which traders could supply, for diminishing game also meant a decrease in skins avail-

[23] *Ibid.*, p. 268.

able for traditional clothes as well as a decline in traditional food sources. Being dependent on trade goods meant, in turn, being subject to the demand to bring in as many pelts as possible, and therefore the depletion of game was even further accelerated. Like other tribal groups, the Micmac had to cover considerably more territory as time went on in order to bring back enough furs to survive according to the terms of the trade system. Speck and Eiseley, writing on Northeastern Indians and the fur trade, concluded that:

Neither is it so clear that the fur trade made it possible for the people to subsist in a smaller area by barter, because trade placed enormous opportunities for economic exploitation in the hands of whites who leveled outrageous prices in terms of skins. Simple wants were expanded until both the native and the white were forced to go farther and farther afield to supply themselves.[24]

According to the report of Denys, writing in the latter part of the seventeenth century, the kind of game conservation which was expected when the hunting territory for the Micmac was generally constant and unchanging was not typical of their new method for capturing game. Denys ends his account of a typical Micmac beaver hunt with: "Few in a house are saved; they would take all. The disposition of the Indians is not to spare the little ones anymore than the big ones. They killed all of each kind of animal that there was when they could capture it." [25] Geographic expansion out of traditional areas into more remote forests was provoked,

[24] Speck and Eiseley, p. 273.

[25] Denys, p. 448; see also Speck and Eiseley, p. 273, footnote II: "Conservation implies a permanent interest in the territory. It may

ironically enough, by a contraction of the fur trade system whose agents were searching out more plentiful sources to the west. The Micmac would soon be left still dependent on increasingly scarce trade goods and unable to fall back upon the full extent of natural resources they had enjoyed before the Whites arrived.

The ability of the Micmac to travel quickly through forests and over waterways, evading the hardship of winter weather, was also important in intertribal warfare. Although relatively isolated, bands of Micmac were known to conduct expeditions against settlements of Montagnais, Beothuk, and Eskimo to the north and to be "in a chronic state of war" with mainland Malecite and Penobscot. As the first group to gain possession of the musket, the Micmac were initially greatly feared, but as the spread of the fur trade brought guns to more Northern tribes, other groups, the Mohawk and the Ottawa in particular, soon acquired reputations as warriors more aggressive than the Micmac.

The introduction of the musket and the rivalries which arose among tribes concerning access to trade routes and claims to profitable "broker" roles in the fur trade increased hostilities and the incidence of intertribal raids in the northeast. For the Micmac, an expedition against the enemy was usually an "affair of honor," a matter of avenging the death of a band member or winning glory for warriors, rather than a defense of their position in the fur trade system. War parties demanded

well be that superior weapons and new economic temptation destroyed or forced into the background for a time a game conservation which is actually aboriginal in origin."

an assessment of each band's and even each family's willingness to commit itself to aggression, given the particular circumstances of provocation or the number of younger members wanting to gain "coups" in battle. In some cases, individual families and even a lone individual would have to seek vengeance for a relative's death when the rest of the community could not, for one reason or another, be persuaded to form a war party.

During the seventeenth century, communication among the Micmac on matters of personal injuries and disputes between families seems to have been relatively efficient. Using the somewhat weighty term "confederation," Biard described the assembly of Micmac which convened in case of an impending conflict:

Now in these assemblies, if there is some news of importance, as that their neighbors wish to make war upon them, or that they have killed someone, or that they must renew the alliance, etc., then messengers fly from all parts to make up the more general assembly, that they may avail themselves of all the confederates, which they call *Ricmanen,* who are generally those of the same language. Nevertheless the confederation often extends farther than the language does, and war sometimes arises against those who have the same language. In these assemblies so general, they resolve upon peace, truce, war, or nothing at all, as often happens in the councils where there are several chiefs without order and subordination, whence they frequently depart more confused and disunited than when they came.[26]

When a war party did assemble, a ceremonial feast was held and a shaman's prediction as to the outcome of the raid was sought and considered as an important fac-

[26] *Jesuit Relations,* Vol. III, pp. 87–89.

tor in the final decision to depart. The Micmac also became very attentive to other omens of the expedition's
outcome:

Omens at the start of a war expedition were matters of great
concern. Gaspé warriors who, by 1661, were in the habit of
embarking in wooden boats purchased from French fishermen, by way of a small gangplank, would abandon their raid if
in this process a man fell into the water or "wetted himself."
Similarly if a boat ran aground or was unduly delayed, the war
party turned back. A remembered promise to a deceased relative, even if recalled when the boats were well off in the Gulf
of St. Lawrence, might cause a man to turn back; in this event
all other relatives of the dead man in the party would also return to the settlement.[27]

Micmac women also conducted mock battles
against warriors preparing for an expedition, and the
victory of the women signified their success. Within the
context of the feasts held for the war party, wives would
also threaten to withhold "lawful pleasures" from those
who returned home without scalps and to give their
daughters only to men who had proved their valor in
battle.[28] The pride with which they claimed their own
importance in internal tribal politics is illustrated in the
following oration given by an old woman to warriors at a
feast in 1644 in preparation for a raid on a settlement of
Malecite:

[27] Wilson D. Wallis and Ruth Sawtell Wallis, *The Micmac Indians of
Eastern Canada*, p. 214.

[28] Abbé Antoine Simon Maillard, *An Account of the Micmacs and
Maricheets Savage Nations, Now Dependent on the Government of
Cape Breton From an Original French Manuscript-letter, Never Published, Written by a French Abbot*, London, S. Hooper and A. Morley,
1758, p. 26.

You men! who look upon me as of an infirm and weak sex and consequently of all necessity subordinate to you, know that in what I am, the Creator has given to my share, talents and properties at least of as much worth as yours. I have had the faculty of bringing into the world warriors, great hunters, and admirable managers of canoes . . . With how many scalps have not I seen my head adorned, as well as those of my daughters! With what pathetic exhortations have not I, upon occasion, roused up the spirit of our young men to go in quest of the like trophies that they might achieve the reward, honor and renown annexed to the acquisition of them: but it is not in these points alone that I have signalized myself. I have often brought about alliances which there was no room to think would ever be made, and I have been so fortunate that all couples whose marriages I have procured have been prolific and furnished our nation with supports, defenders, and subjects to eternalize our race, and to protect us from the insults of our enemies.[29]

Honor and the increase of the tribe were also the concern of Micmac women in their role as custodians of captives taken from other tribes. It was the women who decided whether the prisoner would be tortured and killed as part of the celebration of the warriors' return or incorporated as a "servant" into the extended family. On the one hand, the death of captives increased the possibility of retaliatory raids from their community and the continuation of reciprocal "honorific" war parties. On the other hand, the inclusion of outsiders into the band, which was usual when the captives were children, increased the "wealth" of the extended family.

Rather unlike other Northeastern Indians, the Micmac proved resistant to forming tribal alliances of the kind that arose in the seventeenth and eighteenth cen-

[29] Maillard, pp. 2–18.

turies among disparate native groups seeking a united defense against a common enemy, whether against the hostility of another tribe or against the encroachment of White settlers. One of the by-products of the fur trade, the rise of the Iroquois as a kind of warrior state, effected an increase in Mohawk expeditions to the east in order to plunder Indian settlements there and also to coerce the Montagnais, Penobscot, Malecite, and Micmac to submit to the League of the Iroquois.[30] In 1646, representatives of these Algonquin groups decided to ally themselves against the Mohawk and met "to assert that they all have banished from their hearts the former enmity, in confirmation whereof they offered all these presents [of wampum, blankets, guns, powder, lead, and javelins] to testify their kind affection." [31] The pact, beyond the acknowledgment of the Mohawk as a common enemy, had little subsequent effect on intertribal conflict. If conflict decreased at all, it was more due to the influence of decimation than to any development in tribal-level politics.

Towards the middle of the eighteenth century, efforts were made to bring about an end to conflict between the Northeastern Algonquins and the Mohawk, with the Mohawk as prime initiators of the union.[32] Representatives of the Ottawa acted as mediators and

[30] William N. Fenton, "The Iroquois in History," in *North American Indians in Historical Perspective*, ed. Eleanor B. Leacock and Nancy O. Lurie, New York, Random House, 1971, pp. 92–128.

[31] *Jesuit Relations*, Vol. XXX, pp. 139–41.

[32] Frank G. Speck, "The Eastern Algonkian Wabanaki Confederacy," *American Anthropologist*, n.s. 17, 1915, pp. 492–508.

the Penobscot took a principal role in representing the Algonquin. The Micmac were considered the "younger brothers" in the confederacy and their delegate could look forward to being strapped to a cradleboard for the duration of its meetings in Penobscot territory or, if they neglected to send a delegate, to having the next delegate killed. The confederacy, although it had a political structure on the order of European national alliances, had more to do with substituting positive ritual communication between tribes for intertribal warfare than with creating a forceful institution to counter White settlement. Before the end of the nineteenth century, the Wabanaki Confederacy was reduced to only occasional meetings emphasizing ritual performance.

Soon after the arrival of the Port Royal colonists, the priest who accompanied them, Père Flêche, conducted a mass baptism of the local Micmac, thus including them into French cosmology as "Christian savages" and, inevitably, into European politics as French allies. The Micmac understanding of warfare, as their general understanding of alliances, was consistently on the level of small-scale encounters—surprise raids and forest skirmishes which took place between relatively small groups of men rather than whole "nations" of Indians or Whites. While the Micmac and other Indians on the east coast of North America were drawn into national-level European wars, their participation depended on a translation of continental politics into their own understanding of conflict for the sake of honor and revenge. French military men in Micmac territory made annual presents to band chiefs and, representing themselves as the "warriors of the Great-White-Chief-Across-the-Water," were often able to persuade as many as two hundred Micmac, along with Malecite and Penobscot, to join them on raids against the English.

Throughout the seventeenth century, it was the possession of strategic ports in the Maritimes for which the French and British were struggling, rather than for interior land to be permanently settled. The state of siege which a new colony such as Port Royal was usually in and the number of times which it was likely to change hands during this time were, in fact, only temporary deterrents to immigration and the establishment of permanent colonies. Port Royal itself was destroyed ten years after it began by a small naval force sent from Governor Dale of Virginia who, while England and France were not officially at war, wanted to insure English claim to the first permanent settlement in the New World. French efforts to re-establish the colony were at first successful, but in 1627 it was captured by the British. Two years later, by the treaty of St. Germain-en-Laye, the French took possession of Port Royal and other eastern Canadian ports as well and held them for twenty-five years until a New England expedition commissioned by Cromwell assaulted the Maritimes again. In 1667, when France received new title to Acadia (Nova Scotia proper), a period of relative tranquility set in, one in which the French population grew to several thousands and the hinterlands of Port Royal and Canseau were cleared and farmed. The armed colonists from Boston who captured Port Royal in 1691 had to contend not only with the alliance of French and Indians still operating in the interior but also with the Acadian farmers. Within a brief time, the control of the colony fell back once again to the French, though at this point Port Royal itself was little more than a small collection of wooden buildings, including a Catholic chapel which had been stripped of its few decorations by the Bostonians. Dièreville, a French physician traveling in Acadia in 1699, had this cryptic remark to make about Port Royal: "Je reconnus des bords de l'onde. Que ce port n'était pas le mieux Nommé du monde." [33]

Nonetheless, from the period beginning with King William's war in 1689 until the middle of the eighteenth century, French military officers and missionaries in New France put forth their most virulent defense of this area and of settlements on the eastern coast no more developed than Port Royal. In doing so, they relied on warriors from Micmac bands to join in surprise attacks on New England border towns and to help construct temporary forts on the fringes of Acadian territory.

By 1711 however, the British military had taken effective control of Port Royal and, at least in theory, of Acadia. They made no attempt to cultivate the good will of the Micmac with the customary gift-giving of the French. From the Acadian farmers, they simply demanded and, in part, received a verbal oath of allegiance to the English Crown. In June of the same year, Micmac Indians, aided by a band of Penobscot, ambushed the British garrison in Port Royal and killed or captured some 70 soldiers. The local French Acadians, encouraged by this move, then joined with the

[33] Dièreville, p. 19.

Micmac so that their combined number was about 500 and together they reduced the military force of the British from 450 to 200.

The British retaliated slowly but effectively by rebuilding and reinforcing their garrison with the help of Mohawk warriors, whose ability to intimidate the Micmac was well known by all parties. In 1713, Acadia along with Newfoundland and Hudson's Bay went to England by the Treaty of Utrecht. For the next three decades, from behind the walls of their fort, the English maintained tense relations with the Micmac and the Acadians, both of whom were still in contact with mainland French militia and had French missionaries visiting among them. The French priests remaining in Acadia encouraged both Indians and settlers to raid Port Royal and were known to use the Micmac as a threat against docile Acadians reluctant to take arms against the British. One "warrior missionary," the infamous Abbé Le Loutre, took it upon himself to lead Indian attacks and, from 1740 to 1763, was aided by another priest, Père Germain and the group of Malecite warriors who followed his leadership. These underground efforts eventually failed, partly from a lack of support from the French military, partly because of the apathy of the Acadians, and partly because sustained warfare was not supported by the Micmac notion of conflict. Nor were the Micmac of sufficient numbers to sustain continued raids.

Already reduced in population and with the increase in Acadian settlers affecting their access to rivers and forest lands, the Micmac had to adjust to another dramatic change affecting their survival: the passing of the fur trade. Even before the end of the seventeenth century, staple European goods which the Micmac had come to rely upon were becoming difficult to obtain, mainly because of game depletion in the east and the discovery that a greater yield of furs could be had from Indian hunters far into the interior of western Canada. By the early eighteenth century, guns, especially those of good quality, could seldom be obtained. At this point the Micmac could only seek a compromise position between what they had learned of White ways and what they remembered from their own traditions. A return to Indian trapping techniques and a renewed reliance on coastal food sources undoubtedly sustained the Micmac during the withdrawal of the fur trade.[34] Some hunting by musket was still possible and, although we are left to conjecture on the kind of Indian-White contact which characterized this difficult period, limited barter transactions and some exchange of goods and services probably continued between the Micmac and local settlers.

Meanwhile, at about the same time, the British settlement of Halifax, on the southern coast of Nova Scotia and with close ties to Boston, was beginning to develop as a colony. Although much alarmed by Le Loutre's activities, the English colonists at Halifax, like the English militia at Port Royal, did not employ French tac-

---

[34] Bailey (pp. 46–96) offers a description of the effects of the fur trade and White contact on Northeastern Algonkian tribes and makes the inference suggested here, namely, that the withdrawal of the fur trade necessitated some economic retrenching on the part of eastern Indians and a return to some traditional subsistence techniques.

tics of diplomacy to win local bands of Micmac over to
their side. Instead, they attempted to secure their alliance by legal treaty only incidentally accompanied by
gifts. In 1725, the leaders of the colony at Halifax met
several local Micmac and read to them a peace treaty
they had composed. It did not bring peace, in that there
continued to be occasional Indian ambushes of those
English settlers who ventured into the forests. In 1749,
when the population of Halifax numbered about a thousand, a price was put on Micmac scalps, ten guineas a
piece. Another treaty in 1752, agreed upon by the half-
breed sagamore Jean-Baptiste Cope and four other Micmac men, also did little to prevent Indian and British
skirmishes from occurring, and it was not until the end
of the century that the British considered the Micmac
"peaceful." This was at a time when the Indians were
being considerably outnumbered by successive waves
of European immigrants settling in Nova Scotia in particular and in the Maritimes in general, the informal
segregation of the Micmac commences with the demographic changes which British rule achieved.

Phase Two: Towards Segregation

The wholesale settlement of Nova Scotia under English rule began with the expulsion, in 1755, of virtually
all the thirteen thousand and more Acadians living in
the area from the town of Paradise to the Annapolis
Basin and the Minas Basin area.[35] A plan importing six

[35] R. Louis Gentilcore, "The Agricultural Background of Settlement in
Eastern Nova Scotia," in *Canada's Changing Geography*, ed. R. Louis

to seven thousand settlers from Connecticut, Rhode Island, and Massachusetts was quickly put into effect and, in addition to the land which had been claimed by the Acadians, new interior lands were developed. Lots were drawn and new settlers were given land in each of three categories: marshland, cleared land, and forested upland.[36] At about the same time, Nova Scotia received more than four thousand immigrants from Ireland and Scotland and almost two thousand from Germany. Later, several thousand Tories fled the United States during the Revolutionary War and, with their slaves, set up households in Nova Scotia.[37]

The nineteenth century saw an even greater increase in immigration from Western Europe, immigrations largely of peasant peoples who had no more control over the political upheavals and changes in land tenure there than the American Indians had over the colonization of their country. From 82,000 in 1817, the White population in Nova Scotia rose to 124,000 in 1827 and to over 330,000 in 1867, at the time of Canadian confederation. By 1881, a peak total of 440,000 people was reached, while about the same time, the Micmac population was conservatively estimated at about 1,300 persons living in settlements for the most part located away from White townships.[38]

Gentilcore, Scarborough, Ontario, Prentice-Hall of Canada, 1967, pp. 34–55.

[36] Cornwall, p. 251.

[37] *Collections of the Nova Scotia Historical Society,* Halifax, N.S., Vol. VIII, 1892–1894, pp. 56–57. The Negro population of the same time is given as 104, about half of which was in Halifax.

[38] *Ibid.,* Vol. XIV, 1910, p. 55.

Long before the end of the nineteenth century and long before many western tribes, the Micmac had become, at least informally, "reservation Indians," consigned to separate and more remote parts of the Maritimes in places where their principal reserves can be found today. "Indians and Lands Reserved for Indians" were officially assigned to Canada under the British North American Act of 1867, by which the responsibility to honor treaties with Indians passed from the British to the Canadian federal government. But it was on a local and provincial level that the Micmac and other reservation Indians were initially required to survive as contemporary peoples. As in the case of the relationships between the Micmac and European fishermen in the sixteenth century, there is little recorded history of social interaction between Micmac Indians and White people in the same area from the nineteenth century up to the present. While the missionary Abbé Sigogne, writing from Eel Ground some 150 years ago, bemoaned the fact that Catholics, including his Micmacs, were social outcasts in Nova Scotia,[39] the majority of immigrants coming to the Maritimes were rural folk, farmers and shepherds who were probably less disdainful of fraternizing with the Micmac than the contemporary gentry of the kind who wrote for the Nova Scotia Historical Society. The prevalence of English and French surnames among the Micmac bears some testimony to past relationships. Or, if Brown and Meuse, Maloney and Bouchard are not the names of past grandfathers, but trans-

[39] George S. Brown, *Yarmouth, Nova Scotia. A Sequel to Campbell's History*, Boston, Rand Avery Company, 1888, p. 39–48.

lations or adopted surnames, then the testimony is to the influence of those missionaries who first encouraged the Micmac to take "civilized" names for themselves. An old story among the Micmac concerns a famous medicine man who, when told that he should have a White name, asked to be called "Hell." When the priest refused this shocking request, he changed his mind and asked to be called "Devil." With few exceptions, such as Pictou and Goo Goo, most Micmac have settled for about the same European surnames as their White neighbors and, far from shocking their priests with outrageous nomenclature, call their children Margaret, Louise, Mary, or Patricia, Samuel, Henry, Thomas, or John.

The Micmac language still endures within the tribal community; but most Micmac are fluent in either English or French and sometimes in both. The range of situations in which White and Indian meet probably varies along the lines of historical alliances, from communities in New Brunswick which are reportedly a thorough mixture of French and Micmac to settlements in Nova Scotia which are more representative of the Micmac situation in isolation from White districts. In any event, contact between the two groups has been sufficient for the Micmac to learn English or French even when such contact is unreported or when segregation would seem to act against it.

As for political franchise, federal legislation in 1885 gave the right to vote to Indians on reserves east of Manitoba and to off-reserve Indians "subject to the possession and occupation of a distinct and separate tract of

land with improvements of not less than $150.00." [40]
Whether or not Indians could actually exercise the right
to vote was, however, a provincial matter. In the general
elections of 1887, 1891, and 1896, some Indians in the
Maritimes did vote at polling stations set up on reserves. It is difficult to know the motivation behind such
an enthusiastic and seemingly generous extension of the
franchise. The federal government was quite direct in
its bid for Indian support at the time, as the following
message on an 1887 circular illustrates:

To the Indians: The Queen has always loved her dear, loyal
subjects, the Indians. She wants them to be good men and
women, and she wants them to live on the land they have, and
she expects in a little while, if her great chief, John A., gets
into government again, to be very kind to the Indians and to
make them very happy. She wants them to go and vote, and all
vote for Dr. Montague, who is the Queen's agent. He is their
friend and by voting for him every one of the Indians will
please Queen Victoria.[41]

Anti-federal and secessionist forces in the Maritimes and particularly Nova Scotia were undoubtedly
equally aware of the uses to which the Indian vote,
however small, could be put. In any case, Indian voting
rights (until after the Second World War) remained incidental to provincial politics and hardly an overriding
issue of concern for White administrators on either fed-

[40] *A Survey of the Contemporary Indians of Canada,* ed. H. B.
Hawthorn, Indian Affairs Branch, Ottawa, Vol. I, p. 256. The general
information on Indian franchise is from pp. 255–62.

[41] *Ibid.,* p. 256.

eral or local levels. In 1898, when the federal law was repealed, provincial electoral laws as to who was a "citizen" with voting rights and who was an "alien" without them were formally in effect. British Columbia, Manitoba, Ontario, the Northwest Territories, and New Brunswick barred Indians from voting, while the laws of Quebec, Nova Scotia, and Prince Edward Island did not even specifically mention Indians for exclusion.

Having made no recognized tribal agreement with the Crown to deal with compensation for Indian lands, the Micmac at the turn of the century were nominally wards of the federal government but certainly without the enormous tribal funds or government support which would allow them to succeed as a community isolated from the larger, White economy. In the beginning of the twentieth century, the opening up of new farm lands in Western Canada and the rise of mainland industrial centers began to attract the rural White population of the eastern provinces to permanent moves away from the area, and a general decline in population began. The Micmac were also drawn away from the Maritimes, with the important difference that "down home" continued to be "down home," and their journeys outside the area were usually temporary sorties. As early as the turn of the century, and probably before that time, Micmac men worked building railroads, in lumber camps, on river drives, and in crop harvesting in Canada and the northern part of the United States. Forays out to the industrial centers of New England also began at the same time, and the Micmac, along with other Indians across the country, were continuously being integrated into industrial society as "cheap labor." As the Wallises later reported:

In 1953 the principal source of employment for the Micmac Indians was in the United States. Young people spent the winter in the factories of Hoboken and Connecticut. From Prince Edward Island, at least thirty-five percent of the able-bodied men and boys had gone to New England; the same was true for an appreciable number of Nova Scotia Micmac; while New Brunswick reports Indians working on construction in Connecticut and in potato warehouse and fertilizer plants in Maine "in an increased movement to the United States in search of employment." [42]

As the Canadian government responded to the economic depression of the 1930s with increasing welfare legislation, Canadian Indians, including the Micmac, were (and to a great extent still are) considered the special responsibility of the Indian Affairs Branch and ineligible for the local and provincial support allowed non-Indians. Not constitutionally obliged to administer welfare services, the Branch nonetheless assumed this provincial responsibility and proceeded to direct minimal aid in the form of social assistance to Indian bands via local Branch agents. While assistance programs for the rest of the population expanded to include income maintenance—Family Allowances, Old Age Security, Old Age Assistance, Blind Persons' Allowance, and Disabled Persons' Allowances—federal aid to Indians operated on the principle that relief was not the right of any Indian but was given at the pleasure of the Branch

[42] Wallis and Wallis, p. 279.

to prevent suffering and never in sufficient amounts to remove the incentive to seek jobs where and when available. The expectation that the Indian community should be more self-supporting than any White community continued until the late 1950s. As the Hawthorn Report describes:

An analysis of Branch welfare policy in the immediate postwar years reveals comparisons with the Elizabethan Poor Laws. The insistence on kinship obligations, payment in kind, and service from the able-bodied reflected a continuing adherence to assumptions which, under the impact of pressures from the social work profession, were rapidly disappearing in the White community. The tradition of local responsibility for charity was adhered to by the requirement that bands allocate revenue from band funds for relief purposes. Further, the principle of less eligibility was operative—the ensuring that welfare payments should be beneath the earning of the lowest paid wage-earner. Finally, it is important to remark that the men on the spot—the Agents and their assistants—who operated this system had no professional background as welfare administrators and there were no significant checks on their performance. Indians lacked the vote and were expected to channel their grievances through the Agent, the very person against whom their complaints might well be directed.[43]

Since the 1950s, the move to equalize social assistance to Canadian Indians has coincided with national-level efforts to persuade provincial governments to take responsibility for their Indian populations and to work with Indian band councils and the local branch to administer relief programs. Yet the attitude among provincial administrators, which seems to persist, is that the

[43] Hawthorn, p. 261.

Indians are the business of the Indian Affairs Branch in Ottawa and that the national government in its past mishandling of Indians has created an indigent population which it is now trying to foist off on the provinces. Canadian Indians who have been involved in this decentralization of administration have been equally suspicious of local government personnel and their prejudices, as well as self-conscious about the label "dependent," which is often applied to reservation Indians. Because the reservations are typically places where many of the elderly and women with children take up more or less stable residence, a certain economic dependency is publicly apparent in their relationship with the Canadian Bureau of Indian Affairs. It is, however, minimal. Yearly income for a reservation Micmac averages approximately $180. The Bureau, allowing more per capita to the Micmac than to other Canadian tribes, metes out about two hundred dollars a year over that individual income. Some housing and medical services are available to the Indians in the reservation area, but in the economically depressed and relatively remote Maritimes, the high cost of food and clothing imported from other areas makes this minimum amount of cash seem smaller. The pressure which necessity puts on the young and old alike to seek work away from the reservation is evidenced in the participation of many Micmac Indians in the yearly harvesting of blueberries and potatoes in northern Maine. This enterprise requires living in camps of tarpaper shacks and canvas tents from August through October or November in order to earn migrant labor wages. Some Indians get to stay in the

States beyond the harvest season to work in the packaging and processing plants connected with the food industry. Most, however, are not needed. Those who return to the reservations are faced with the irritation of White administrators who, like the early missionaries bemoaning the misconduct of Micmac hunters, have been known to chide the Indians for this seasonal departure, complaining that children should be in school, not working, that too many young unmarried girls come home pregnant after living in the camps, and that the life of a migrant worker is disorganized, unsanitary, and immoral. Such complaints, which usually fail to cite the negligence of employers in providing social services for the hundreds of Micmac whose labor they profit by, are based on the same ignorance from which the missionaries suffered, ignorance of the exigencies of survival in a fundamentally racist society. When seen in the context of the larger structures which require Indians to live poor, they can hardly be blamed either for their dependence on the Canadian government or for doing the kind of work left to them.

The core of the Micmac community, by which I mean most adults in good health and relatively free of the direct responsibility of maintaining a large, child-oriented household, is able to avoid the label "dependent" by dissociating itself from permanent residence on the reservation. In response to economic pressures, it directs itself towards urban job markets, keeping the reservation as a haven in hard times and as a focus of sentiments, as a home. How the Micmac eventually fare with provincial administrators will be affected by the fact that conventional politics requires the stable physical presence of citizens in much the same way that years ago property ownership was required. The recently-formed Union of Nova Scotia Indians and the equally new Union of New Brunswick Indians, like other progressive Indian groups, must deal with the mobility of their members, especially young people. Their difficult task and the task of tribal councils as well is to develop a stable leadership which is recognized by Whites and at the same time genuinely represents the interests of all the Micmac people. This means battling racist attitudes from without while organizing the mobile population from within.

The 1968 statistics on the Micmac population indicate that about one-third of the adult population of registered Indians were living off the reservation *and* outside Canada at the time of the census. From infancy up until the age of 19, there were 2002 males and 1948 females on the various reservations, 364 males and 386 females off. From age 20 to 49, there were 1018 males and 919 females in residence on reservation land, 663 males and 659 females off. In the age range of fifty and older, there were 379 men and 328 women living on the reservations, 173 men and 136 women living elsewhere. This approximates the figures arrived at by the United States Bureau of Indian Affairs which show that at least a third of the American Indian population can be found living in urban areas.[44]

The traditional band organization of the Micmac is nominally recognized by the Bureau of Indian Affairs,

[44] Mimeo., Bureau of Indian Affairs, Ottawa, 1968.

but whatever political transformations it might undergo, transformations in the direction of Indian autonomy, are also affected by the spread of the Micmac network of social relations over an area larger than the Maritimes. As a result of European settlement, most tribal bands have long been dislocated from the traditional places which gave them their names. The official Ottawa Agency listings reflect the dispersal of bands to different areas of the Maritimes—Miramichi Agency: Burnt Church, Eel Ground, Fort Folly, Indian Island, Pabineau, Red Bank, Eel River; St. John River Agency: Kingsclear, Oromocto, St. Mary's, Woodstock; Eskasoni Agency: Eskasoni, Whycocomagh, Chapel Island, Sydney, Middle River; Shubenacadie Agency: Shubenacadie, Truro, Pictou Landing, Anapolis Valley, Bear River, Afton, Acadia; Edmundston Agency: Tobique; Prince Edward Island Agency: Lennox Island. Government efforts in the early 1940s to concentrate small settlements of Indians at two main reservations, Shubenacadie and Eskasoni, became a more recent force towards producing an admixture of bands in Micmac communities. What is interesting is that the bands themselves have persisted as named groups instead of dissolving under external pressures past and recent. More accurately, an individual Micmac Indian knows his band affiliation as information which locates him in a potentially larger group outside his kindred. Aside from electing band council representatives, people from the same band might never operate as an organized group, though individuals meeting for the first time can use their common band affiliation as an excuse for developing a friendship.

At Shubenacadie and Eskasoni one of the indirect, and one might almost say inadvertent, benefits of the move toward consolidation was the establishment of on-reservation primary schools and the introduction of the possibility of an Indian education for Indian children. The education made available to American Indians in general has almost always been based on the premise that White civilization must conquer aboriginal failings. Micmac children growing up prior to World War II were either sent away to boarding school to endure direct administration by Whites or expected to attend a local school and endure more diffuse racial prejudice. The third alternative, of not going to school, occurred to many Micmac but not apparently until they saw themselves as adults more ready to take their chances in the wider world than in school. Protecting young Indian children from the taunts of White students and the presumptions of White teachers is the marked improvement which reservation schools can offer. But for a Micmac to be educated on a higher level requires that he enter an unfamiliar, often hostile White institution where the expression of prejudice is meant to antagonize and exclude. Faced with these circumstances and feeling the imperative to participate in the cash economy, young Indian men and women are quickly propelled out of school and into the cheap labor force. It is, of course, true that those White teenagers who harass their Indian peers feel the same economic imperative to leave the Maritimes. The point of difference is that society's message to the Indian is much more clear and direct, and complete; it admits of no proper place for him but at the bottom. In its educational system, institutionally separate from the political and economic sectors, Western society teases the lower-class White with promises of reward, success, and acceptance, which a sterner economy can seldom fulfill and to which an indifferent government feels little commitment.

The clarity of society's message brings from two to three thousand Micmac to the Boston area, where they live, work, and travel. They cover the distance between Canada and New England with more personal resourcefulness than money, and their enterprise, while a response to economic fact, is cultural, not simply pragmatic, in origin. The patterns of behavior, the customs and beliefs which are the concern of this book are fundamentally answers to the complex question, "How will our people survive?" The Micmac have coped for hundreds of years with balancing the internal cohesiveness of their tribe against apparently destructive White forces. Their various solutions, from an active response to the fur trade to the passive endurance of large-scale immigration, have been proof of an unusual cultural flexibility. This is no less true in their survival as urban people today than it was in the past.

CHAPTER II

The Tribal Community in Industrial Society

Tribe and Social Network

Throughout the years of their transition from hunters and gatherers to industrial laborers, the Micmac have endured as a tribal people and, more to the point, have endured largely because their tribal organization was flexible enough to meet external pressures without sacrificing the integrity of the group. Culture loss is a theme which frequently arises in discussions of contemporary American Indians, as if, after being museumized, tribal groups began to suffer an inevitable decay of custom. Every deviation from tradition can be seen as breakdown or loss, but greater credit is given to living Indians when the possibility of cultural adaptation and cultural gain is admitted as an explanation for social change. No group is capable of a perfect functionalism; yet when a people survives over generations, the first questions asked should be about continuity, not discontinuity. There are few Micmac today who hunt full-time or make canoes or live in wigwams; for their economic behavior to suit the demands of industrial society it is much more appropriate for them to know how to drive and repair a car, how to live in small houses and apartments, and how to find work for cash. There are no great sagamores or forest warriors. Courage and endurance have instead found an urban arena, so that contemporary Micmac political activity is divided between tribal contests with imposing bureaucracies and a traditional egalitarianism sustained by the tribal network. Today, Micmac bands no longer gather for ritual celebrations. But the traditional principle that kinship orders behavior is at the very core of tribal organization, the goal of that organization being, as ever, to insure the perpetuation of the people.

To think of a tribal group operating in contemporary urban society is somewhat difficult. In the United States, native tribal groups are accorded a legal status which harks back to the Roman roots of the word *tribe* as a civic unit. Yet Biblical and nomadic connotations of the same word make of it the kind of human organization which belongs to less secular times than our own times when simple homogeneous bands could wander the earth. Because urbanization is usually considered as a force which moves society towards greater complexity and so-called higher levels of organization, it is often assumed that less complex forms are destroyed by it.

Urban industrialization has not, however, been ultimately hostile to tribal forms of social organization. The literature on tribal groups in the new industrial centers of Africa make this very clear.[1] Because American Indians are a numerically small minority and because an era of thoroughly corporate postindustrialism is apparently upon us, the existence of tribes in an urban setting is obscured and the functional aspects of tribal organization go unnoticed. The social structure of the Micmac, for example, who are generally representative of American Indians, is elastic enough to permit the geographic mobility of workers as an expansion of the perimeters of the tribe. The community remains a community even as its network of affiliations is spread over the physical distance between reservations and cities. It is subject to some stress and open to some change but its flexibility and the fact of tribal affiliation assure its continuity.

The nature of the tribal network, with its unique combination of centripetal and centrifugal energies permitting homogeneity and elasticity, is such that it must be contrasted with other social networks which are accurately associated with urban life but which describe more arbitrary and specialized associations. Studies of

[1] See, for example, A. L. Epstein, "The Network and Urban Social Organization," *Rhodes-Livingstone Journal,* 1961, Vol. 29, pp. 29–62; Philip Mayer, *Tribesmen or Townsmen: Conservatism and the Process of Urbanization in a South African City,* Capetown, Oxford University Press, 1961; and A. W. Southall, "Kinship, Friendship and the Network of Relations in Kisenyi, Kampala," in *Social Changes in Modern Africa,* ed. A. W. Southall, London, Oxford University Press, 1961.

social networks are motivated by curiosity about the principles by which people associate informally. In an urban society such as ours it makes very good sense to inquire into the reasons for social interaction, making no assumptions about the necessity for adult social relations beyond those required in the corporate context of office work. The severity of urban *anomie* is alleviated by employment in government and private industry so that, at a minimum, one has to keep to a fixed schedule of interaction with coworkers in return for a private life characterized by the freedom to choose or reject friends. Since there are no claims on a bureaucrat's time except those of the bureaucracy, it becomes necessary to ask basic questions about kinship, age, residence, and status as factors which might but do not necessarily have to motivate social interaction.[2]

The kind of network of social relations which is typical of American Indians is maintained outside the influence of corporate institutions, although the network articulates with larger systems at lower levels of industry and by contact with government agencies. The patterns of organization discernible in a tribal network are cultural imperatives operating to maintain cohesion in the community. While individual members may at times interact with non-Indians or with Indians from other tribes, all associations are directed by cultural goals so

[2] Philip Slater's *Pursuit of Loneliness: American Culture at the Breaking Point* (Boston, Beacon Press, 1971) is one of the most concise if informal descriptions of the extent to which the choice of social alienation is not only possible but valued in the dominant American society.

that interaction with fellow tribesmen is more highly valued than relationships with outsiders. This is perhaps the most important fact to realize about a tribal network: its apparent flexibility supports a maximum level of interaction among members beyond any issue of complete freedom of choice and beyond the notion of the right to privacy.

The second most important fact about tribal networks follows from the first insofar as the community, and not individual goals, dictates the nature of the group's boundaries. The apparently total freedom in the informal relationships of a conventional White is limited only by personal preference. An individual may theoretically interact with anyone and the frequency, purpose, and quality of interaction, and the number of people interacted with can vary by choice. An adult may have a small stable network or may travel impersonally through a series of unrelated networks, only occasionally checking in with former friends. A married couple, as a single social unit, may claim this same interactional freedom. Their children, if raised to independence, will probably claim the right to choose their own friends and provide the parents with the classic dilemma between their belief in freedom of association and the fact that the autonomy of their children will infringe on their own right to control interaction. Again, theoretically, there are no boundaries on the networks of so-called free people who, as the song goes, have "nothing left to lose."

Ideally, freedom should make it possible to explore an area of informal ties within which everyone is equal or should be treated as if they were. In contrast to this, the internal hierarchy of institutions presents the only legitimate structuring of inequality, the only system of ranking which is impersonal enough to let individuals escape the pain of personal evaluation and simple enough in its requirements to give security to thousands upon thousands of its managers. To admit inequality in the informal, private sector is so taboo that most respectable people limit their social relations in fear of meeting and having to treat as equals those inferiors without economic security and without corporate commitment. This theoretical freedom to travel through infinite networks gives an illusion of choice; but we each have a great need to control social interaction, to keep ourselves from different others who threaten our single-mindedness with the suggestion of other value systems.

A tribal community, on the other hand, has the boundaries of a traditional community with a relatively stable membership. Its membership can be identified by first-hand testimony, so that the question of who is a member, if it should arise, can be quickly settled. For American Indians, the natural boundaries of the tribe have added the restraints imposed by racism. That is, while the natives might prefer each other's company, there is really little intrusion from the outside on the part of non-Indians wanting to associate with them as equals. Although their rank in the racial hierarchy varies from one locale to another, depending on what other minorities they are compared to, Indians are usually close to the bottom. Prejudice further insures the strength of the tribal community's boundaries, as does the formal and equally demeaning treatment which government agencies give Indians.

Yet, within community boundaries, truly egalitarian

associations occur naturally and without fear, so much so that the interpersonal contests and conflicts between people are continuous and continuously resolved, much more than among those who use their freedom to avoid social interaction. The tribal network also provides multiple bonds between individuals—kinship, reservation ties, and a shared history of human relations.

The idea of an urban network is useful in the study of tribal people for two reasons. First, it allows their forms of social organization to be compared with those of other urban people, including non-tribal ethnic groups. Second, the concept releases them and other groups from the need to have community identified with geographic stability, because the concept essentially treats patterns of communication as social structure, or at least allows that possibility. The definition of community with which the social sciences have been most concerned is that of a geographically stable population which, because of its fixed locale, permits observation. A Yankee City, an Elmtown, and a Street Corner Society can be physically located and their physical structures seem to assure us that community social organization must have a material base or in some way exist only within physical boundaries. Even used metaphorically, the network concept permits a definition of community that can put aside the usual concern with place and property and instead consider enduring patterns of culture spread over time and space. In societies like our own, minorities have been urbanized for generations, yet remain a people apart, without the establishment of conventional, land-based communities. There are ghettoes and slums, places for marginal people, but these cannot be understood simply as pathological communities any more than they can be dismissed as chaotic dumping grounds. An urban minority community, whether or not the label *tribal* is properly affixed to it, is inevitably a network of relationships among the propertyless, among people for whom the city is a backdrop, a setting, and for whom survival often means maintaining a high rate of mobility beyond any initial migration to the city. The urbanization of minorities has failed to be the transformation of individual country bumpkins into alienated cosmopolitans; it has been typified instead by the development of a variety of social networks which have defensive characteristics as well as an internal social organization. As Fredrik Barth writes on the social organization of ethnic groups,

Stable inter-ethnic relationships presuppose such a structuring of interaction: a set of prescriptions governing situations of contact, and allowing for articulation in some sectors or domains of activity, and a set of proscriptions on social situations preventing inter-ethnic interaction in other sectors, and thus insulating parts of the cultures from confrontation and modification.[3]

Racist prescriptions and proscriptions make the dominant society appear as the chief perpetrator of minority culture. My own belief is that the human tendency for cultural diversity is shaped rather than created by racism. While academics speculate about the universality of an urban Culture of Poverty, minority

[3] *Ethnic Groups and Boundaries*, ed. with an intro. by Fredrik Barth, Boston, Little, Brown and Company, 1969.

groups recognize and act upon the cultural differences they perceive between one another. For Native Americans, an individual's tribal affiliation is extremely important. In New York City a native of Harlem and a former Jamaican consider themselves members of two different cultures. For a Spanish-American, the village his family comes from may be crucial in locating him in a specific network and excluding him from others in the urban community. Of course there are similarities in the ways in which many of the poor have accommodated themselves to the economic demands of urbanization. Still, it is necessary to balance that comparative overview with an understanding of the "flavor" of culture, as Kroeber called it,[4] the group's total communication to an individual that he is among the people who speak, look, feel, and act in ways most deeply familiar to him.

For most Micmac, associations with other tribal members make up a primary network in which one is much more likely to stay with one's own kind than to cultivate relationships with non-Micmac. This varies somewhat from individual to individual, but, generally speaking, a child is raised to be aware of the difference between his own people and the strangers of whom one has to be suspicious. As an adult, he or she is still likely to regard as outsiders both the local Whites whose towns neighbor the reservation and the other "ethnics" and lower-class people who live nearby in the city. In addition, the middle-class people who represent corporate service organizations in the Maritimes and in in-

[4] A. L. Kroeber, *Configurations of Culture Growth,* Berkeley and Los Angeles, University of California Press, 1944.

dustrial centers are considered peripheral to the Micmac interpersonal network.

The institution of a formal reservation system and the simultaneous draw on the Provinces for labor to service New England has had two important effects on the tribal network. First, there was an increase in communication between diverse subgroups of the Micmac influenced by some geographic consolidation of dispersed bands, especially in Nova Scotia, through efforts on the part of the federal government to promote a more efficient administration of a single, localized bloc of people. In addition to the larger settlements, such as Eskasoni or Shubenacadie, there still remain small groupings of Micmac people outside reservation boundaries. Even their isolation, however, has been minimized by the effects of industrialism. Improvements in transportation, particularly in travel by bus and automobile, and the possibilities for earning a wage in industrial centers attract Indian sons and daughters from every hamlet and reservation. The community is today quite knowledgeable about the extent of its own tribal boundaries. Each member in the course of a lifetime is likely to meet up with many other Micmac who are relatively difficult to place in an immediate kinship network and yet look, speak, and act Micmac and have to be accounted for. There is no such thing as a stranger, because information about any individual's alliances is widespread and a part of general knowledge. Who he or she is related to and has been friends or lovers with is counted as a factor, provided the intermediary person is identifiable as kin, friend, or enemy within one's own group. How an individual has declared himself or herself in past dramatic events also figures in assessing how he or she will be placed. "Were you in that big brawl they had up at St. John? Did you see Charlie Francis there?" These are the kind of opening questions an Eskasoni man might ask of an Eel River man with an eye to learning whether this person was one of the antagonists who helped beat up his cousin Charlie or one of the friends who dragged him away. A woman will be similarly identified by the company she keeps and by her alliance in a noteworthy feud or fracas. Each Micmac newcomer, whether he shows up for the first time at a party on the reservation or in a barroom in Boston, carries a history of associations which makes it fairly easy to locate him in the tribal network.

Kinship is still very important as a means of classifying others who are outside the extended family household and yet still associated with it, perhaps as a third or fourth cousin or as the person who married in at one of the more remote branches of the family tree. Kinship can often be a very neutral way of acknowledging the social existence of others. Older people and younger children, for example, were often described to me in terms of their family ties (sometimes irrespective of their kinship to the speaker) while adults of the same generation were much more likely to be identified as friends or rivals, whether or not they could be counted kin.

For both men and women, talking about their own generation (which was also the generation of their siblings and numerous cousins) prompted much reference to rivalries, confrontations, and adventures in which various *personae* emerged clearly as allies or enemies throughout a personal history. For men in particular, the details of what was happening among younger people or what had happened among adults of the parent generation were of less interest, unless, of course, they involved a close relative. One night at a gathering, I sat talking to a Micmac man in his middle fifties when a young woman of about twenty passed by us, someone whom I had met but whose name had slipped my mind. I asked the man if he knew her. He described her benignly, and, as it turned out, inaccurately, as one of Leroy Cleaver's daughters who had just married into the Samuels family. Interestingly enough, he had the correct form of a kinship designation without the correct content. When it came to talking about his own age group, the same man had a great amount of information to recount and a considerable fund of accurate detail.

For an adult the ties of kinship mean the designation as a certain member of the family that comes with birth and endures until death. There is very little that has to be worked out in matters of alliance between grandparents, parents, and children, between siblings, between nieces and nephews, or between aunts and uncles who have lived together within the same household or stayed in close contact with the family. Beyond kinship, there exists a whole range of people, discounting children and the elderly, with whom issues of amity and enmity have to be settled. Because the status of a Micmac adult lies in an individual's strength within the tribal context, the friendships, confrontations, courtships, and sundry adventures which involve most Micmac between late teens and mid-forties are the events within which power and will are rested and personal reputation augmented or tarnished. In a life history perspective, the family and usually the extended family household provides an initial vantage point from which a child considers and then enters into relationships, friendly and less-than-friendly, with his peer group. Of the Micmac I met during my field work, most were either born in the reservation area or, if they were born in New England, raised in the Maritimes. The experience of Micmac under twenty-five who have come as children to visit Boston and other cities contrasts with the more abrupt rural-to-urban shift their parents' generation underwent when they first ventured into the city as youths of nineteen or twenty. Nonetheless, while adults consider it good for children to get an idea of what city living is like, the preferred place for children to grow up is "down home" in the Maritimes, and the reliance on relatives who remain there to help care for children born in the city makes it still a first experience of the world.

Reservation Communities and Household Organization

When Sidney Mintz wrote in 1953 about the development of a certain kind of rural community within the contemporary plantation system, he could also have been describing the kind of economically peripheral

community which typifies an Indian reservation, provided that a hunting and gathering tradition is substi-
tuted for an agricultural one:

The same forces which have molded the rural proletarian community into an unexpected analogue with the ideal folk society have also been those which have made it more "urban."
Independent freehold primary production has been replaced
uniformly by plantation estates; exchange labor, tenancy, and
sharecropping have been replaced by cash labor; cash is used
exclusively to buy essential commodities; personal relationships between employer and employed (or between
owner and tenant) have been supplanted by purely impersonal relationships, based on the work done, and with a standard payment for that work; home manufacture has practically
disappeared; consumption commodities have been standard-
ized; and outside agencies of control and service—medical,
political, police, religious, military, and educational—have developed. As a result, the rural proletarian community associated with the modern plantation system exhibits a character which is superficially folklike in some ways and yet might
be labeled "urban" in others. But actually such communities
are neither folk nor urban, nor are they syntheses of these clas-
sifications. They are, rather, radically new reorganizations of
culture and society, forming a distinctive type not amenable to
the folk-urban construction.

One cannot understand reservations without rec-
ognizing the greater economic structure which makes
them segregated by class as well as culture. At the same
time, one cannot understand reservation communities
without an appreciation of their dependence upon and
support of a mobile urban population. To look at a map
of the Maritimes and to drive through the reservation
area could lead one quickly to the conclusion that the

Micmac or at least some part of the tribe lived in quaint rural isolation. The ties which connect the reservations to urban industrial areas are, of course, people, and to deduce the nature of Micmac social organization from the evidence of social interaction is much more appropriate than to take the physical plant of the reservation as primary evidence. Its appropriateness lies in the fact that the Micmac consider relationships among themselves more important than the setting in which they take place. Because of this, human urban and rural settlements where people provide the context are preferred to natural contexts. The forests on and adjacent to reservations are still used for hunting and fishing by some Micmac men. Rather than having a full traditional reliance on nature, however, the Micmac simply allow their forests and waterways to be. They use them more in times of economic recession than in times of plenty, yet always with the understanding that nature has its own incontrovertible rules, some of which provide man with resources, others of which operate irrespective of human wants. As a Micmac Indian who worked as a guide put it, "Going out into the woods here is a dangerous thing to do. You've got to watch and listen and remember everything. Then you can make your catch and get home." The White men who hired him for his knowledge of the forest did not need to understand nature. They just returned home with their game after a good hunting trip. It is an unusual Micmac who goes for poetic, solitary walks in the woods or who seeks to get away from it all by isolating himself for communion with nature. The biological force of nature, like the bio-

logical fact of humanity, is accepted by the Micmac; the
former fact is not abstracted and violated by subjection
to human ends, no more than the latter is denied and
depersonalized as an atomistic machine. In any place
where Micmac tend to congregate, such priority is put
on social interaction that the locale as an objective physical entity apart from or even reflective of the community literally never arises spontaneously as a subject of
conversation. For example, I would often mention to Indians that I met that I lived at Shubenacadie. The universal reaction was to respond to that fact in terms of
people, referring either to those who were relatives or
friends who came from there or to those who were old
enemies from past confrontations. When I would press
the matter further and ask, "Well, what do you think
about the homes there?" the response was invariably to
mention people known who had worked on the construction of government houses or to dismiss the question with a shrug and, "Could be worse." It is a telling
fact that when I encountered missionaries or local
White people or Bureau officials and made the comment, "I've been staying at Shubenacadie," their responses were almost always about the "things" which
made up the reservation landscape: houses in better or
worse repair, the size of the school building, the proliferation of abandoned cars in the last twenty years, a
new road, the size of the reservation forest. With bureaucrats, people were a kind of secondary subject, incidental to the place in which they could be found or, at
least, explicable and even determined by what could be
seen there. The most sympathy for Indians was ex-

pressed over the dilapidated condition of many homes, especially the tar-paper and wood shacks which characterized some of the settlements.

To a stranger, the aura which pervades the locale which is labeled a Micmac community is one of dispossession. The tar-paper shacks set up on a flat of cleared land are one- or two-room affairs with small metal chimneys on top and washlines strung on poles outside. The government-built houses are large and solid by comparison—four- or five-room frame dwellings lined up along a narrow road, each on an identical patch of land. For every two that are being lived in, another has collapsed into its cinderblock foundation, its roof spilling over onto what was to have been, theoretically, a properly tended green lawn. While I heard more than one local White deplore the way the Indians let those "free" houses slide into disrepair, there were simply not that many Micmac who could afford to stay on the reservation; it was the familiar predicament of "just passing through" which had, in a good number of cases, allowed houses to deteriorate a bit more after each family's temporary retreat to the reservation. The houses in good repair belong to those who have been able to find some kind of steady work in the area, in a paper mill for example, or with the Bureau itself, and even these families number only a minority in any Indian community.

More often, the reservation area is a place to which one retreats in hard times until opportunity beckons elsewhere. In a government-built house that was completely bare of furniture except for beds, a kitchen table and two chairs, a living room couch, chair, and lamp,

Kathy Meuse, a middle-aged woman born and raised at Eskasoni and married to a Micmac man from Shubena-cadie told how she and her seven children had come back to live on the reservation.

I been in better places than this, you understand. My husband was in Korea, in the army, and he done right well with them. Then he got throwed out 'cause of a fight with one of them officers. But he did okay after that. He did carpentry and electrical stuff all around the place. Sometimes me and the kids, we'd follow him around, spend a year in Montreal, then go to the States, down as far as near Philadelphia. Then there got to be too many kids. Charlotte and Roy [the two eldest] I sent for a while [two years] to stay with my sister at Eel Ground. I always like to keep the little ones near me, but that wasn't always for the best. The children's grandma [on their father's side] took them on here at Shubie the year before last when I had pneumonia real bad. Now this time, things got so bad that I thought we'd better lay low for a while, take all of us down home while Eddie looked for some work. He's in Boston or thereabouts.

What the reservation actually supports in the way of a stable household is a conglomeration of "home bases," that is, extended families which will host individual adults and children for longer or shorter periods of time, depending on what a visit is prompted by: ill health, good luck and a desire to make a munificent display, or bad luck and the need to put up somewhere for a while. The extended family includes three or even four different generations. A married man and woman or a married woman alone are typical heads of the household. The many children in the household are often only about one-half to two-thirds their own, while the rest are informally adopted from near and distant relatives. In the case of Kathy Meuse's family, she and two of the the older children joined her husband in Massachusetts before a year had passed; Charlotte and the five youngest were accepted into the homes of relatives in Shubenacadie and Truro, as, it should be noted, a temporary and not necessarily unpleasant solution to economic ups and downs. The extended family, in fact, survives on the understanding that such favors are only lent, and on the assumption that the more people associated with the household, the greater its chances for present and future support. The child left with relatives is still the concern and ultimately the responsibility of its parents, who will send funds, if they can, to help out. The elderly grandmother who is taken in by a son or daughter will let it be known to her other children that extra cash should be given to that household. The adult (man or woman) who is between jobs and sleeps on the couch is expected to remember whose hospitality was enjoyed. There are always some "bad debts," some whose fortunes never peak, some whose memories are poor when it comes to remembering old favors, some who simply do not live long enough to do a service to the family. Nonetheless, it is understood that the more people a family can claim as allies in kinship and draw into a reciprocal network of specific obligations, the better its chance of survival from one generation to the next.

The interiors of such extended-family homes are more filled with the presence of people than dominated by things. The furniture available through social assistance is characteristically discount-house plastic, from upholstered chairs to night-tables to lampshades. Many bedrooms have iron beds and heavy, framed mirrors from another generation and, occasionally, a patchwork quilt of the tiniest triangles made by an old grandmother or aunt years ago. Almost every home has one or more little bric-a-brac shelves with family snapshots placed among the ceramic statues of puppies and ballerinas. A television set, sometimes working, sometimes broken, is typically found in the living room.

The more people of all ages there are around, the more it seems that the material things in the home—the lamps, the chairs, the T.V.—dissolve as entities which make demands on human beings (e.g., needing to be dusted, polished, washed, not stepped on, treated with care, etc.) and become subservient to the random demands of people. A sofa which might last a conventional nuclear family two years (speaking hypothetically, for most welfare furniture is hardly of the quality most conventional families would choose), will serve many more Indian people and in a much shorter period of time show signs of tears and chips and cigarette burns, the natural marks of wear which are not blamed on any one person. In a similar way, a television set, which might otherwise be understood as a thing which makes exclusive demands on individual human consciousness and demands, now and again, mechanical repair, becomes subservient to and acts as a kind of amplifier of the social interaction which is already going on in the living room. For example, while nine or ten people are talking with each other, a child or an adult might decide to flick on the T.V. as just another visual and auditory input. Rather than distracting from the social interaction, it provides a kind of background rumble and roar, adding no new information to the scene than its particular light and noise. The person who turned the set on wanders away; children sit down in front of it and begin to play "Slap Jack"; a grandmother shifts her chair and inadvertently blocks out the screen from the view of most others in the room. After some time, the baby of the family will switch the channel, perhaps find something familiar or amusing such as cartoons, and fall asleep on the floor in front of the T.V. Later still, an adult will reach past the grandmother and turn off the set. The social use, not the abuse, of property leaves its mark on every material thing.

Socialization

Growing up in the midst of this kind of family, with many other children around, with many adults dropping in, which sometimes moves from one household of relatives to another, is a common experience of childhood for many Micmac. Peter Dunn, born in Bear River in 1931, described his family in the following way.

My mother had twelve children in all, well really fourteen but two are dead. Sam, Claude, Ann Mary, and me were the closest. Her brother's two children, Betty and Leonard, lived with us for a long while after their mother died. Then there was her own mother who came from Bear River and had a lot of her family there. Well, my father also had a brother who he'd go hunting with and he lived in a little shack right close to our place and he'd eat with us. Then he got took away 'cause he had t.b. My cousin Henry lived with us too, he's my age. My mother's younger brother, Joshie, used to come and stay and me and Henry and Sam would have to double up so's he could have our bed. That's a lot of people already but we always seemed to have room. Then there was the babies, the little ones, Pauline's [Peter's older sister] boy Alfie and Zeke who came to us when he was just a baby. His mother took him back when she got out of the hospital and got married again. And, of course, Martha and Elmer [Peter's two youngest siblings].

Being in charge of a "home base" in the reservation area is a role which fairly conservative women seem to opt for, e.g., a woman who has never left the area and has never wanted to, a daughter who tried out the city for a while and did not like it, an older woman who considers her days of traveling behind her. The male head of such a household need not feel constrained or tied down to home ground. He might be relatively less mobile than men his own age who travel the circuit from reservation to city, but a man always has good reason to be independent in his "business" from the affairs of women and children and, particularly for reasons of finding employment, will go off with his friends on jaunts which take them away from the home for varying lengths of time. The household, with many children and visitors, continues in his absence.

Cooperation among women remains an important part of running a household, particularly among women of different generations. A woman who is the head of a household will be helped by her mother, even if she only lives nearby and not within the household itself, and by her older daughters. In an established home base household, there is, however, typically only one woman in charge and she is likely to be the only woman of her generation in the home. Sisters-in-law, friends, and sisters visit and even send their children to be cared for without ever intruding on the hierarchical structure of the household. Competitively claiming the responsibilities of a married woman is less a factor in their adult years than the release of other women to participation in the economy.

Arnold Lefebre, born in New Brunswick in 1938, gave this description of his family:

My mother never could've managed without her own mother living right in the little cottage next door. I got four sisters older than me too and they was a great help, I know that. My dad used to fish and every once and a while he'd bring home a deer and we'd have some right good venison. He was very quiet and he didn't bother anyone too much. He and a few of my mother's brothers would go out fishing a bit in a wooden boat. Sometimes I'd get to go for a ride. When one of my father's sisters got t.b., her three kids came on to stay with us. But they were already big, sixteen and seventeen, as old as that and they didn't stay around. They come back even now though just to say hello to my mother. My father's mother lived with us just before she died. She had a gift, she could see the future and ghosts, too. We always had people dropping by to talk to her. We had family everywhere, too, it seems.

In households such as these where people of several generations live together and in a community where human relations makes up nine-tenths of the subject matter of conversation, the facts of sex and death are, relative to our society, demystified. Children laugh among themselves at their own contrived jokes about

the "mic" (penis) and the "wekitc" (vagina). Sexual relations among people in the community are of consum-
mate interest and generally discussed, even in the company of young children. At one time, a man who worked
in New England left his wife for a long while on the reservation. He came back to find out that she was about to
give birth to a child that could not possibly be his. Everyone else in the community had been following the
details of the relationship between the married woman
and her lover, the real father of the baby. A group of
children, some of them in the early years of grade
school, filled me in on the details, adding that, as a matter of fact, this was the second time poor Mr. Brown had
been "fooled."

A Micmac house has its separate bedroom with a
double bed where the mother and father of the household usually sleep. Yet, with the changes in number and
composition of the household, the bedroom is usually
not a secret domain and may have to accommodate visiting relatives, an assortment of children, or an elderly
person who has taken ill.

Death as a subject is about as open to discussion as
sex, although instead of humor, the subjects of illness
and dying are usually accompanied by ghost stories and
references to a realm of spiritual power which can be
seen as either beneficial or frightening. Mary Dunn, a
teenager, described how her mother's mother passed
away:

You know the room where Stevie, Ida, Johnny, and me sleep
in? That used to be my grandma's room. She had a bad cancer,
in her stomach, I think, and she used to complain that her
mouth was always feeling bitter, sour-tasting. I'd make her

some warm milk and carry it in to her. She didn't say nothing much to me, but I knew she liked me to sit next to her while she had her milk. My mother really had the most work with her. She'd have to get up at night and make Grandma stop moaning because it was keeping everyone awake. Johnny was real tiny then. One day I brought in the milk as usual 'cause I heard her [the grandmother] calling, that is, making them little noises in her throat. I brought in the milk and grandma put her hand on my arm and kind of pulled me near her. I said, "What is it?" She whispered to me that she would come back after she died and give me special help. I wasn't even sure it was her talking because she had lost her voice for a few days. I told my mother what she said and she got afraid. She told me to stay away from grandma after that. She died the next day. My mother and my aunts washed the body and dressed it. After the funeral, my mother didn't want to put me in that room. I wasn't afraid. I was only twelve at the time but I told her that Grandma had promised to help me, not to frighten me.

Sex and death, while demystified, are perhaps the two most fundamentally important areas of community concern, for they have to do with its reproductive continuity and the generational cycle from birth to death within which all Micmac participate. As such they are devoid of associations of romantic love, which we tend metaphorically to link with sex, and of violence, which we associate with death. The polarities of euphoric love and the destruction of nuclear war which count for so much in the dominant society mean much less in a tribal community and are, in fact, concepts unavailable to most of its members. The interactional realities of human conflict make up the very life of the community and it is in the larger households that a child is edu-

cated into the continual ebb and flow of human relationships.

While reservations are hardly considered ideal
places to live, most Micmac women agree that a child is
better raised there than in a city environment. Once
again, this is a judgment made for interpersonal reasons,
not out of disdain for the physical setting. In the city, a
young child has to associate and go to school with
Whites and risk the conflicts which that contact inevitably engenders. The reservation household can offer protective care at least until the child reaches his or her
teens and becomes independent. One woman, Maureen
Paul, who was born in 1945 in Boston, was raised at
Eskasoni in a large household managed by her grandmother and then her aunt:

It would be hard, right hard to say just how many there was in
the family. My grandmother was always trying to keep us in
line but there were a lot of kids, a whole lot of us little bas-
tards running around. Sal [Maureen's brother] and me were
about the oldest, though there was Francine that my grandmother brought up and she was about three of four years older
than me. But she left and went to Halifax when she was about,
oh, fifteen or sixteen. She run away but she come back later,
all grown up and with a job. Anyway, after Sal and me there
was Eveline and Debbie, my mother's sister's children, that
was Aunt Helen, and there was the twins, one of them nicknamed "Popeye" cause he had one eye blue and the other
brown, the other was Matthew who I told you about got Es-
telle's girl pregnant. The twins was from my father's side of
the family. Their mother was a close cousin of his and Seda
[Maureen's grandmother] took them in when she couldn't care
for them no more. Let me see, then there was Uncle Alfred
who stayed at home when he came in from the States and

Aunt Dee who lived with us and kinda took over when Seda died in 1962. My mother took me and Sal down to the city with her in about 1953, but that was just for a short time. Sal would get into fights with the boys there and they were real tough. So we were sent down home, to Seda.

Even as a reservation household protects children in a physical sense, it gives them an Indian identity which emphasizes individual autonomy and personal strength. The ideal Micmac adult has the will and spirit to travel, to make spontaneous choices, to be aggressive and assertive, to take risks—all within the context and with the approval of the tribal community. The power of an individual does not exist in a vacuum; it is the group which continually witnesses, verifies, and makes comprehensible individual behavior, putting limits on individualism and optimally preventing autonomy from becoming isolation.

In the socialization of children, the personal strength which is encouraged has two aspects. One of these is an aggressive physical hardiness or toughness, the other is a sense of unique access to spiritual resources. The two aspects are so interconnected that the presence of the former is taken to indicate the existence of the latter, physical endurance being the proof of spiritual power.

Among the Micmac, childhood is considered a biological phase through which human beings pass naturally and without conscious educational efforts on the part of adults. Childhood is seen as an adequate state in itself, rather than merely a path to the final goal of adulthood. Children are not expected to talk or think like adults and they are not rewarded if they do. To the contrary, a child who tries to assert himself during a conversation between his elders is misbehaving. The individual child is, however, encouraged to assert himself in his own league, among other children. The adult in his prime of life has maximum access to the ideal of physical and spiritual fortitude. The child, like the old person, has an appropriate arena for performing according to the values of the community. When a small child stands up to a bully, he is courageous, not simply acting courageously and mimicking adult behavior. When an old person boasts about long-ago adventures, he is acting within the value system in a way which fits his physical limitations. The child is not rushing toward another state; he is living in the present reality of a child's body. The old person is not chagrined by the loss of a youth he expected to go on forever; he is living with the biological fact of his body.

From the time a Micmac child is very young, he or she is encouraged to be strong. A father or uncle or older brother will show a toddler of two or three how to make a fist and jab with it like a boxer. An older sibling will affectionately urge him to fight and then feign retreat under the miniature torrent of punches and kicks and even four-letter words. The women in a family might verbally protest such aggression, but nonverbally, with smiles and without taking action to intervene, show pride and approval. When a young boy acts fearless of physical retribution from older children and from the women in his family, his behavior is generally condoned. If he begins to get too aggressive with the men in the household, his behavior will be checked, not to make him fearful but to communicate to him that taking on an adult male is more presumptuous. I observed one incident typical of how this message on the limits of aggression is communicated and how the household cooperates to do it. A sturdy boy of three decided that he was going to try out a few punches on his father who was sitting at a table talking with some friends. The father tolerated some pummeling and then pushed his son away. The boy came back and his father gave him a slap which was hard enough to make the child cry. Instead, the boy, with his face very red, held back the tears that were in his eyes. An older sibling, a girl of about thirteen, came to the rescue with a good-humoured invitation to spar with her. The friends of the father remarked on the boy's courage in holding back his tears and he proudly nodded in agreement.

Any child, boy or girl, who takes to whining and crying will be ignored by the adults and mocked by other children as a weakling and a sissy. Infants are cared for and indulged by an array of people who meet their needs so as to avoid the necessity of their crying. When infancy is left behind, there are still the other children and adults, who anticipate individual physical limits and take on the responsibility for tying shoes and buttoning coats, for reaching high shelves, finding lost toys, and giving up indulgences like candy or some trinket to a young child. Micmac children learn by observation and are not subjected in a family to intense verbal instruction. Younger children are expected to imitate their older siblings in the basics of eating, toilet training, and general physical dexterity without individual instruction, and the expectation is apparently justified. The reason a child who whines is despised is that he would seem to deny a correct ratio between the care offered by the group to a dependent child and his limited, but real physical autonomy. The whining child says, "I'm not getting enough" and the group says, "we're giving you what you need for your age. The problem is with you."

The solidarity which exists among children in the same household is complex. Blood relationships count and the child with remote or no real kinship ties, the child actually liable to be transient, is acknowledged as a less permanent member of the family, unless, of course, the parents legally adopt him or her. This is an unusual step to take, because in the great majority of cases, the circulation of children is kept informal and flexible.

Age and sex differences are important additional factors. There is a point at which closest siblings become part of a larger adolescent peer group and will see each other both in and out of the family setting. Because the whole function of the peer group seems to lie in the proliferation of social ties it offers and because independence is a strongly supported value, siblings coming into their teens at about the same time tend to keep some distance between themselves. It is very unlikely that two brothers or two sisters would ever openly fight with each other, but they may avoid each other in the larger peer group. The quick defense of a sister or brother, especially a younger one, is a common reaction which persists from childhood all through life and which, despite adolescent autonomy, can be elicited in a crisis. If a quarrel arises, for example, over the matter of flirtation and stolen affection, brothers and sisters will defend each other. A brother is most protective of a sister, younger or older, while a sister is likely to defend her sisters and the younger children, both brothers and sisters. A hierarchical bias in the large household makes all other children assume responsibilities of caring for younger children, responsibilities which are not directly reciprocal when children become adults. A young man is likely to be protective towards the older sister who cared for him and the younger sister for whom he cared, but he is likely to view his brothers as somewhat independent rivals. A young woman accords her older brothers the same autonomy and feels a lifelong solidarity with her sisters and younger siblings. Themes of competition and caring figure strongly in the relationships between children of the same family and through life there is a general bias of males towards the former and of females towards the latter. Adolescence as a phase in life requires movement out into a wider peer network and for a time the de-emphasis of all kin ties in favor of a more competitive individualism.

The socialization of Micmac girls prepares them for this phase even as it prepares them for a later, adult phase of increased mutual support and caring among family members. The show of physical strength that is encouraged in boys is rewarded in girls as well, although in girls stoic endurance, more than physical aggression, is praised. Young girls seem to get into just as many fights where blows are exchanged as boys and are similarly expected to hold back their tears when hurt or frustrated. A child's physical hardiness, much more than physical attractiveness, and personal independence, more than passivity, are characteristics in which adults take delight.

The physical vulnerability of Micmac females is admitted to in an interesting, indirect way. It is women who are preoccupied with the subject of medicine, with accounts of accidents, and, more frequently, internal illnesses, their symptoms and their cures. Folk medicine has been supplanted by remedies available in drugstores but, very importantly, a cure is only assured by a combination of human products and human spiritual resources. A woman has the cultural license to approach the problem of illness, her own and others', with speculations about the specific motivations behind the fact of sickness: are there bad feelings in the kin group of the sick person; is there an old enemy who has reappeared on the scene; is the sick person, for a lack of spirit, ready to die? There is no formal witchcraft or sorcery among the Micmac but there is an understanding that explanations of the physical fact of illness must include information about human relationships and, further, that humans must be understood as embodiments of spiritual forces, never machines. The area of competence within which a girl works is the home and her sense of responsibility in helping with younger children, the old, and the sick helps enormously in the operation of the household.

No professionalization of the female's housewife role,

however, is really possible in a large Micmac family. Specific responsibilities vary with the number of people around so that there is no formal possession of chores or control of space, no chance for a girl to play at being her mother and thus arrive at a total occupational understanding of the role of housewife. The mother of the family orchestrates the carrying out of domestic tasks and relies particularly on her daughters to accommodate themselves to a shifting array of responsibilities. It is the ethic of responsibility, not pride in having accomplished a task, which makes the home run smoothly, and a young girl has to get used to working gracefully along with her sisters, mother, aunts, and grandmothers in a system within which work is not divided but shared. The verbal directives to assume responsibility are very few, leaving the initiative to the child. By the time a Micmac girl is eleven or twelve, she has learned to be basically noncompetitive about family responsibilities.

In Micmac society and, I believe, in other minority communities as well, the women in a household and any old people who are around socialize children in a way which allows them to deal with more than the internal value system of the Micmac. As every student of colonial literature knows, few people know the oppressor better than the oppressed and it appears that verbally instructing their children in the ways of White society is as much a tradition among Micmac women as the communication of tribal culture. The role of men in socializing children is extremely important but most of it lies, as does much of the role of women, in an area where the ideas of a child are shaped by an informal mixture of nonverbal and verbal communication concerned with what is happening in the present tense within the kin group. In addition to that fundamental education, Micmac women make a special point of enunciating the abstract tenets and "respectable" values of the dominant society. They tell their children that they should stay in school, that they should go to church, that they should get legally married before having sexual relations, and that they should in general act "right." Very few Micmac have lived or even could have lived according to these tenets. Prolonged education is hardly feasible, legal marriage implies a completely different family system and relationship to property, and the participation of most Micmac in institutionalized religion amounts to a nominal Catholicism. The demands of life for the Micmac have very little to do with so-called civilized behavior and even a radical transformation of their tribe into respectable folk would not alter their position in society.

What women are doing when they tell children to act right is articulating the differences between two value systems, that of the Indians and that of the dominant society. They urge the young to look at themselves from the point of view of the White man and to understand the behavioral limits which are imposed upon them from without. To tell a child to act right according to White convention is, in reality, to give a warning, to communicate the fact that a Micmac would have to make an effort to become acceptable to the dominant society, and the fact that one's natural, culturally sufficient way of behaving is not widely approved. So it is that women who are most respectable in White terms become the heads of large reservation households and raise children who in no way accommodate themselves to White institutions. Nor is it by accident that women, children, and older people on reservations have an access to respectability not shared by the rest of the community. Most of the children will repudiate that access to school and church and legal behavior before they are twenty, as their grandparents did, and find it again when they are old and less mobile and have grandchildren themselves who will need instruction in the ways of the world.

All Micmac women are self-educated experts in the ways of the dominant society. In each stage of life, in every interaction with a bureaucrat, they perceive the nuances of communication from behind a polite, if impassive, mask. Good demeanor keeps Micmac girls in school for a longer time than their male peers; and this gives them the opportunity to learn thoroughly the value system of the oppressor. Women of all ages go to church more frequently than men and have again the opportunity to pick up bureaucratic categories and metaphors. As it turns out, a woman is good when she is respectable, not because she meets a White model of behavior, but because she brings information into the Indian culture which adds to the defenses of her children against the total society which keeps them at its periphery. It is only in her public performance that she appears to have capitulated; among her own, she has only to phrase the legal value system and let the perception of its variance with Indian reality fall to the children, a variance which very few children fail to perceive. It is interesting how educational and religious institutions, which always seek to reform, inevitably only inform, their abstractions being reworked by cultural imperatives.

The endurance of a traditional Micmac language is a vital part of the socialization of children and a well-protected aspect of Micmac culture. When questioned directly about the survival of their language, many Indians deny its continued use and their own proficiency in it and claim that the old people still speak Micmac but very few others remember the language. Basically the same claim is made about traditional myths. But in fact, the use of Micmac, more than being a second language to English or, in parts of Quebec, to French, is common within the household. Denials of its importance stem, I believe, from several sources. First, the researcher who asks about the Micmac language implies that there is a known grammar and vocabulary to some extent rigidified by tradition. What the Micmac are speaking is a living language which has dropped some words over time and included others, notably English words for technological inventions, car, T.V., transistor, etc. A man or woman might speak fluent Micmac but not feel expert enough in it to live up to the standards of linguists. Second, denial of fluency in Micmac may come from an individual's need to present himself as a civilized rather than a savage person to an inquirer from outside the community. It takes a great sense of humor on the part of Indians to put up with anthropological expectations of a traditional, museumized culture; such expectations usually postulate a maximum distance between the ways of the Whites and the antiquated, primitive customs of the natives. It is not surprising that any Micmac given that choice should try to associate himself with contemporary ways of acting and disclaim knowledge and practice of tradition. Third, as with mythic images, language is a part of culture which the Micmac, to refer to Fredrik Barth's description, insulate from confrontation and modification. It is truly the language of the family group which strangers passing through are not likely to hear. It is the form of communication used in conflict and in courtship across family divisions. It is the language which is absent when Micmac Indians find themselves on the boundaries of their community in interaction with Whites, unless aggressive exclusion of non-Indians is intended, for the great majority of the Micmac are bilingual and can speak the language of the dominant society.

Mythic Images of Power

The physical strength and fearlessness praised in children is idealized in Micmac tales of giant folk heroes who walked the land long before Indians or any other human beings existed. These mythic characters were not only strong in body but possessed great supernatural strength. They had power enough to create islands by simply tossing huge rocks into the ocean and, in addition, they had the power to transform an enemy into a tree or cast a fatal curse on a malefactor. In real life, the Micmac often take the physical strength of an individual as an indication of special access to spiritual power, although the subject of magical practices, except as an activity which properly belongs to the realm of folklore, is greatly underplayed. It is acceptable to describe the supernatural gifts of mythic giants or even of Micmac Indians who lived a generation or so ago but reference to a living person's ability to deal in supernatural cause and effect is strongly avoided, at least in the presence of non-Indians. Nonetheless, it is admitted that some Micmac have magical power and are to be feared for what they might do in anger and, on the other hand, protected against the anger and suspicions of others. From their earliest years children are watched for signs of special communication with the spirit world and with the dead. The child who claims to have talked with a deceased relative or received a message from a ghost is taken seriously and never dismissed as over-imaginative. It is impossible to will or earn favoritism from spirits. Extraordinary magical abilities are innate, and then are developed over time.

Simply being born a Micmac, however guarantees an individual his share of spiritual resources. Ordinary *keskamzit* or the kind of good luck that gets one out of risky situations is claimed by everyone. The ability to "think" evil on another person, not in the specific sense of causing disease or death, but in the general sense of adding to another's store of bad luck, is also at the disposal of every Micmac. Between these ordinary powers and the adventures of folk heroes lies the full range of preoccupation with the outward appearance of power and the possession of inner strength. Both of these are appropriate concerns for any people who, like the Micmac, have to maximize their defenses against a hostile environment. The tales of the Micmac, whether old or new, deal with this duality of human resources and, conversely, with the basic issue of human vulnerability and weakness.

The stories about the past present a blend of personal and historical information which indicates that the French, English, and Mohawk became incorporated into mythic structures as occasional enemies who gave the Micmac reason to demonstrate their physical and more-than-physical powers. In future generations there will be other categories of enemies—Canadian Mounties, city police, other minorities—who will exist in Micmac adventures as a similar category of *provacateurs.* Wallis, in his first field trip to the Maritimes in 1911–1912, recorded this explanation of how Micmac mythology evolved to its present mixture of historical reference and exploits, which includes a sense of the past as a single category "collapsing" discrete eras into one:

Among the first generation of old-time Micmac there were no stories. The second generation told a true story about the first generation. The third generation made a story about the second, and added it to the other. The process continued and today a great many stories are known to us all.[5]

[5] Wallis and Wallis, *The Micmac Indians of Eastern Canada,* p. 11. See also Père Adrien "Conservatisme et changement chez les Indiens Micmacs," *Anthropologica,* Vol. 2, 1956, pp. 1–16, for a defense of the persistence of belief in the supernatural among the Micmac in Quebec.

Mythology among the Micmac exists less as a set body of traditions than as a means for presenting images of power in situations which are linked to "real-life" history. If one asks a Micmac Indian today about traditional stories, the reaction is invariably one of vaguely concerned interest in the "old ways" about which it is sadly remarked not too many Micmac really know very much. One will be sent down the road to an elderly person who knows all the old tales everyone else has forgotten. But if the same researcher, having gone through the arduous process of recording a few tales in isolation with an old person, stays close by the Micmac families he has come to know, he soon discovers that there is a more natural context for folklore in the family. In a casual moment, someone will bring up the subject of ghosts and this will lead to a recitation of wondrous tales of supernatural forces. The figures in such stories are either decidedly traditional, such as the giant *Gluscap,* or they are individual Micmac with the special physical power of a *ginap,* or with the witchcraft power of a *buoin,* or more commonly a person with *keskamzit.* The figures may also be ghostly apparitions of once-living Micmac which have, even in death, physical and magical powers of their own. Whether a giant or specially-endowed human, the Micmac in each story demonstrates great strength, sometimes over lesser beings such as ordinary humans and animals, as is the case with *Gluscap,* sometimes in competition with others of nearly equal power.

The Micmac culture hero *Gluscap* exists in the mythological past, in the time of other giants and of the first Micmac Indians. *Gluscap's* origins are more natural than supernatural. He claims Bear as his mother and Sable as his younger brother, with fishers and martens as his kinfolk. The paternity of *Gluscap* is sometimes linked to Turtle, but more often left ambiguous. Instead of being a god who created the Micmac, *Gluscap* organized and ordered the natural and moral world within which the Micmac were living. He directed natural species to their correct habitats, whether woodland, lake or ocean. The Micmac he instructed in the construction of tools, weapons, and canoes so that they, like the animals, might fit their environment. He also acted as a judge in conflicts among the early Micmac, encouraging them to share with each other and taking it upon himself to punish the selfish and the proud. Along with his enormous size, *Gluscap* had the power to change men into natural, inanimate forms as a way to immortalize them and is said to have left monumental evidence of this power in the Maritime landscape.

The most interesting thing about this culture hero is his disappearance, which seems to coincide with the English phase of colonization. The dislocation of the Micmac from their natural economic environment is reflected in mythic history by the retreat of *Gluscap*, who has no cultural solutions to offer, although he attempts to the end to use his transformational powers to absorb, i.e., culturalize, the British. The following story, told to me in Nova Scotia during the summer of 1970, illustrates the style of *Gluscap*'s retreat.[6]

[6] This and the stories which follow were recorded during fieldwork in various settings both in the Maritimes and in Boston. For other sources of traditional Micmac myths, see Silas T. Rand, *Legends of the*

At Cape Breton, there is an island made by *Gluscap* from a whale. First he gave the muscles from the whale to all the Micmac so that they would be strong and would not be afraid of the whale. He gave muscles to all the animals as well. Then he put the whale in his canoe, which was made of stone, and he paddled out into the bay and pushed the whale into the water. It is an island there [at Broad Cove] today. One day, a long time ago, a Micmac man asked *Gluscap* for a favor. He wanted to live for many years. *Gluscap* said that would be all right and he turned him into a big tree. Another man asked *Gluscap* to keep him and his family from starving. *Gluscap* gave him plenty of animals to hunt. When the French came, he was very kind to them. When the English came, he had to leave. He told the Micmac that they would get their land some day in the future but until then he could not live with the English. *Gluscap* was so big that he could walk from one end of Nova Scotia to the other in just a few minutes. He could stretch out one leg and touch Prince Edward Island but wouldn't step on it because he might sink it, that is, squash it down. He could stroll over to Quebec and New Brunswick. When the British came he left. There is some red agate in the ground around here that used to be British soldiers. *Gluscap* raised his arms and they turned into red agate, to stone. Then he left to live high on a mountain [Mt. Katahdin]. *Gluscap* picked up some rocks and threw them into the ocean, right off Halifax. That's Five Islands. One of them has a cleft made by his hand. You can see that today.

Gluscap has an aggressive counterpart in another mythic giant, *Kitpusiagana,* who sometimes appears in stories as his twin, sometimes as *Gluscap's* rival. *Kitpusiagana* was influenced by an awesome giant from the west, *Djenu,* the Cannibal, which explains the se-

Micmac, New York, 1894; and pp. 317–493 in Wallis and Wallis, *The Micmac Indians of Eastern Canada.*

verity of his vengeance and the ferocity associated with his warrior image. With colonialization *Kitpusiagana,* like the more benevolent *Gluscap,* must retreat, even as the Micmac must become peaceable, and he seeks refuge beneath the ground just as *Gluscap* sought refuge above it.

Kitpusiagana knew all along that his mother was killed by the grandfather *Djenu.* When he was just a little baby he knew that. This was in the days when there were enemy Indians here who would kill women in a village. They took *Kitpusiagana* and raised him as the chief's son. He had an older [step-] brother in the family. As he grew bigger and bigger and when he hunted with his brother, he would kill a lot of moose, and bear, and deer and carry them all home, while his brother carried his special big bow-and-arrow. Finally, when *Kitpusiagnana* was grown, he killed the chief and ground his bones into round stones which he placed into the ground. Then, he came upon his grandmother and grandfather sleeping and killed them both with a sharp knife. His brother helped him in all this. Afterwards, *Kitpusiagana* had many adventures. One day he disappeared into the earth and buried himself because there was another giant bigger than him who chased him out to Cape Breton. Now he lives under the ground.

The retreat of the aggressive *Kitpusiagana* is directly connected with military defeat as, for example, when the giant who chased him to Cape Breton is described as a Mohawk. *Gluscap*'s exit is much more dignified and is based on a kind of prior knowledge of the difficulties White settlement would inflict on the Micmac.

Gluscap knew that the Micmac were going to have trouble with White people. He himself could not be hurt. The English tried to kidnap him and bring him to England but they could not. *Gluscap* knew that the French would lose their king many years before it happened. He knew that the hunting and fishing he taught the Micmac would not be used much today. He had a big hound of his own that would howl in the woods to tell the Micmac *Gluscap* was coming. When *Gluscap* decided to go away, he turned that hound to stone and he left. He didn't die. He was just very angry with the English.

The culture hero, in a sense, abandoned his people, leaving behind the land and his marks upon it. The people have not, however, abandoned the culture hero. The direct reliance which the Micmac once had on the land has become much more diffuse and difficult for a non-Indian to understand because it cannot be explained in pragmatic, economic terms. Micmac land, a fraction of the land of giants that it once was, has endured along with the people. Their participation in industrial economy has made hunting and fishing only occasional ventures; but the rule of the bureaucracy has not dislocated the Micmac from the fact of the land itself. Whatever legal definition can be given a reservation, an Indian cultural definition can supersede it and surpass it in power. A corporate, managerial understanding of a Micmac settlement is always an abstract projection which functions for the convenience of the corporation. A Micmac knows the reservation as an insider living the reality of that environment; it is his own turf, it is home, and historical forces have, kindly enough, left it thus far in relatively undisturbed condition. *Gluscap,* it must be noted, is not dead, only on retreat. I have been assured by a good many Micmac storytellers that when White people have gone away, *Gluscap* will return once more and the Indians will again thrive. This prophecy never seemed to me a vainglorious fantasy of Indian re-surgency. The Micmac have never really had anything more than an unassuming, even diminutive claim on survival. The return of *Gluscap* is, to my mind, a meta-phor for another truly postindustrial age when, corpora-tions having disintegrated, everyone will be required to search out human-scale solutions to existence; we shall all be Indians then.

There is in the tales of *Gluscap* and *Kitpusiagana* and sundry other giants an emphasis on physical size and strength which, tied in with spiritual gifts, reflects contemporary Micmac values. In the mythic past the enormous physical size of the heroes is underscored. When a middleground between mythology's era and the present is approached, the heroes cease to be giants and become mortals of rather ordinary human size. It is their supernatural powers, as forces which can be directed against other human beings, which are underscored. Physical strength continues to be an important corollary of psychic power but heroic dimensions are dispensed with.

The transition between the category of giant and the category of human being is expressed in the Micmac concept of a *ginap*. A *ginap* is a particularly strong per-son, one who lived in the past, with the power to travel quickly over many miles, to defeat enemies with a wish, a shout, or a mere raising of the arms, and sometimes the power to work magic. The knowledge that someone is a *ginap* is supposed to be suppressed during his or her lifetime; if such information were widely broadcast, the *ginap* would fall sick and the family would suffer a great loss. *Ginap* stories reveal a concern with physical strength and the innate power of the individual to cross the boundary from merely human to "giant." The Micmac tell a story of the prototypical *Ginap* whose origin goes back to precolonial times. This figure is larger in size than most other Indians but seeks to hide the fact and even refuses the acclaim that falls to him when he performs wondrous acts.

The first *ginap* was Micmac who lived a long time ago, before the French came. He was very big, bigger than most any other men, but he wore a special shirt that his mother made for him which kept people from seeing his size. He was so strong that he could fight the Mohawk and kill all of them that came to his band. He wasn't the chief or anything like that. He was ordinary-looking. His wife's family didn't know just who he was. They thought he was just ordinary. Then one day he went out into the forest in the winter and brought back a bear in just a few minutes. The next day, he brought back a moose. He asked his wife's people if that was enough. The next day he brought back another bear and told his wife to skin it. Then he rested because he didn't want her people to get suspicious. After that, some Mohawk came. Everyone in the village ran away. *Ginap* stayed and when the Mohawk came in, he just held up his arms in the air and they all fell down. When the people of the old village came back, they saw all the dead Mohawk lying around and they wanted to make him a chief. The old chief [his wife's father] agreed, but *Ginap* said no.

Some *ginap* tales, like giant stories, refer to the historical conflict between the Micmac and the English and imply that he not only had an ability to kill with an angry gesture, but a vision into the future and an understanding, like *Gluscap*'s, of the inevitability of White intrusion. As an example,

Over at Miramichi, there was a *ginap* who fought the English. He was sitting and smoking his pipe in his house [wigwam] when some French soldiers put in by boat. They said that they were getting ready to fight the English. The man's mother told him not to go. But he went anyway. He showed the French which way to go. They surprised the English as they were sleeping. The *ginap* made a wish and called out with a special cry. This made the English soldiers fall down. Then he went back to his own house. Later all his people found out that he had killed thirty English soldiers. They thought that would be enough, that the English would stay away. The *ginap* knew that they would be back. He told them that and he was right.

Ginap stories require some distance between the storyteller and the person with *ginap* powers. A temporal distance of one or two generations back is common. A distance of place is often interposed between the locus of the storytelling event and the reservation or settlement where the *ginap* lived. It might seem as if this distance of time and place unburdens the speaker and his audience of scientific consideration of the factual reality of magic. It does, from a Western point of view, but the issue of factual proof is not admitted and, being unadmitted, is hardly a burden. The belief in a magical realm where the normal laws of human existence do not hold is a given. A good storyteller, man or woman, postulates a certain remoteness of time and place structurally equivalent to the remoteness of a magical realm and uses recitation to effect a rapprochement between what is experientially distant—time, place, and the supernatural—and the audience.

The belief that a contemporary *ginap* can be killed by a broadcasted reputation reflects the necessity of a culturally correct and structured presentation of verbal information on the delicate and dangerous subject of man's access to the supernatural. It is as if the person who tells a tale of magic reaches up to a shelf for a mythic package, turns and presents its contents for reflection to the group, and then puts it back on the shelf where it can later be found again.

The benevolent strength of the *ginap* image is tempered by a poignant vulnerability. Often a child prodigy, the male ginap is skillful as well as strong and an asset to his family which tries to protect him from being discovered. The following story is typical in its theme of great strength toppled by general knowledge.

My grandmother told me that she almost married a *ginap*. But that she was afraid to after she found out. He lived at Burnt Church. He could pick up three or four men at the same time and spin them around. One day, two Mohawk Indians came to Burnt Church. They met this man but they didn't say they were Mohawk. He knew anyway and he put one under each arm and carried them back to Montreal and then came right back himself. He knew the trouble the Mohawk had given his people. Another time, when he was still just a boy he made his own fishing boat and brought it into the water and was gone for a whole day. No one paid him no mind at first. No one made a fuss over him. Turns out, he married another girl but he fell sick after awhile. Too many people knew about his being a *ginap*. Even when he was getting sick, he'd still be able to chop wood and all. He had a special trick of picking up a wood-burning stove. But he died when he was still right young and my grandmother wasn't sorry she hadn't married him.

The sickness which kills the *ginap* is seldom attributed to a specific cause. It is implicit that the jealousy of other families might bring about the death of the *ginap*, to equalize advantages within the community. It seems fitting, too, that an oppressed Indian group should continue to be concerned about secret strengths and the vulnerability which attaches to exposure of knowledge.

The female *ginap* is usually presented without great emphasis on physical strength; her powers always seem a bit more mysterious, though not unrelated to survival. For example,

Fleur Martin was a Cape Breton woman who was a *ginap*. She could light a fire without any matches, just by wishing. If she wanted to have a rabbit or even a deer, she would just go into the woods and reach for one. People would come to her house for a visit and she would say, "Wait a minute." She'd go into the woods and get a rabbit and hand it to them as a present.

A woman who is a *ginap* might be benevolent but she is pictured as an isolated figure whose motivations are less than clear and who may be literally subject to flights of fancy as the following description points out:

A woman, Mary McDonald, from Miramichi, was a *ginap*. She would be standing in the yard one minute and her family would see her disappear the next. She would be gone to Cape Breton and people would see her there, walking along the road. My uncle said he saw her once and he said, "Hello, Mary." He found out later that she had disappeared from Miramichi and traveled in just a few minutes to Pictou Landing where her family was from.

Just as the benevolent *Gluscap* has an aggressive counterpart in *Kitpusiagana*, the benevolence and vulnerability of the *ginap* finds structural opposition in the role of the *buoin,* a person with magical powers who seeks to control others. The traditional *bohinne* was described in the seventeenth century as a medicine man who also acted as a dispenser of justice and keeper of public morals for the community, using his power to punish the greedy, the proud, the unfaithful. Today's *buoin* is a much more ambiguous figure, one which operates almost totally in the area of supernatural practices. Like the stories about the *ginap,* tales relating to the *buoin* are located in a time intermediary between the mythic past and the present and usually at a spatial distance as well. The skill of the male *ginap* in manipulating the physical environment, and the unearthly and undirected gifts of the female *ginap,* contrast sharply with the wizardry of the *buoin,* whose concern with survival goes beyond craft and skill and whose strength often provokes conflict. The medicine a *buoin* deals in comprehends the human spirit and seeks to use it against the body. Jealous of the power of others, a *buoin* might take the natural form of a bear and attack someone of equal supernatural strength. In the following story, a female *buoin* transforms herself into a bear, converting some of her magical strength to physical strength, and directly encounters a male rival.

There was a man who lived at Cape Breton who fought all night with a bear that came into his wigwam. He knew this wasn't an ordinary bear but the spirit of a *buoin* that was trying to kill him. He fought all night until he killed the bear and then it disappeared. He knew then that his power was greater than that of the other *buoin.* Whenever he had trouble before, he knew it was that woman who was trying to kill him. Finally he made up a special medicine. He made a little birch-bark canoe and put the medicine in it and pushed it out into the water. It must have gone like a bullet through the water because that very day the other *buoin* was knocked to the floor while she was cooking and soon after she died.

A *buoin* is much more likely to be a woman than a man and to use a means of manipulation much less direct than the one above. The former *bohinne* association with medicine and morals seems to have shifted from men to women so that the latter are frequently represented as aggressive and punitive, people who can kill by wishing to kill, as this tale illustrates:

When I was a little girl [at Lennox Island], there was an old aunt of mine who used to know all about medicines and plants from the woods that would cure just about anything. She knew a lot more than that. There was one family in the village where she lived that was mean to her. One day the mother in that family came down with a terrible fever. The rest of the family ran to this old aunt and begged her to stop. She told them that she had bad feelings she wouldn't do nothing about. They brought her to where the dying woman was and begged her to cure her. But that old woman wouldn't give up and the other woman died after all. It came back on her though because no one would go near her after that, except to get a potion. One day, she said that a man she used to know had fallen into some water and drowned. A little while later, this was found out to be true. Another time, she told a woman that her child would be born with a red mark on each hand. This also happened. Still another time, she asked some men for meat after they had been hunting. They said no and while they were walking home, they saw the ghost of a man who had died the year before. They were so afraid that they dropped their guns and meat and ran away. When they came back, the meat was gone and their guns were all bent and rusted. That was what this *buoin* would do.

The punishments a *buoin* can mete out often seem quite arbitrary. It is one thing to frighten two hunters who have been ungenerous; it is quite another to let angry feelings bring on death. Yet such arbitrary intent is allowed because it is assumed that the *buoin,* like everyone else, is embroiled in interpersonal relationships and is going to feel more kindly towards some, more competitive with others. In myth as in real life, there is really no accounting for interpersonal preferences and no expectation that a figure sitting in judgment on the community's behavior should be rigorously objective.

A *buoin* is commonly involved in affairs of the heart, making love potions and working magic on unfaithful lovers and spouses. She will act quickly and competitively to defend nearest kin from unwanted intrusions on the family. This next story is typical in that respect and, in addition, implies the transmission of *buoin* powers within the extended family.

There was a woman who lived at Big Cove in my mother's time who was a famous *buoin.* Any time anyone needed a cure or a love potion, they would go to that woman. The priest used to be very angry that anyone would go to her instead of praying. But her ways were just Indian ways and she would never bother the priest. One day, her son fell in love with a girl from Pictou Landing. The old woman didn't like the girl and even though she was far away, she made the girl get sick. She took some feathers and wrapped them in a little bundle and dipped them in tar. The girl told everyone that her whole body was weighted down. The son went home and told his mother that he would marry the girl. She said, "All right." Then she took her magic off the girl. The girl's people were afraid for her because she would have a mother-in-law that could not ever be made angry. The son promised that his mother would behave. But they were also afraid that he had magic powers as well. Anyway, they got married, but everyone said that all the children had very strong power and that if they wished a bad thing to happen to someone, why, it would happen.

The mythic association of *buoin* powers with a woman is somehow appropriate to the real-life concerns of Micmac women and the role they play in the tribal community. Much more than men, women are involved with notions of physical vulnerability, especially with childbearing and with illness (as opposed to accidents). Out of their involvement comes a concern with curative remedies and a willingness to consider other-than-scientific explanations of poor health. The Micmac as a group do believe that anger has the power to cause physical harm. They also believe that competitive individualism within the group and the ongoing conflict which comes out of it is a healthy social condition. Some expression of anger is permitted in face-to-face encounter; the residue may be transformed into another form of energy and cause illness or accident. That some individuals might have good access to the spiritual realm and easily turn their anger to that medium is a good possibility. Women take on much of the social responsibility for speculation on the causes of misfortune, on medical remedies, and on estimates of just who is angry about what and what his or her range of power is.

Compared to the men, the expression of anger by Micmac women is less direct, although relative to many other societies, Micmac women would probably seem quite aggressively demonstrative and unafraid of conflict with their peers. Perhaps verbal identification with the respectable values of the ruling society adds a taint of suspicion to a woman's role. Certainly, a woman who acts with too much polite restraint needs to be watched as closely as any isolated hag.

The physical and supernatural powers of culture heroes, *ginaps,* and *buoins* are thematically satisfying to the Micmac because so much of their own existence is caught up with the testing of strength, with the endurance of the body and the will of the spirit. The larger society with which their community is associated is corporately and informally hostile to its survival, perhaps even more so as the expendability of unskilled labor seems imminent.[7] Micmac resources for survival lie squarely within the community, in individuals' fortitude and the human-scale organization of the group. It is no wonder then that, to stories about more remote eras, Micmac Indians add their own adventure stories which are, after all, claims to the same kinds of wonderful powers as those held by mythic personages.

To claim the special good luck of *keskamzit* is the prerogative of any Indian who overcomes the obstacles to survival which poverty inflicts. It is the most innocent boast, usually made by unassuming older people, and implies a special rapport with the dead. The following excerpt from my field notes ends with a classic evasion of the claim to more active access to the supernatural.

Noel Ginnish told me today that he's surprised he's lived as long as he has (63 years) because his "luck" was so special that he might have died just from having so much power. When he was young, he told me, he used to see ghosts. Before

[7] Sidney Wilhelm in *Who Needs the Negro* (New York, Schenkman, 1970) argues that the combination of racism and advanced technology makes Blacks as vulnerable to extinction as Indians were in the last century. My point is that American Indians participate in smaller numbers but with an equal liability in the present hostile system.

the local parish priest died, Noel saw his ghost walking down the road to the graveyard, going into it and picking out a place to lie down. Then it disappeared. Three days later the priest was dead and he was buried in that very spot, although no one knew it was going to be that spot because it was written in a letter to be opened when the priest died. Noel also saw his grandmother's ghost and he knew she was dead before the news came from Eskasoni. She was walking by the house in her nightgown and, since he was only a small child at the time and did not really understand his own power, he told her to go and get dressed. Then she disappeared and he had a very strange feeling about what had happened. Noel also was afraid of trains when he was young. His mother wanted to take him traveling on a train but he cried so much, she left him home. That train went off its tracks and people got hurt, but not Noel or his mother either. Once, when he was working in a fertilizer factory in the States, his boss told him he could go outside and smoke a cigarette for a few minutes. Noel had suddenly a terrible shaking feeling take over his body and he told the boss he would keep on working. About a minute later, a truck crashed into the wall just where Noel had the habit of taking his cigarette breaks. If he hadn't stayed in the factory, he surely would have been killed or injured. I asked Noel if he ever used his power against other people. He didn't answer. He just looked away.

Even a younger man than Noel would have evaded a direct admission of supernatural power. But he would have emphasized his own physical strength and courage more than just good luck. For men to take risks and dare to push situations to extremes is as important to Micmac survival as the women's gathering of information at the boundaries of the community. A man's physical prowess, fortitude, and even foolhardiness are appropriately extolled in storytelling sessions, whether on the reservation or off. The telling of each adventure is an education for the young into culturally approved aggression based on a spirited sense of one's individual power. There is an element of boasting involved in recounting adventures yet most of the stories are verified even before they become standard fare. Information about the exploits of men travels quickly among the Micmac so that, while a man is allowed some room for exaggeration, his audience is already acquainted with his story and only awaits being satisfied by the exciting details. Men in their prime of life are culture heroes in the sense that they live so close to the line that issues of power and vulnerability are constantly being tested. The issues and the tests are presented in contexts such as these field notes describe, at a time when a handsome young man from the city came to visit his sister's family on a reservation.

During the rainstorm this afternoon, most of the family, with the exception of Noel who was over at his grandmother's across the street, were sitting in the living room. Anne and Patrick were playing cards on the floor; Martin was out in the kitchen with his mother. I was teaching Carrie to knit while the dog kept jumping up on the couch and licking our hands. Uncle Eddie came in the back door and after talking with Louise (the mother of the household), he came in and sat down in one of the armchairs. He turned on the T.V. and then started to chat with me. As he began telling me about where he was living now in Boston, Louise drew one of the kitchen chairs up to the doorway between the kitchen and the living room to listen to what Eddie had to say. . . . In the course of his description he told this story about how he got the long scar on his scalp:

"Me and Elmer and these two girls were on a date. One of them was kind of big and heavy and dark. I didn't know her too well. This colored guy in the bar had it in for this girl. I don't know why. He said that she was a Lesbian. That made me and Elmer awfully mad. She was a White girl and we didn't know her that well but, even so, that was an insult to us. I went up to this colored guy and told him to fuck off. He was big. I'm almost six feet but he was bigger than me. He had some friends around. I just had to tell him off, no matter what. Then me and Elmer and the two girls was leaving the bar. The two girls was in front. I had the feeling they weren't so happy about the evening and were going to go home or something. Elmer was right in front of me. I was just going through the door when I got this bang on the head from behind. I didn't know what it was. I was so angry I didn't care. I turned around real quick and there was that sonofabitch colored guy with a big smile on his face. I was so angry I went for his throat with my two hands. I knocked him down and started beating his face with my fists. He was so surprised he hardly did anything. I went crazy. Elmer had to drag me off him before anything worse happened. I mean, he probably had friends all around who were going to wake up and jump on me. You know that fellow had hit me over the head with an old iron pipe. It was at least six inches around. All I knew was that I was angry. I leapt right back on that guy. You can ask Elmer. He took me over to Mass. General to get my head put back together. There was forty-two stitches. I told Elmer that if I saw that fellow again, I'd get him for good. As it was, I'm lucky to be here."

The most flamboyant stories men tell often seem related to the kinds of conflicts possible in a barroom setting or to the physical risks involved in driving a car. In the former, fights with non-Indians are most sensationally represented. In the latter, the danger shared by the group and their common Micmac *keskamzit* is given full play. The competitive conflicts which go on among Micmac men are de-emphasized in storytelling; there is talk about enmity but no thrill in a man's giving it a dramatic presentation. The social distance between an Indian and a Black, for example, functions in the present tense in the same way that time and place can function to structure a distance between a mythic event and its recitation. The narrator works to bring issues of competition and power from the racial boundaries of the network to the rest of the community. There are stories, too, about encounters with the police and about adventures in military service which are fundamentally concerned with risk-taking and which stress a great will to transcend physical vulnerability. The messages in these are similarly related to an understanding of how strangers to the community can be counted on to react towards the Micmac and, out of that understanding, how the community must defend itself.

The most dramatic claims to power a Micmac woman is likely to make have little to do with physical strength. Instead, unusual knowledge and power in the crucial areas of childbirth, disease, death, and ghosts makes up the content of a good contemporary tale. Ghost stories, like claims to good luck, allow the narrator a passive and innocent association with the supernatural. A ghost or *skadegamutc* will give direction for some action or by its appearance signify a coming event. Older men as well as women can easily get an audience for stories of their personal encounters with spirits. When it comes directly to the subject of physical vulnerability, claims to power have to be made with some subtlety, for the ability to do harm to others is implied in too much knowledge of how the human body is affected by spiritual energy. Nonetheless, the subject is approached. A benevolent competence is the easiest to claim, for example, that by a special combination of traditional herbs and aspirin, one has cured a boy of tuberculosis or stopped the prolonged bleeding of a woman after childbirth. Claim to an aggressive and punitive use of special knowledge is usually reserved for tales of conflict with non-Indians, in much the same way that the most dramatic physical competition occurs between a Micmac and a stranger. The following account from field notes has to do with a stormy relationship between a Micmac woman, Belinda, and a White man:

While Belinda and I were having coffee in the kitchen, before the children came home from school, she told me about how she "scared" her most recent boyfriend. She had a feeling that he was cheating on her, so she told him that if he went around balling anyone but her, he was going to come down with something terrible "right where it would hurt the most." Sure enough, before the week was up, he broke out with a terrible rash on his prick and balls. He went right away to the doctor who couldn't recognize it as any disease he knew. He gave him some penicillin that did no good at all. Then the boyfriend came to Belinda and begged for forgiveness. Belinda made him swear to be faithful but she wouldn't cure him right away. The rash was really painful but she wanted to make sure he knew who he was dealing with, "not just any bitch off the street." Then she told him a number of things to do to make the rash go away. He had to change the kind of shorts he was wearing (which were of all different colors) and wear only white ones, he had to take a bath every night for three nights in Ivory Snow and he had to put on plaster of wet leaves which Belinda gave him for the infected area. In three days, he was all cured. Frannie Harper came in as Belinda was finishing this tale. I asked her if this really happened. At first she said she didn't know anything about those things and gave Belinda a most reproving glance. Belinda countered that Frannie had powers of her own. Frannie, having fixed her own cup of coffee, admitted that she knew that if she wished evil on people, it often happened. In addition, she and Belinda both can tell when "a girl, any girl, is pregnant, even if it's only a few hours old."

All women have to live with their physical vulnerability, their embodiment, as it were, and the Micmac women directly approach this fact, embellish it with special knowledge, and dramatically present it to others. This is in contrast to the incidents men describe, which represent a searching after their own physical limits, which limits almost always are extraordinary. Perhaps women live with an immediate understanding of those limits and men must seek the contexts which will communicate their physicality back to them. In any case, images of power, interwoven with themes of conflict and cooperation, are perhaps the best visions for a Micmac man or woman to have in beginning the adult life of an urban Indian. Through a whole range of images, from traditional myths to contemporary accounts, the Micmac educate their own in a defensive set of values, one which emphasizes individual physical and spiritual strength within the context of the community. The actual testing of that strength and endurance starts in adolescence, in those first forays away from the family, and takes a lifetime to prove.

CHAPTER III

The Urban Tribal Network

About Jobs and Money

The kind of work history which a Micmac Indian accumulates over the course of a lifetime includes an enormous variety of jobs, all of them on the order of unskilled or semi-skilled labor. The jobs range from dirty-work to work requiring at least physical daring. Indian men and women commonly work for low-price restaurants and cafeterias where they wash dishes and floors, wait on tables, and clean up the trash which gets littered under tables, in the kitchen, and in the back alleys where garbage cans are stored. There are also jobs for the Micmac doing cleanup work for large institutions, such as hospitals and private industries which have incinerators that need tending, cafeteria floors that need washing, and various odd jobs that need to be done. In Boston, the lower levels of public institutional employment are fairly well preempted by those with contacts higher up in bureaucratic organizations, so that most janitors, for example, who take care of public buildings seem to be native Bostonians of Irish descent with relatives and friends in the city administration. Whatever jobs are beneath the concern of a janitorial staff, and these tasks are unequivocally dirty work, can fall to outsiders like the Micmac or to members of another minority group. In private industry, there is more opportunity to pick up work ranging from odd jobs to the factory assembly line. Factories in the greater Boston area have employed the Micmac to put together everything from door locks to curtain rods to the inner soles of sneakers and electronic equipment. Micmac men have sought out the heavy physical labor which industry still demands, such as warehouse truck-loading. Depending on what construction is going on in Boston, they will also try to apprentice themselves as painters or roofers or carpenters by appearing on a site with a direct request for work. The kind of training, formal and on-the-job, that it takes to become a skilled blue-collar worker is usually not available to the Micmac, unless the whim of a foreman or a union member permits it. Indians in Boston get some mileage out of being *bona fide* Native Americans. However, they take a great interpersonal risk in walking up to a group of White construction workers and asking for work. As the Micmac are aware, the Iroquois long ago cornered the American Indian high-steel construction market and presently have union status few Micmac enjoy. Nonetheless, with no claim to a special "human fly" disregard of heights, Mic-

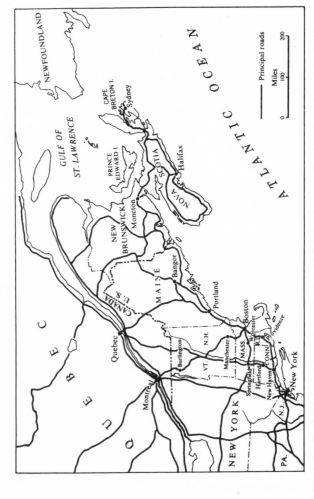

Map 2. *The Urban Turf of Contemporary Micmac Indians*. Rather than being confined to reservations, today's Micmac community extends from the Canadian Maritimes to industrial centers in New England and Canada.

mac men have worked on both the Prudential and John Hancock buildings and other skyscrapers in Boston at floor levels and vantage points above which insurance companies refuse coverage. Their pay, which sometimes went as high as seventy dollars a day, was earned by sheer courage.

Individual Indians with the same spirit of adventure will latch on to unusual jobs which provide the source material for good stories. One man went out west to join the rodeo circuit although he had never been on a horse in his life; he was just curious to see the America that Indians were most associated with and, in the process, he met an assortment of Sioux and Navaho and other Indian people, none of whom he got along with or liked. Another Micmac man became for a time the bodyguard of a wealthy man in Philadelphia who had been convinced by a medium that he needed an Indian around for good luck. One woman traveled south to Florida because she had been shown pictures of its beaches and palm trees and was curious to see them with her own eyes. She drove her car part of the way until it broke down in Maryland and then rode buses and hitchhiked the rest of the journey. When she got to Fort Lauderdale, she picked out the biggest hotel she could see and successfully offered herself as a housemaid to earn money for a bus ticket back to Boston. Another woman, with a girlfriend, decided to see Las Vegas for just about the same reason and in just about the same way made her way to Nevada and took a job as a waitress to finance her return trip.

In addition to the variety of work situations in

which an individual Micmac can be found, the interim
between one job and another can vary greatly. This is so
partly because the economic scene changes. In June the
cheap labor market becomes flooded with young people
out of school. In the winter construction tends to slow
down. And there are national economic recessions and
depressions which hit hardest the people who are most
economically expendable, the poor and minority groups
who all seem so alike, so interchangeable, and so insig-
nificant. When strikes or lay-offs occur in industry, the
first people to lose their wages are those who, like the
Micmac, are generally without union protection and
work at the level of cheap industrial labor.

There are other reasons why a Micmac work history
will have both variety and random interims between
jobs. One of these has to do with the nature of work at
the fringes of industry.

In his book *Socialization and Social Class,* Alan
Kerckhoff typifies the kind of work available to the poor:

Such jobs require no particular intellectual effort, but they do
require conformity to externally imposed specification. The
worker is told what to do, how to do it, and when to do it. He
is neither required nor permitted to use his own judgment, nor
is the quality of interpersonal relations on the job seen as rele-
vant to getting the work done.[1]

The kind of work which the Micmac ordinarily do
requires a real subjugation to industrial goals. There is
no intrinsic value to the work being demanded, whether

[1] Alan C. Kerckhoff, *Socialization and Social Class,* Englewood Cliffs,
New Jersey, Prentice-Hall, 1972, p. 179.

it is washing a cafeteria floor or working on an assembly line. The laborer is valuable only for the contribution he makes towards someone else's enterprise or towards the life of a corporation. The personal initiative and sociability in which a Micmac is trained has really no value in his work setting, so that, as in approaching a public institution, an Indian usually has to mask his real self and hope to escape with his pride intact. Walking on girders twenty stories high is a sufficiently dangerous and well-paid job to make it interesting. For a woman, waiting on tables puts her in contact with other people in a way that reduces the drudgery of work, provided she too has the kind of personality which thrives on the risks that come out of dealing with strangers. The tedium of a job, more than how dirty it gets one's fingernails, is the hardest for the Micmac to take. Aversion to tedium, the ups and downs of the market, and inexperience basically account for the variety in Indian work histories.

For example, Eveline, Maureen Paul's cousin, came to Boston in 1966 when she was nineteen. She had already done cleanup work in a hospital in Halifax and heard through her brother that a hospital in the city had advertised for cafeteria help. The job never materialized, but when Eveline arrived in the city, she found work in a commercial cafeteria, preparing food and doing after hours cleaning. Her boss told her she was too slow at her work and fired her after several weeks. This depressed her somewhat and so she returned to the reservation for about a month before trying to get another job. When she got back to Boston, a relative told her about work that was available in a curtain factory in

Quincy. Eveline put off going to ask about the job until she was really in need of money. After about two months, she left for New York with her boyfriend, leaving Boston, the curtain factory, and Maureen and her friends behind. In another six weeks, Eveline re-emerged at her brother's place in the South End and in a few days found herself another factory job. By 1969, she had gone through two years and eight work situations in the city. Her philosophy:

I'll take the money when the money is good. I don't turn down no work I can get. I lead my own life. I need the money for that.

Most Micmac Indians try to avoid working alone at new jobs. Having a friend along, even if he or she is stationed in another part of the factory or given another task to perform makes work much more social and much more bearable. The Micmac bring their way of impassively observing new situations to each job and usually remain outsiders to the general social interaction that helps more numerous groups, Whites, Blacks, and Puerto Ricans, find their employment tolerable. Having been brought up to value both individual initiative and group cooperation, the Micmac seldom find their best social selves in working for cash. Many Micmac have the courage to put themselves into unfamiliar situations where a foreman's Boston accent is difficult to understand (as theirs may be to him), where the details of the work are new to them, and where there are many strangers around. Eddie Park, who came to Boston in 1967, described his first job experience this way:

A friend of mine had a job in this place that made machine parts. He told me one day that there was a job for me too. I went over and I signed the paper to ask for the job. I had to stand at this belt and fit two parts together and the guy next to me would do something else to it. I never got it too clear what the thing turned out to be. I think it was used in elevators. There was a lot of noise. I could go for a smoke break but not everyone there spoke English. There were French-Canadians and Puerto Ricans, a lot of them. There was a supervisor who told me what to do and he'd walk around checking up on what everyone was up to. Sometimes he'd come up and say something to me. I couldn't understand him all the time and I'd wonder if I done something wrong or what. I felt like one of the old people but I don't have no trouble with English. He just talked fast and went away. What the hell. The noise of the machines would still be in my head, hammering away.

In a similar vein, Annie Pictou, a young woman who came to Boston in 1968 when she was twenty, told of one of her jobs:

My girlfriend Patsy told me about this plastic factory where her cousin was working. I took myself over and landed up working in this big building, in the part where the cutters were, with them machines squeaking and squawking the whole damn day. I was living with two girlfriends at the time, right here in Boston. I'd get on the MTA every day and ride over to Revere. But I just couldn't take that shit. It was a long ride. The work had me going. I'd just get up every morning and run right off. I thought I'd have a nervous breakdown. I really almost did.

Sustaining the motivation to keep at work frequently seems too great a personal price to pay for the money earned. When the factory situation becomes so dehumanized that the machines seem bigger than the people who run them and human priorities are lost, the old urban nightmare of the nineteenth century would seem to persist in Boston's industrial-age factories. If we look again at Kerckhoff's description of the kind of job available to the unskilled, it is similar on some levels to most white-collar work, the point being that standardization, whether in a factory or in an office, reduces human priorities to a minimum. This is important to understand if one is trying to make any sense out of the common reality shared by different groups in this country and make intelligent comparisons as well. The corporate manager works to abstract specifications, his behavior is ordered by the tasks of his office, and his individual integrity and efficiency always has priority over on-the-job interpersonal relations.

Speaking generally, the real difference between factory work and managerial work is that the latter is an abstraction of the former. It has security, is better paid, bestows status, and supports corporate goals. The successful bureaucrat, in fact, merges his private and working life so as to become totally public, totally at ease with institutional values because they are his own. The abstract level at which institutions operate makes this kind of identification dangerous, for it is often impossible to see the corporate machine, to sense how indirectly one is affected, and to feel the extent of dehumanization which organizational goals can demand. In most small factory settings, such as those the Micmac work in, the message is clear: human beings are expendable. It is signified in grey walls, a broken soft drink machine, deafening noise, a strict schedule, and an institutional indifference to the fate of individual workers. It might be argued that some institutions are kinder than others, yet it is in the nature of corporate structures to subvert all ends, including human ones, to the end of self-perpetuation. To control this tendency, every bureaucracy requires human vigilance. The employees' lounge might be cheerfully decorated and the retirement benefits might be generous while the corporation, like a machine in the abstract, grows larger than the people who run it and strays farther and farther away from the human services it was designed to perform efficiently.

What, then, is the real difference between managerial work and the work available to the poor? The decision-making powers and autonomy we associate with a good job are scarcely to be found in this society of almost total incorporation. It is increasingly difficult in government and in private industry to find out who, if anyone, has power and the responsibility which goes with it. Power, it seems, rests more and more in the corporate body on which individuals rely and to which they are subject. Realistically speaking, the individual white-collar worker is likely to be as subjugated by a dehumanizing system as an Indian gluing furniture on an assembly line. He will, however, be better paid for his time and energy and, in trading loyalty for security and status, be less aware of and more susceptible to institutional standardization and routine. The Micmac and others who are outsiders to the system get only money for their work and less of it than the managerial class. The factory or restaurant or public building within which they find employment is always someone else's turf. Routinization and standards of efficiency always exist for the benefit of the institution and those who serve it. Efficient with his own energies, a Micmac invests less of his private self in work and will act on gut, physical reactions to a job to protect that private and, at the same time, very tribal identity.

As an outsider the individual Indian is almost immune to the confusion of personal and institutional goals. When routinization threatens to make a machine out of him, he quits his job, even when, from a conventional point of view, he cannot possibly afford to. As more than simply an economic unit, his primary responsibility is to keep himself a viable member of his community. Work which requires his or her own mechanization, and work in which there is little socializing with other Indians, is only tolerable for short periods of time.

It is important to remember that the fact of economic marginality does not suddenly dawn on a Micmac Indian after two or three years of shifting from one job to another and from being employed to being unemployed. For generations the Micmac have dealt with being positioned as outsiders denied the compensations of economic security and social status in the great society. Yet, looking at a single work history, which looks like a string of jobs randomly spaced through the course of a life, it is almost impossible to perceive any definite pattern of employment. This is so because the economic strategy of the Micmac is communal and cannot be understood except as an aspect of their culture. It has sought to maximize the multiple compensations which come out of human interaction. The effect of this has been to keep economics in its proper social context, embedded in rules of human responsibility and cooperation. The amount of time spent on a job and the interim between one job and another is determined by social imperatives. Kin must be responsible to kin and friend to friend. Socializing, contests and conflicts, and communications of all kinds must continue. Out of the social activity of the community comes its solution to economic marginality.

The general socializing that goes on within the Micmac community allows several important economic functions to be fulfilled. First of all, communication about jobs is always circulated through the network. Men and women alike are consistently curious about who is working where, although each sex handles giving out the details of employment and job opportunities in a different way. A Micmac man, for example, is much freer with information about the wages he or his friends are getting than a woman, who will tend to be more competitive with those facts, sharing them only with the relatives and friends to whom she feels committed. Similarly, when there is a job opening, a woman will spare herself no pains in getting the news to a younger sibling or to a close friend. Men tend to hear more about new work because they are relatively more involved in being on the market but also because they are basically uncompetitive about economic information. If they run into a son or nephew or see a daughter or former girlfriend, they will spontaneously relay news about jobs where they work or where their buddies work. Men expect and usually get the same openness from each other.

Second, if women are more selective in passing on job information, they are also more predictable in their determination to provide themselves with allies when they go to work. A Micmac man might boldly walk into a warehouse or factory and ask for a job and even occasionally a woman will go alone to a diner and ask to be employed as a waitress, but it is much more typical for a Micmac woman to try to make applying for work and being on the job a joint endeavor. Information about a factory job is not simply passed along to a younger sister; the two women will go to the job site together, helping each other in filling out forms, and probably stay on the job for the same length of time. If they can, they will try to have another woman or two they know work at the same place. Men do more of the risky investigative work involved in finding new jobs and yet they, too, prefer to work in teams, especially as a means by which more experienced workers teach novices the ropes. Formal requirements, such as filling out an application sheet, understanding the schedule which orders work, knowing where to get coffee or eat lunch or pick up a paycheck and get it cashed are simple issues only to those who have gone through the paces themselves and it often helps a newcomer to have experienced fellow Micmac from whom to take cues. The emphasis on the value of human interaction which is characteristic of the Micmac community functions to produce a spill-over from the social network into the job situation, easing the debut of a young person as a wage-earner and generally acting to humanize work.

To note a third function, it would be almost impossible for the Micmac to survive if their homes were not open to each other. Child care in private homes is an economic service which few parents of any group can afford to purchase outright. To have the security of knowing that one's child is being taken care of by one's own kind, by people who, as members of the community, have a vested interest in his well-being is a service beyond purchase. In addition, Micmac adults mutually oblige each other with extra beds and couches, sometimes expecting remuneration, very often not. The longer a visitor stays with a household, the more he or she will be expected to make a direct contribution to it out of wages. The debt incurred by accepting hospitality, however, is never settled by money. Instead, a similar favor is expected in the future which, in turn, incurs a debt of service.

To give an illustration from one man's history, "Bear" Knockwood came to the States in 1957 at age sixteen to work in a factory in Maine, where he lived in the home of a cousin of his whose husband worked in the same factory. Bear gradually made his way down to Boston to another household, that of his mother's younger sister. He did some odd jobs around the Boston waterfront and could not seem to find any better work. Through one of his friends he heard of a new chemical plant outside of Boston that was looking for workers. With the help of a twenty-dollar loan from his aunt, he drove with three other men and two women to the town where the plant was. For about four months, Bear roomed with a sister of one of his friends who was also employed at the factory. Over the next five years, passing through various job situations but remaining pretty close to Boston, he was in a position to reciprocate the favors he himself had received from his cousin, his aunt, and his friend's sister. Both of Bear's relatives had teen-age sons who turned to him for help when they were looking for their first jobs. Bear was directly instrumental in getting one work as a repairman for the city's transportation department. The other he "adopted" as a traveling partner, sharing rides to other towns offering jobs and to Maine for the blueberry and potato-picking seasons in the early 1960s. When his friend's sister decided she wanted to move her family back into Boston, Bear made arrangements for her dependents to room with his girlfriend until she could find an apartment of her own. In numerous other ways, the first favors extended to Bear when he was young have been returned, and a new chain of mutual obligations has begun with every move to another job, communication of news about a job, or extension of hospitality.

It would almost be as difficult for the Micmac to earn money without sharing transportation as it would be if places to live in Boston and other towns were unavailable. They rely on each other for rides to get from the Maritimes to the city and, while there is work available in the general area of the South End, they maximize their chances of earning money by extending the tribal network and its system of communication to other, smaller industrial centers. It is very rare to find a single Micmac riding alone in his or her car. Relatives and friends have the right to ask for a lift for distance of anywhere from two blocks to seven hundred miles, and the owner of the car can, as in other social situations, expect to have the cost of gas, oil, tolls, and repairs (if the car should break down on the road), shared by his passengers. There is considerable expertise on the subject of cars to be found among the Micmac, so that someone like Bear, for example, who it seems spent most of his reservation adolescence under the hood of a car, often gives maintenance and repair service in return for transportation.

In addition to the economic importance of the automobile, the Micmac invest it with an important social significance. In the sparsely populated Maritimes as well as in urban New England, having a car or good access to one is a mark of admirable style. An automobile lets one travel around, see people, do things. It does not really matter what it looks like as far as body condition; dents and rust are considered incidental to the ability of a car to operate well and for a long time. What is fundamental is the size of the car. An automobile is meant to take a lot of people on a lot of trips in and around the city and back and forth across the Northeast, so a small car just will not do. The layout and public transportation in Boston being what it is, it is equally important to have a car if one is going to remain in contact with one's fellow Micmac who reside outside the core city. The interpersonal network of most Micmac Indians is so dispersed that it requires travel from the Maritimes to Boston, from Boston to secondary centers and smaller groupings of Indians in Worcester, Springfield, Leominster, and Portland, and then travel back again up to the Provinces to insure frequent communication between its members. This communication does take place, not because any one individual is constantly on the move, but because most Micmac individuals between the ages of nineteen and thirty-nine are involved in a life style which alternates between moving around for several weeks and setting up camp, as it were, for several months. Older and more settled Micmac men and women are also good letter-writers, and will take the time to pass on news or gossip to relatives far away. Within the city, anyone who is comfortable enough to have a telephone often receives and transmits information about a whole assortment of other Micmac to and from Indians who have only a pay phone at their disposal. Face-to-face interaction is more desirable than letters and telephone calls, which have their limits as far as assuring the rest of the community, and in particular the family, that one is an interested and participating member. For this, having a car is especially important.

To be without a car is to miss all the socializing which goes on among people in dispersed areas. Sometimes it also means that one's peer group lacks an effective retaliatory weapon. One day in the summer of 1970, a car full of belligerent local White teenagers stopped by a small Indian settlement in the Maritimes and, leaning out of the car windows, announced that they had come for the "squaws." A handful of Micmac boys began pelting them with rocks and succeeded in chasing them away. Nonetheless, the chagrin of these young reservation Indians was enormous because they were still too young to have a car of their own. They could only contemplate the joy of trapping their foes in one of the back roads of the reservation and giving them their just deserts. One of the most common sights on a reservation is a group of five or six adolescents working on a car to get it in running condition, not only because it is their ticket to economic viability, but because it is also a mark of their social status and the means to a reputation. Anyone who owns a car inevitably has its descriptive details associated with him and a lot of interest centered on the fact of ownership. There is a constant commentary on the order of the following:

"You know Frankie, he's got that blue Impala, '65." "Pull over, I think I just saw Henry's car. Isn't that Henry's Biscayne with the busted-up back fender?" "Ellie's picked herself up a new car, a 1959 station wagon, Ford. She's coming right over to take us for a ride." "What kind of car do *you* have?"

The Micmac, both men and women, drive with a real appreciation of the risk taken by getting into a powerful machine and navigating roads full of other people similarly armed. There are, after all, some superhuman aspects of commanding a great engine, of being motorized. The potential for great speed with a minimum of exertion is a thrill which is not lost on the Micmac. With the kind of older car most of them drive, they seldom forget the mechanical basis of that thrill and are constantly reminded of it by weary batteries, worn out carburetors, mufflers precariously wired to the underside of the car, and misfiring pistons. Both men and women, but men more than women, confront the danger inherent in driving a car and boast of the brush with annihilation experienced in careening down a midnight country road or over a super highway. For example, Richie Gabriel, his friend Popeye, and two other men were driving in central Massachusetts when their car lurched out of control, rolled over twice, and landed upright with two of its wheels only an inch or so from the edge of a deep ditch. Fortunately, none of the men had more than a few bruises. The story of their near-miss has been told over and over again with other dramatic accounts of the same kinds of adventures. Like Richie and his friends, the survivors always count themselves particularly lucky and therefore particularly powerful people. The acceleration allowed by a car has its fascination and, as with drinking and fighting, pushing the boundaries of experience too forcefully and too frequently results in death for the unlucky.

Between taking risks and dealing with mechanical failures, the Micmac do an enormous amount to humanize the experience of traveling in a way which is totally congruent with their culture. Not only do groups rather than individuals ride together, but the privilege of doing the actual driving is shared on short and long trips alike. To travel with great purpose from one destination to another is almost an impossibility because of the priorities put on social interaction. Five people might hear of work in Worcester and, in making what is an hour's journey from Boston directly west to Worcester, will take a whole day of side excursions to visit friends along the way, adding new members to their party and losing others. There is always reason to stop to eat and drink, or someone will have to relieve himself or herself by the side of the road. En route, people keep talking, mostly about other people. Or, if the journey is long, country-and-western songs with their themes of heart-break and of the pain and excitement of always "movin' on" will obliterate the need for talk. The automobile, in addition to being a vehicle for traveling from one place to another, is used for spontaneous diversions from the straight path to a given destination, so that it is subject both to the economic ends and the social ends of the group.

Money, like the automobile, is subject to the social values of the Micmac community. Access to it through working for a cash wage is strongly affected by friend-ship and family ties. The Micmac will just as soon leave a job as take it, according to what their feelings about the rightness of the social situation dictate. If two or more Indians prefer to work on a job together, the de-parture of one of them can also motivate the others to leave work. Sickness or death, a wedding or a baptism, is sufficient cause to make a Micmac Indian disappear from a job site, especially if the labor required is drudg-ery. Sometimes it can be just a feeling that he or she should return to the reservation. There are older people there, children who are growing up, men and women who in their inability or refusal to travel represent the more traditional, rural roots of the Micmac. On the res-ervation one is surrounded by the familiar and is, in a sense, on furlough from the battle of urban living.

Even as the Micmac are expendable, cheap labor on the job market, they often return an employee's lack of commitment for an employer's indifference, countering the solely profit-making ends of an enterprise with their community's social goals. There must be legions of White employers who, when faced with a black-haired, black-eyed, brown-skinned Indian, hired someone else or hired him only as a last resort and only for temporary work. The individual Micmac cannot change his economically marginal position by acting like a career man when, in overalls and a flannel shirt, he is hauling garbage or loading trucks. Instead, he works only to get money and does not waste his time and energy lavishing loyalty on work which renders him no security. It would be impossible for the Micmac to survive in urban society if money (like information on work, places to stay, and transportation) were not shared. A man or woman can obey the impulse to leave work, shifting attention from earning money to investing time and energy in the community, precisely because the basic economic strategy of the tribe is communal. The constant facilitation of access to work allows an individual to drop out and even absorbs the impact of his or her being fired. In addition, money is diffused, particularly through the generosity of men who, in order to gain a good reputation, are expected to be free with the wages they earn. A Micmac man can scarcely control when he will earn money and how much he will earn. With a certain fatalism, he refuses to hoard today's gain because there is no predicting tomorrow's feast or famine. His current woman or wife is going to put immediate pressures on him to give her money for food and rent and the children's needs. His mother and sisters, if he should visit them, expect presents and he also gains prestige by playing the role of the beneficent uncle to his sisters' children. A man is never more a man, however, than when he spends his money on good times for other Indians, a seeming luxury which is actually an investment in the community itself, yielding many times its cost in social solidarity. It is such men who make a great display on payday of buying drinks in a bar, or who pay for the food and liquor that make a Christmas gathering or a reunion on the reservation a feast for many. The money a man has in his wallet on a Friday can turn a whole weekend into a party. He adds to his reputation by this generosity and, as the community shares in his plenty, its morale and optimism are revived because one of its own has done well.

Peter Maloney, who spent about ten years at odd jobs, at last in 1970 found lucrative construction work. He treated his good fortune like a windfall and spent his first paycheck in a South End bar. As he expressed his sentiments at the time:

What's the money? The money is to spend, ain't it. If I got it in my hand, it's goin' go right through, it won't stop. So I'm making sure all the time I got it, it goes for good times. I get a Friday check and I'm poor on Sunday. You wanna know why? 'Cause I'm gonna buy whiskey and I'm gonna have everybody drink with me. I don't buy women. The women'll be there. As sure as hell, that money will go.

His exaltation was short-lived when, after only a few months on the job, an economic recession forced a slowdown in construction work and Peter was fired. But he had his moment.

The generosity of men and the prestige they get from lavish spending is complemented in turn by the pecuniary vigilance of Micmac women who are more directly responsible for mundane household expenses and weigh more closely the cost of good times against domestic needs. The woman who is managing a reservation household with many children in it has the most dour reaction to the spendthrift ways of men. Her interest is specifically the endurance of her menage. She depends a great deal on remittances from the city, the amount and periodicity of which are out of her control, and on the sense of responsibility to household needs felt by her husband and other men associated with her home, a responsibility which she unrelentingly demands. In the city, a woman, although usually responsible for rent and other costs of maintaining a place to live, is also likely to have fewer dependents and more adults helping with expenses. Consequently, she puts no damper on a party. After a week of doing her share of work, she puts her paycheck towards more mundane bills and enjoys whatever celebration a man or several men can stage.

Living precariously at the edge of the economy, it is an interesting social statement when the Micmac invest their money in one sensationally good bash. They celebrate their own existence in the face of brutal poverty, in the face of a society which, if it did not succeed in exterminating them, did not fail from trying. There is more optimism than fatalism in spending rather than hoarding money and, in watching a Micmac party in progress, one cannot help but be reminded of the "festins à tout manger" which their ancestors, already beleaguered by European intrusion, held hundreds of years ago. The

Micmac community now, as then, performs in ways which seem like madness to White observers precisely because the goal of their Indian behavior is communal, not individualized. When the Micmac of the seventeenth century feasted on their total supply of game, they praised the skill of the hunters who provided for the band and as a community rejoiced in their survival at that point in time. The spirit of solidarity they gained must have stood them in good stead, for they continued to survive when even the most diligent conservation of food would not have deterred the impending force of colonial expansion. The Micmac man with money to spend has power only for the moment, whether he chooses to save it or share it; his economic marginality is a structural fact which no amount of individual parsimony can change. In terms of his own morale and feelings of worth and well-being, he can make no better expenditure than on a celebration with people who make up the social context of his life, the people who have the power to give him a good reputation.

The Micmac prefer to put their money towards a good experience more than towards the purchase of things and would rather have their good times in the present tense than save for the uncertain future. For example, most of the furnishing of a city room or apartment has been handed around from one Indian to another. If a man or woman dies outside the reservation, the body will be shipped back to the Maritimes for burial, and bed, clothes, and personal effects will be distributed among family and friends as need and convenience dictate. One woman in her sixties, having made up her mind to retire to a reservation in Nova Scotia after living many years in Boston, took a small satchel of clothes, a few china dishes, and a patchwork quilt that her Dutch mother had sewn and distributed the furniture from her small apartment to her younger relatives. A couch, which no one seemed to need, she sold to a Micmac woman from New Brunswick for ten dollars. She reduced her small stock of possessions without regret, commenting that she would have to requisition a bed through the Indian agency when she arrived down home, a strategy for acquiring furniture which she, like most Micmac, never learned to use on local welfare departments.

The disinterest in owning and maintaining property, which is apparent on the reservations, is just as apparent in the city, where in many ways the clear-cut dispossession of the Indians is more fully evident. A reservation, for all its tarpaper shacks and dirt roads, is still Indian property, and this fact can deceive an observer into forgetting that, in an age of urban industrialism, having remote acreage and no capital cannot possibly change the cheap-labor function of a people like the Micmac. The reservation functions as an outpost and a haven from the urban scene where the adult battle for survival really takes place. In either place, Indians must be with other Indians, constantly involved in a network of social relations, often on the move, keeping the network of communications alive by circulating over time and space. This business of socializing is more important than property ownership, and the mobility it requires makes investment in material things like furniture more burdensome than profitable. Men are always on the move and are content as long as they can find shelter when and where they need it. Women have more of an urge to decorate the places they rent but even they have to be flexible enough to move themselves and their households around.

Even a most sedate Micmac woman, one of the first Micmac Indians I met, had to move herself and her three dependents four times between 1968 and 1971, either to get a better deal on rent, or to be closer to a job site, or because there was conflict between one of her children and his White classmates. Women decorate their temporary homes with photographs, souvenirs, and little knick-knacks which can be easily packed into a cardboard box or shopping bag. They hold on to the essentials of beds, tables, and chairs when they move but personal and purely functional possessions are kept to a minimum. In addition to the photos hung in frames or pinned to a wall, most Micmac women accumulate a great many snapshots which are kept in old shoe boxes or cookie tins. Few have any dates or names written on the back to identify the people who were photographed. It takes the woman who collected this store of memorabilia to organize it and present it as a chronicle of her own life. The faces that stare solemnly back from pictures of boarding school pottery classes, wartime shipyards, logging camps, the front stairs of reservation houses, car windows, and country fairs—these faces are dead and lost images to the outside observer until the woman who owns them supplies her narrative. The parents, sisters, brothers, boyfriends, girlfriends, and children represented are perfectly real to her; she is the only one who can see past the picture to the life from which the image is abstracted.

Micmac women and men dress in Boston much as they do in the Maritimes, with an emphasis on the functional rather than on the fashionable. The men wear drably colored work clothes of heavy cotton, occasionally don a plaid flannel shirt, and weather the winter in woolen lumber jackets, with sweaters or an insulated workman's vest underneath. Their shoes vary from heavy leather boots which tie just above the ankle to inexpensive black plastic men's shoes of the kind that can be gotten at a discount store. An older man usually has his best blue suit folded away in a box in his room for use on a special occasion such as a funeral (even his own) or a wedding. Younger men consider it a sufficient effort to put on a tie for a dress-up event. Young women pay the most attention to fashion and style and will buy more clothes than any other group. Yet they wear only simple cotton slacks (never dungarees) and brightly colored sweaters for much of the year and will make inexpensive clothing—dresses, shoes, coats—last through as many years and as many relatives as possible. Older women will wear the same kind of plain cotton housedress from one year to the next, and in the colder months put on the same type of heavy, functional coats and jackets as their men.

Anyone studying the importance of machismo and reputation among other urban minority groups (not only American Blacks and Spanish-Americans but urban migrants in Europe, Africa, and South America) must give important consideration to the way in which men and women dress themselves and must finally ask the question, "For what audience or audiences are the people dressed?" It is noted over and over again in the literature on Caribbean and Mediterranean cultures that a flamboyant sense of style in clothes and the obvious expense of silk shirts, alligator shoes, and custom-designed hats are part of the social presentation of a man of good reputation. This style is appreciated by others in the same group but it is a presentation of self which is often also directed to the wider society, communicating both a nonconventional understanding of dress and a consumer status which flies in the face of poverty. American Blacks, with a long history of direct subjugation by White society, have made an art of the high style of social presentation. The more public the occasion and the more coverage guaranteed by the media, the more aggressively is their dress fashioned and the more blatant the fact of its cost. When a trio of Black singers appears on television or when the crowd at a Muhammed Ali fight is covered by the news, dress is in the imperative mood, commanding attention to the fact that whatever happens tomorrow, each performer has gotten it together tonight, defeating oppression and poverty in a stylish flash. There is a special wit to Black performance. Its emphasis on conspicuous consumption fairly collides with the fleeting nature of public performance, irritating most of those who believe that money should give one a hold on immortality. Because conventional notions of what to do with money emphasize the accumulation of capital and property as security for the

future, wealth is often used as if it could purchase tomorrow. The Black who drives a Cadillac or sports an
ermine coat is frowned at by Whites for not being more
sensible with his money, yet he is conscious of the truth
that the present tense, not the future, is where we are
living.

When W. E. B. DuBois, in *The Souls of Black Folk*,
wrote of a Negro "double-consciousness, this sense of
always looking at one's self through the eyes of others,"
he was describing a public notion of self which the Micmac, as an ethnic group early isolated from the dominant society, do not generally have. Their double invisibility, as reservation Indians and as urban migrants,
has worked to make them more aware of being Indians
than of being seen as Indians and this is reflected in the
plainness of their dress. As individuals, they do not decorate themselves any more than they would bank their
earnings in order to accrue capital. Their understanding
of what to do with money is, instead, shaped by tribal
needs. A Micmac in the prime of his or her life, physically strong and with ready cash, is a consumer who
divides money between the basic essentials of clothes,
food, and shelter and the dispersal of money by giftgiv-
ing and celebrations. There are sanctions against hoarding money and there are sanctions against making great
expenditures on such nonessentials as clothes in the lat-
est fashion, a car that looks too fine to use, or furniture
that is too precious to withstand human use. The Micmac neither convert money into property, nor do they
parody, as Blacks do, the vain attempts of the dominant
society to do the impossible, i.e., to purchase immortal-

ity with cash. Their earnings and their energies are instead concentrated on the tribal community. By responding to its present needs for basic necessities and good morale, they ultimately insure its continuity.

The City As Adventure

The industrial buildup engendered by World War II marks the beginning of the most contemporary phase of American Indian participation in urban economics. Starting in the early 1940s, Indians from Western tribes were drawn in large numbers to Los Angeles, San Francisco, and Chicago; numerically smaller Eastern tribes likewise sent their people to New York, Montreal, and Boston. The Micmac, like the Iroquois and northeastern Indians, responded to industrial expansion by extending the perimeters of their community to include cities. Boston, as the largest and most diversified employment market in New England, attracted and continues to attract many Micmac Indians from the western and southern reaches of the Maritimes, an area in good proximity to New England and linked to it by a common history of White settlement. The Irish and Scotch immigrants who came to Nova Scotia and New Brunswick in the nineteenth century had fellow countrymen by the thousands in New England.

The eighteenth-century migration of Tories to Nova Scotia and the British recruitment of New England farmers to settle the land vacated by the French Acadians produced almost a recreation of colonial American society on Canadian soil. During the latter part of the nineteenth century, the arrival in the Northeast of Irish immigrants and "two-boaters," those who arrived in Boston after having stopped and worked for wages in Halifax, increased the ethnic similarity between New England and the Maritimes. Even though they cross an international border to come to New England, the Micmac stay within a region where the dominant language, English, is the same as it is generally in the reservation area. The physical appearance and the behavior of the dominant society basically remains the same; that is, a second or third generation Irish or Scotch-Irish population is conspicuously in evidence on both sides of the border. When the Micmac meet welfare workers or policemen in Boston or in the Maritimes, the chances are very good that most of them, regardless of national allegiance, will speak English and be descendents of immigrants from the British Isles. In the same way, the local folk of the Maritimes and the city folk of much of residential Boston share the same European heritage, the physique and habits of peasant agriculturalists whose individualism and sense of patriarchal authority allow a strong identification with corporate goals, even when political and economic institutions turn on them or exclude them.

The relationship which the Micmac tribe has had with French settlers in the Maritimes has been, at least in the more remote northeastern section, more amicable and influenced by the fact that the French, like the Indians, are a political minority in eastern Canada. The common outsidership of French Canadians and Indians is less apparent in urban areas, however, where French institutions—economic, political, and social—paralleling those of the dominant English-speaking population have arisen and some access to rule is possible. For this reason, the journey of a French-speaking Micmac from a rural settlement in New Brunswick to a bilingual city like Montreal is a socially complex transition. The fact of being Indian puts him or her at the bottom of the pile, for the French Canadians are, after all, White men. If the Micmac speaks only French and not English as a second language, he bears part of the discrimination which exists towards French-Canadians, in addition to being discriminated against for being an Indian. There is no particular hope that French-Canadians in the city will be his allies for, as they become politicized, the ethnic differences between themselves and other groups are emphasized and French solidarity works against other minorities, not simply the British. So it is that an Indian can be refused a job in a French-run factory because he is non-White and refused a job in an English-run factory because he is an Indian who speaks French. Many Indians I spoke to during the course of field work nonetheless included Montreal and Ottawa as way stations in their travels. The presence of other Indian tribes—Iroquois, Montagnais, Cree, and others—in both cities was a source of irritation rather than common cause. The Micmac, when they come to a city, generally operate with a sense of their own tribal solidarity, without embracing the abstract notion of pan-Indianism. They distrust the Iroquois and will cite historic reasons for their enmity. They consider western tribes inferior and do not care to associate with them. Closer to home, the Micmac generally distinguish between themselves and their neighbors, the Malecite and the Penobscot, but are sufficiently close in language and customs as to allow more or less friendly relations. There is some intermarriage between all three tribes. The Micmac, however, are very careful to stipulate when, by common residence or by legal marriage, one of their own has crossed the tribal boundary to join another group. It is considered a rare and rather unfortunate occurrence, as if one's son or daughter had taken up with a cripple.

The preference the Micmac have for their own culture is most explicitly stated when the different others in question are other Indian tribes. In an urban scene, for example, when several Micmac men find themselves in a bar with several Iroquois, the Micmac will not hesitate to irritate their ancient foes with loudly-stated insults and to provoke physical combat. As the largest Indian group in Boston, they are most aggressive on this, their own turf, to Indians who come in from the western mainland.

It is very difficult to be critical of the ethnocentrism of the Micmac because it is a fundamentally defensive stand. They have no ambitions to impose their way of living on others, as correct as they believe it is, because their culture, what makes them Micmac, cannot be abstracted from them and spread to others. The tribe can adopt a few strays from other groups but only to a very limited degree. Like *Gluscap*, the Micmac culture proved unable to incorporate Western expansion and still defends itself against outsiders.

Geographic proximity and a recognizable, almost familiar dominant population have influenced Boston's becoming a major center of the Micmac population. The crucial difference between the precolonial situation of the Micmac and their contemporary one is that they and not the White settlers have become the immigrants. The change of roles is more than a simple reversal, for the Micmac, like many other Indians, have little motivation to colonize the places to which they travel. Their tribal notions of property, including land, make them individually disinterested in territorial expansion and resistant to settling down. Even the reservation settlement called home will be used by an adult Micmac as a stopover. The expression "to put down one's roots" comes out of a European agricultural tradition foreign to mobile tribal groups such as the Micmac, whose migration is a continual journey.

The nomadic, tribal aspect of Micmac culture affects their approach to Boston and the social relations they have with other minorities. When young Micmac Indians come to Boston they search out that part of the city which is most open to minority transients, the South End, and there find in remote pockets many of their friends and relatives from the Maritimes. A physically distinct section of Boston, the South End has wide, treeless, rather desolate boulevards where numerous bars and sundry food shops are located. The boulevards are intersected by narrower residential blocks. These are

lined with red brick town houses, graced by old black
iron railings and bow-front windows, remnants from an
elegant era in the last century when the South End
housed solid upper-class families. Many townhouses
have been converted into rooming houses and small
apartments and have an uncompromising air of physical
degeneration about them. With encouragement from the
Boston Redevelopment Authority, other townhouses
have been restored, some by the personal initiative of
individuals, some by investors interested in capitalizing
on the residential proximity of the South End to inner-
city offices, and some by the Boston Redevelopment Authority itself in an attempt to provide some low-income
housing for minority families. During the 1920s, the
South End underwent a similar resurgence which terminated with the Great Depression when individual investors failed. Optimism about recreating the South
End, and efforts towards improving housing, schooling,
and medical facilities, were at a height during the latter
part of the 1960s when, as happened forty years before,
the initiative of fairly well-off Whites was stirred. At the
present time, corporate influence rules the South End.
The powerful and relatively autonomous B.R.A. orders
the demolition and erection of buildings in ways which
often appear arbitrary to people living there. The municipal government so effectively controls services to
the community—education, health and welfare, police
protection, etc.—that efforts by South End residents to
take political charge and administer those services to
themselves are diminished by the machinery of the corporate government.

The South End is a culturally heterogeneous part of Boston. Blacks make up the largest minority, with Puerto Ricans as a more recent and important group.[2] Bordering on the city's Chinatown on the east, the South End has a considerable Chinese population which, partially displaced by the construction of the Massachusetts Turnpike, has had to expand beyond the traditional boundaries of Chinatown. Smaller, dispersed groups of Armenians, Greeks, and Syrians also live in the South End, along with much less apparent bands of Gypsies who, to the annoyance of the Micmac, have been known to go begging as poor American Indians among the White office workers in the center city. There still persists in the South End a population of older Irish-Americans, a remnant group cut off from their families and from another, younger Boston.

The Micmac fully realize that, in a city of more than a half million, a few thousand Indians are indeed a small minority, in fact, a minority among minorities. Their uniqueness is a source of pride and, in conversation, they frequently contrast their Indian heritage with the negative qualities of other groups. Blacks are feared because they are thought to be more physically aggressive and hostile than the Micmac and disliked for being political manipulators who get what they want from the Whites. The latter image is one picked up from the news media, while the former is a reflection of the fact

[2] In round figures, the total population of the city of Boston is about 640,000; about 25,000 live in the South End area, almost half of whom are Black and about a quarter of whom are Puerto Rican (United States Census of Population, 1970).

that Black men are most in evidence on the streets of
the South End and apt to be antagonistic and threatening to any stranger who passes their way. Their aggression, the Micmac say, is right at the surface, meaning
that long before an Indian would draw a knife on a foe,
a Black would have run him through and left the scene.
Conflict as well as any positive socializing between the
Indians and Blacks in Boston is truly minimal, considering their close proximity to each other in the South End.

The Micmac are much less extreme in their assessment of Puerto Ricans, although, once again, they project an extreme hostility on adolescent Puerto Rican
gangs whose members, male and female, are sometimes
represented in Indian stories as cutthroats. The Micmac
also resent the frequency with which their children are
taken for Puerto Ricans by teachers in Boston schools.
Although they have no particular investment in the
school system itself, their ethnic pride is offended in
any corporate context that assigns them to another minority. Despite resentment, some socializing goes on
between young Micmac men and Puerto Rican girls.

The local Irish-American population in Boston is
one which the Micmac regard as least hostile and least
exotic in their behavior. When Micmac women, as
sometimes happens, become "spin-offs" from the tribe
by inter-marriage with Boston Whites, the spouse is invariably of Irish or Scotch-Irish descent. Even the Ital-
ian-American population, as another White group, is
looked on with relative suspicion and lumped in a common category with the Jews, Armenians, Greeks, and
migrant French Canadians who can be found around

Boston. A Micmac woman can satisfy her class ambitions by marrying an O'Connell or a Murphy, but not by wedding a dark-skinned "foreigner." A Micmac man, on the other hand, if he is going to venture outside his group, will usually avoid socializing with Irish-American women and pick his mate from among any other group than that one. It must be said that no good is thought to come of any marriage outside the tribe. A woman who thinks she is improving her situation by marrying a White is often resented for her decision to separate herself and her children from the community. A man's relationship with a non-Indian woman is apt to be much more casual and yet, when it becomes more than an adventure, it is looked upon with disapproval.

There are so many ways in which risk-taking is essential to the survival of the community, that Micmac culture seldom restrains individuals from exploratory adventures, except at that point when the community chances to lose new members, i.e., the children born of legal unions with strangers. Otherwise, the continuity of the community relies on the lessons learned as each generation matures. For many young Micmac, coming to Boston is a necessary adventure. To make the transition from child to adult requires moving out and away from the family to a wider peer group which, to be economically and socially viable itself, must have strategies for city life. There are lessons to be learned from older generations which have survived urban America; but each new generation of Indians has its own reconnaissance mission, its own testing of the boundaries between itself as a group of social outsiders and the dominant society.

Even as adults act to minimize the dangers of the city for their adolescent kin, the business of the young is exploratory risk-taking and adventure, by which they gradually come to a first-hand appreciation of tribal strategies. The experience of every new generation is also a way in which subtle shifts in those strategies are effected. The expansion or contraction of the tribal network and the strengthening or weakening of boundaries between the Micmac and strangers are determined by the responses of each new generation.

An adolescent coming to the city has another important task, that is, to take his place as an adult among other adults in the tribal community. Over time, an adolescent peer group eventually merges with previous generations, so that the identity of each individual is brought from a specific generational context to the context of community. Before this happens, a Micmac teenager is actively exploring the issues of special power and vulnerability; he takes physical risks to discover his own personal limits as well as the rules of survival in urban society. The energy and courage it takes to pursue life's lessons and come to cultural and individual solutions by adventure and risk is enormous. Most Micmac young people, like young people everywhere, are eager to leave childhood behind and, for the most part, look forward to the adventure of going to Boston as a move towards adult status. Even as adults, the Micmac never cease their explorations and adventures. It is really only the very young or the very old who can afford to be abstract about life's demands. The rest of the community is engaged in a battle to endure and must remain, as a group, sensitive on the issues of communication with the wider society and internal cultural resourcefulness. The physical strength and energy of an individual can hardly be separated from his group's successful cultural organization, for the biological continuation of the community, whatever the abstract content of culture itself, is its primary goal. When a people no longer has the energy or inclination to carry out a defensive investigation of the social and natural environment, and lacks the motivation or strength to reproduce, that people ceases to exist. A Micmac adult is almost as likely to risk a physical fight, a sexual encounter, or a run-in with municipal authorities, as an adolescent fresh from the Maritimes. The difference is that the adult man or woman can pick and choose when he wants to make a show of strength, whereas a teenager is in the process of learning about his own resources and the appropriate boundaries of behavior.

There is tacit agreement between adults and adolescents on the importance of concrete experience so that older individuals, realizing the pitfalls which await a young person just learning about the city, offer simply their patronage to young relatives and are generally tolerant of their independent peer associations and misadventures. Peter Dunn, who told of growing up in a Bear River household, gave this typical account of how he relied on an invitation from his father in Boston to leave the reservation area, and of the loose and easy, yet exhilarating, way he and his friends made the journey:

My father came up for a wedding that summer [1950]. He brought his girlfriend with him and he had a lot of nice presents for everyone. Seemed to be doing right good. He asked me to come down to Boston and promised me that he could find some work for me seeing that I was out of school and just screwing around. So after he was gone, Terry [a boy-friend] and me went over to Shubie [Shubenacadie] and we found Wilson Brown working on an old Ford that was looking just fine and about ready to go, except for a little carburetor repair. So we waited at my sister's there for a few days until Wilson had the Ford in shape and him and Terry and me and two other fellas from Shubie piled in and started out for Bos-ton. I had my father's street number and all, so I knew where I was heading and Wilson had a girl in Boston who was from home. We picked up my cousin Will at Bear River. The car must've broke down seventeen times between Shubie and Amherst but once we hit Maine we were sailing right along. We were sailing so much that this state trooper gave us a ticket for speeding. Wilson was mad but he didn't say nothing and he drove a bit more easy, more like eighty or so, when the trooper was gone by. We hadn't bought liquor yet so we were lucky. It took us two days to get here. We stayed with Wilson's girlfriend for a few days and Terry and me went and stopped by the apartment of a girl my grandmother raised. She was like a cousin and she lived over on Summit Avenue. I got real cozy with her roommate and a bunch of us did some nice partying. Then I went to find my father. There were some people from down home over at his place but he was off on a job outside the city so I just waited for him to come back. I was kinda ex-cited about being in a new place and all, so it was good just to have a place to wait and not go outside for awhile. So I just slept it off. When I woke up, it must've been the next day. My father was back and he brought me to this warehouse to get a job.

The experience of coming to the city can be a fear-ful and heady one for any young man who is on his own for the first time. In addition to the support a parent can provide, maternal uncles and older sisters often attempt to structure the transition from dependence to independence. The promise of a bed and meals and a lead to a job are more than sufficient incentives, yet once a young man has come to the city, warehouse or factory work is seldom enough distraction to circumvent a rambunctious exploration of unfamiliar urban turf. Simon Knight arrived in Boston in 1967, when he was seventeen, on the invitation of his mother's younger brother who, at thirty-one, knew his way around the urban scene. He offered his nephew a place to sleep and arranged for him to do crating at about $1.50 an hour. Simon gave this narrative of his first days in Boston.

I knew it was a rough place, with some real bums around but I knew it would be better than down home. We all knew the stories before we left, really rough things like knifings and people getting beaten up and shot. My uncle, he was working for a contractor. He went all over the country building buildings. He sent for me. I lived with him and then I went and stayed with some relatives of mine from Bear River who were over on Concord Avenue. My uncle, he got me this job hammering boxes together but I quit it after the first day and just went off on my own, with a friend of mine, Sam, who went to school with me. I got really drunk and my uncle came walking by and saw me lying on the ground right outside the Royal [Lounge] and he gave me a kick in the ass and just kept right on walking but I don't think he was out looking for me, I think he just found me and just had to kick the shit out of me. He saw Sam the next day and kicked his ass too.

Simon's uncle continued to pass on information about jobs to him and took no more punitive measures than the swift kick described above. Because a balance has to be achieved between an adult's giving protection and stifling independence, most adult Micmac familiar with the city proffer their support casually and reserve judgement on the activities of the young. The city is a rough place and one which has to be discovered anew by each generation so that they will have an immediate understanding of its nature and of the slight changes in that nature which might be imperceptible to older, relatively less exploratory Micmac. There is an understanding among the Micmac that youth are not to be harangued for their behavior. The lessons on assertion and cooperation have long been taught and adults assume that each individual will eventually accommodate himself to the community and the larger social reality in which it exists. Even an older sister who is likely to share her city home with a young sibling resists directly preaching conventional standards, letting the newcomer work out his own understanding of adult life.

This individual accommodation and working out of an adult status takes place mainly in the social context of the peer group, which enthusiastically agrees that Boston is where the "action" is and which is willing to risk such independent forays as coming to the city without adult contracts and support. Billie Sark, one of Peter's cousins on his mother's side, told how he came to Boston from the Maritimes in 1959 when he had just turned seventeen. His story exemplifies the spontaneous reliance on friends both as fellow travelers and impromptu hosts which makes mobility more than just a pragmatic search for wages.

When I was fourteen, I broke out of school. Couldn't run fast enough. My uncle was up doing lumber in Maine so I went with him and my mother's cousin there. I was already a man at that time. Then I went home a while [Eel Ground] when a friend of mine from Eskasoni [Leonard] told me he been down to Portland and Boston. In my mind, I knew I wanted to get down there, so I asked him to let me know when he was going back. We left that night, right quick. There was a car of Henry's [Leonard's brother] and hardly no gas, so it was stoppin' and goin', stop and go, all the way to Old Town [Me.] Well, we knew people there and I met Patty's sister there. She was living with a fella there but she went back to her people at Shubie after. Portland I didn't see that time cause we went direct down to Boston. I took one look at that place, over the bridge, and I said, "I gotta get outa here." Buddy, who was driving, he's gone now, dead, went right up to Clara Francis' place on Winter Street. It was night and a police car came shootin' by and I said, "More Mounties! Gee-zus!" Buddy didn't care and he came whooping out of the car and I came whooping right behind him. We had, must have been twenty bottles under the back seat. We didn't care, we got up the stairs, and they let us in, Clara and her brother and his girl-friend. Next day, I was saying to myself, "This must be the goddamnedest noisiest place on earth." But Leonard knew his way and Buddy, too. So I kinda put my hands in my pocket and stuck with them. Shit. But it was all right then.

Billie's survival in the city came to depend on the patronage offered to him by Clara's brother, who was at that time in his mid-twenties and thoroughly conversant with the rules of urban living. After a week or so in Boston, Billie also came in contact with one of his mother's foster brothers, a man in his early thirties who for several years after provided Billie with news about job openings and a fold-out bed on which to sleep.

The young Micmac women who come to Boston rely on a similar combination of family support and the company of friends to ease their transition to city life.

They are much more likely, however, to stay close to the relatives who sponsor their arrival and to be conscientious about good performance at the jobs that come their way. The fear that they have of the city as a place populated by crowds of strangers and full of noise and confusion often brings on a depression in the first months of being in Boston. Sadness and melancholy can direct a young girl back to the reservation or make her leave a job and retreat to the circle of her relatives in the city. The great comfort during this first foray is the presence not only of relatives, but, even more important, of girl friends who have the same fears and the same desire to overcome those fears and be independent. One woman, Mary Ginnish, told the story of how she first came to Boston in 1962:

I was the third girl in the family. My two sisters are still down home. One is married and works as a hairdresser in Truro. That's Margo. Ellie is with my mother. She's more quiet. When I left, there was Edward who was fourteen or fifteen at the time and then the younger kids, Claude, Henry, who's dead now, Patsy, and then the children Mom was caring for, first little Helen and then Fleur and Joseph, but his mother's folks came and got him and took him back to Eskasoni. Well, I really did want to go. I was good at home but I knew there was a lot of action in Boston and my uncle and aunt came up one time and they said, "Mary, you can come stay with us." I got my clothes together. I borrowed some things from Margo. Me and Elsie Dunn and Maggie Sark decided to hitch-hike as far as we could and try to make it to Portland to the bus. We was lucky in that a friend of Eddie's took us to Amherst. From there we got a ride with a truckdriver, kind of a nice fellow, into Maine. He wasn't going to Portland, though, so we had to stand out on the road and wave our thumbs. It was night. We didn't have no money to put up at Portland, so we had to count on getting a late bus. Everything worked out all right. It was scary, but it worked out that we got down to Boston by the next day. We got off the bus and called my uncle's. I stayed with him for almost six months. At first I'd look out the window at the trains [the Washington Street elevated] and I'd be so sad, I'd go and lie down. Elsie and Maggie and later Maggie's sister came over and cheered me up. I got a factory job. Then we all decided that we could get a place together.

Mary's factory job and her whole adventure into city living would have terminated very quickly if it had not been for her girl friends. Her uncle and the woman he lived with were kind but not a sufficient support to offset the new and isolating experience of working all day in a mattress factory among strangers who really did not care about her. Without her friends, Elsie and Maggie, Mary would have returned to her family in New Brunswick instead of sticking it out in the city. Their friendship and her gradual integration into a larger peer network in Boston made it possible for Mary to avoid being overcome by city life and eventually, after some serious bouts with drinking, to become an active and competent adult in the Indian community. Like many young women newly arrived from the Maritimes, she eventually had to reject the individuation imposed by urban economics and treat her factory job as a temporary trade-off for cash. Again, like many other young Micmac, she had to invest her energy in peer group activities so as not to be personally overwhelmed.

The things a male or female peer group does together accumulate, event by event, into their common history. Every individual who makes a show of his or her own special powers, every individual who takes a risk, however awkward or dangerous its repercussions, is adding to a kind of honorific stockpile. Young men and women do this in very different ways. For example, when Mary's younger brother Eddie Ginnish came to Boston for the first time in 1966, he did not like the people he saw there or the way the city looked. The numbers of Blacks and Puerto Ricans on the streets, compared to the more sparsely populated Maritimes, looked like hordes of enemies, even though he had arrived in the winter, when most of the South End population stays indoors. After a few months, Eddie worked up the courage to trespass on Black turf. He would coolly walk by a bar patronized exclusively by Blacks and pass through the crowd of young men who hung around outside it. One night, with great daring, he ventured into the bar and ordered a beer. Some four years later, a veteran in the city, he told the story of what happened.

I walked right in. I said, "Gimme a beer." The bartender said, "What?" I said, "A beer, you sonofabitch." This colored gal was standing there and she let out with a big laugh. She said something like, well, on the order of us getting together. I was just going to have my beer and get out. It was black in there, blacker than outside. There were some big guys right next to me, really big colored guys who kept edging close to me. I put my elbows down on the bar and didn't move.

The dialogue and Eddie were probably not quite so tough as he represented them. His sister Mary finished off the account with an emphasis on her brother's inexperience: "The bartender asked Eddie for his license and Eddie beat it out of there fast." Even so, the risk that Eddie took on strange turf at the tender age of seventeen was appreciated by his friends who singly and together involved themselves in a testing of the city environment. At their most extreme, they would antagonize and fight with Black and Puerto Rican youths, although the results of battle with gangs who were city-bred are bound to be disastrous for the Micmac. During the summer of 1970, a Micmac teenager was found stabbed to death in a Boston Railroad yard, a casualty of his own involvement with and provocation of city gangs. By the time the story of his death reached the reservations in the Maritimes, it was embellished and gory and, I believe, fictitious details of torture and maiming and transformed into a moral lesson of what happens to a person who seeks too much fame with too little caution.

Micmac men have a certain reputation for being very uncompetitive among themselves. It is said that when baseball teams are formed on reservations, the Micmac would rather play with White teams than face off against each other. There is a great solidarity among men who have grown up with each other. However, Boston attracts people from every settlement, so that the tribal community includes within itself men and women who are familiar to each other first by the category of a common tribe and then by family and residence categories. A young Micmac man, as much as he feels solidarity with his immediate peer group, might occasionally pit himself physically against another young

Micmac Indian less familiar to him, provoking a minor risk-taking escapade. But when a young man arrives in the city, it is more the difference between himself as a Micmac and the other groups in the city that he seeks to explore than the unfamiliar faces within the community network.

Before that exploration begins, there is a whole range of activities by which to know the city. Eddie and his friends, for example, would "borrow" cars once and a while to go on a joy ride, or drink too much and go prowling around the alleys of the South End. They'd tease a Black prostitute until her pimp showed up, or practice how to disperse effectively when a patrol car cruised by. Sexual prowess, although not as openly boasted about as physical conflict and brushes with the law, was and is a typical enterprise whereby the young demonstrate their ability to brave new contacts in the urban scene.

All young Micmac are essentially trying on adult behavior, which, like a suit that fits them better every year, is often worn awkwardly at first. The reputation that young men are trying to acquire, starting from about the age of fifteen or sixteen, will take another ten or fifteen years to be worn with ease, although fundamentally the same high value on risk-taking and the same exploratory behavior characterizes both the man in his youth and the man who is moving through the tribal community as an adult.

The kind of risk-taking and adventure which young Micmac women pursue has more to do with sexual competition and conquests than with the direct physical conflict and aggression by which their male peers test the urban environment. The discipline of adolescents within the reservation family is not so strict that it makes the city a scene of new sexual freedom. Among the Micmac, a young person's physical autonomy is sufficient license in itself to override the restraints which adults might want to impose on teenagers. A conventional morality is verbalized, yet the restrictions on behavior which would prevent a young man or woman from freely associating with peers, and the punishments which would bind an adolescent closer to the family, are lacking. An individual Micmac's physical maturity is followed so quickly by economic and social autonomy that it proves nonsensical to insist on the childhood of a thirteen- or fourteen-year-old when in a short time he or she will be an independent agent in a new generation of adults. The exploration of peer relationships in early reservation adolescence is only a brief preliminary to the issues of sexual union and reproduction, which are investigated most seriously when young Micmac are on their own in the city.

On the reservations, young teenagers are divided into friendship groups of girls and boys. They are actually quite shy with members of the opposite sex and are subject to romantic crushes which make them vulnerable to teasing at home. This sexual division of the peer group remains throughout life, with the kin ties and the social ties created by a sexual union the only strands which cross it. As the sons and daughters of a family move into their middle and late teens, what they do with their friends becomes more and more of a private matter, a set of activities separate from the family and generally inaccessible to the rest of the community. Most of the adults prefer to leave young people their private adventures and, unless some crisis turns an adventure into public knowledge, barely take even a vicarious interest in the subject. An unfortunate car accident, an unwanted pregnancy, or a teenage brawl are cause for comment and gossip, although these public events are not taken as proof of the reprehensibility of all adolescent behavior, only as some of the extremes possible in an otherwise normal range of activities.

This is not to say that some adults, particularly old folks, do not have the right to worry about young people and express anxiety over their inevitable struggle with the realities of adult life. But such anxiety is more a nod towards White conventions than a deterrent to youthful antics. One old Micmac woman went on for days bemoaning her fifteen-year-old granddaughter's predilection for riding around in cars with other young reservation Indians. Having seen the young girl leaving the settlement's teenage hangout (a soda shop *cum* pool hall), the grandmother warned the whole family of the dangers to feminine virtue brought on by the automobile. Shortly thereafter, however, the same woman was showing this researcher photo after photo of the many boyfriends she had had in the course of her sixty-three years, beginning with a man by whom she had a child when she was seventeen.

In the city, a young woman enjoys an even greater independence from conventional White mores. And the lessons of cooperation and personal resourcefulness

learned in childhood will stand her in better stead than
the dominant society's norms. After initial fears and depressions are over, many women, like Mary Ginnish,
put a distance between themselves and their older relatives by renting an apartment with a few very close girl
friends and perhaps a sister. Without leaving these
friends and without cutting off ties with her family, a
young woman will begin to socialize more ambitiously.
There is still at this point a competitive edge to her relationships with other women, even though a few close
friends and sisters are admitted allies. When she has a
boyfriend, the details of their affair—the good times, the
love-making, the fights, the other woman or man who
intrudes—are faithfully reported back to her girl friends
and hours are spent discussing these first adventures
into adulthood. The most important witnesses to a sexual conquest are other women, both those who share in-
timate details and those rivals who are chagrined by it.
Pearl Rivière, who came to Boston from New Brunswick
in 1948, gave an interesting account of her first years in
the city and some of the relationships she had:

We had family in the city, both Barbara and me did. We was
most interested in what was happening around the town. If
there would be a party. If one of the boys had picked up some
stuff to drink. I worked steady at the time. I didn't have no
kids. Barbara and me and a few of the other girls would find
out about a get-together and off we'd go. I had a boyfriend
with arms as big around as a tree. I called him "Peewee." He
was from Sydney [N.S.]. Once he got so jealous of me that he
parked his car outside our room on Market Street all night
long. Barbara couldn't believe how that man loved me. If he
had money, well, it was mine, too. Maybe that's the one I

should've stayed with. I would have, but that dirty lezzie [lesbian] Patsy Mayhew started flirting with him and when I heard about that I said, "It's finished, that's it." I had another man. He's up in Montreal now. I saw him only a little while ago when I was visiting my relatives. Him and me was from the same place [Richibuctu]. Once when we had a big fight, he got sick. He got pneumonia, I think. His people were angry with me 'cause they believed I done that to him. I might've given him lice but I never let no man get pneumonia! One boyfriend I had was real mean. He could get very angry and rough. Barbara and me shared this room on Tenth Street right up until the time that Henry was born, which must have been almost three years. Henry's father is dead now, you know, but at the time he was visiting me where I lived.

Every new affair brings a risk for a young woman, and the sense of conquest she gets from having a new boyfriend is not unlike that which men get from competitively fighting with each other. On the most obvious level, someone like Maureen or Pearl has a lot at stake in maintaining an image of being in control when it comes to affairs of the heart. Young men usually assume an indifferent air when the subject of love comes up, preferring to emphasize a more impersonal, detached image of emotional control. Women approach the issue directly and talk of capturing and keeping the affections of specific men and controlling the duration of the relationship. Any bad treatment from a man on the order of nonsupport, or physical violence, or going out with another woman, makes a woman lose face with other women. It follows, too, that a young woman who ventures into a casual relationship with a non-Indian takes the greatest risk of all, because she is attempting to control the affections of someone who just might operate by another set of rules in the game of male-female encounters.

On quite another level, a young woman in each new affair risks creating an enduring new link between two families, that is, a child, before she has much comparative sense of men, let alone families in the community. Very few young Micmac women seem to use contraceptive devices and rely instead on their own families and reservation households as a retreat for themselves and their infants if indeed they do become mothers while still in their teens. The possibility of pregnancy makes affairs with non-Indians even more risky, for while direct support from a Micmac man might not be at first available, the Micmac child can grow up in a tribal context where his relationship to his father's kin can one day be claimed. But the non-Indian father is much more likely to disappear and take with him that part of the child's family context.

As time passes, the social network of people like Pearl Rivière and Eddie Ginnish expands from a narrow group of friends and relatives to a social world which includes a wide variety of contacts in the tribal community. The sense of exploration and risk-taking, which in the first years of living in Boston was a primary means of learning the rules of survival in the city, continues. Once some basic lessons are learned, the investigation of community boundaries becomes balanced by an investment of energy in the internal social functions of the tribe. Bumping up against the legal sanctions of the dominant society and colliding with other groups in the city are necessary encounters with reality, no more to be avoided than birth or death. At the same time, sexual encounters and physical conflict between men and women and competition between members of the same sex operate to familiarize young adults with each other, increasing their awareness of the tribal network. Each new relationship between members of different cliques opens up the possibility for entirely new sets of relationships between people previously only indirectly involved. Noel Harper, the father of Maureen Paul's first child, was known only slightly by her brother Sal and cousin Popeye. Through his relationship with her, he became their friend and traveled with them on rides to other towns and cities in search of work. Maureen's cousin Eveline had an affair with one of Noel's best friends. Still later, she married a man from Noel's group. In another case, Peter Dunn's younger brother Claude became involved in a brawl with a Micmac man from Quebec. After the fight was over, friends of Claude began to go out with women from his former adversary's clique, and his own sister, Anne, began a long and serious relationship with a close friend of the Quebec man.

The concentration on social relations with members of one's own generation gradually gives way, with age, to an intergenerational emphasis, as when an individual finds himself the parent of an adolescent who is about to take his or her place in the adult community. By the time most Micmac reach their late thirties or early forties, the fast pace of mobility and action-seeking is beginning to slow down. Since being on the move has also meant a maximum availability for work (being able to pick up a job that opens up almost anywhere in the New England area), becoming less mobile is also a signal of one's decreasing participation in the job market. Generally, dropping away from the most mobile part of the community comes with a physical inability to continue at that kind of pace. The incidence of tuberculosis, pneumonia, and other diseases is as high among the Micmac as among any other American Indian population and the life expectancy is about as low (between sixty and sixty-five). Becoming less active and mobile usually means that one becomes more sedentary, more attached to one locale (for instance, the South End or the reservation), and more visible as far as institutions are concerned.

There are also some Micmac Indians in the Boston area who, while they are not as visible as the Indians in the South End, are less mobile for other reasons, i.e., they are more economically stable and more concerned with maintaining households in the city than most of the other adults. Their families are usually smaller and less stable than the home base which the reservation area supports and their location in lower-class residential areas outside the core city sets them apart from the action of the city, although there is pressure from enough relatives and friends in need of a place to stay to keep them involved. The two less mobile groups in Boston, those individuals in the South End and household members outside the South End, are potentially the most visible to White society in that they are easier to locate and to observe in a single location. The more active and the more socially viable members of the Micmac community are those who, in their mobility, have remained invisible to the conventional records of social existence.

Social Relations in the City

The boundary-testing which is characteristic of young newcomers to the city is also characteristic of more accomplished city-dwellers. Yet because of the tribal organization of the Micmac and because of the heterogeneous social organization of the city, the social contacts made with non-Indians seldom accumulate. That is, relations with other minority groups and with urban bureaucrats rarely work to incorporate an individual Micmac into an entirely new social network or corporate system. The Micmac are a transient people whose mobility makes them unavailable for long-term relationships with outsiders. Also, the mobility of other minority groups who live in and around Boston is perhaps underestimated. To be economically marginal to industrial society requires all the cultural flexibility of a hustler and, logically, the capacity for serving multiple job markets. If a boxer in the ring has to be graceful, quick, and on his toes, think how much more adept minorities must be, given the nature of their continual struggle for survival. The Blacks, Puerto Ricans, Gypsies, French Canadians, and others who operate outside the corporate support of the dominant society are undoubtedly as resourceful as the Micmac in their separate cultural strategies. The question which remains to be answered is whether, at this point in history, any one city offers sufficient support to such outsiders to make them a relatively settled population at any level of social stratification or if the poor are actually compelled to be mobile.

The economic opportunities in the greater Boston area far outweigh those of the Maritimes, but in order to live the Micmac have had to extend their tribal network, which is also an informational network, to industrial centers in the general area of New England and southeastern Canada. Their whole social organization, in fact, responds to the fact that, in the eyes of many, they are just another expendable minority competing for "dirty work," to use Everett Hughes' term.[3] The mobility of adults and the flexible sharing of child care responsibilities are in tune with the exigences of urban economics, as they apply to minority groups. A similar response seems generally characteristic of other urban minorities which, like the Micmac, invest most of their energies in the development of successful cultural strategies and generally go beyond their respective group boundaries only to gain information to update and therefore increase the efficiency of their cultural solutions. If one looks closely at such ethnographies as *Tally's Corner* and *Soulside* and at the literature on Caribbean families and peer groups, the seemingly random organization of urban households and social networks reveals itself as an efficient means for maximizing

[3] Everett Cherrington Hughes, *Men and Their Work*, Glencoe, The Free Press, 1958.

the participation of adults in a cash economy while providing for the care of children.[4] The institution of a
large, flexible household unit, and the existence of multiple alternatives for raising the young, releases the energies of men in particular so that they can be about the
business of job-finding. It also allows many adult
women to do the same, without sacrificing the biological
continuity of the group. For example, the so-called ma-
trifocal Black family and the "satellite" position of men
in regard to it is actually an efficient way for a group to
divide its cultural labor, given the demands of economic
marginality. When a group is without property, its main
resource becomes people, and its most successful strategy lies in cooperation, including the mutual dependence of peers and the tendency of male and female
groups to be complementary.

This heavy emphasis on the efficiency of minority
cultures would make less sense if the wider society
dealt less harshly with them and if, instead of enduring,
each became extinct. If, for example, the social reality of
the Micmac were tempered by respites from the struggle to earn a cash wage, or the sting of racism were

[4] Elliot Liebow, *Tally's Corner*, Boston, Little, Brown, 1967; Ulf Han-
nerz, *Soulside: Inquiries into Ghetto Culture and Community*, Co-
lumbia University Press, 1969; see also Edith Clarke, *My Mother Who
Fathered Me*, London, Allen and Unwin, 1957; Oscar Lewis, *Five
Families*, New York, Basic Books, 1959; Keith Otterbein, "Caribbean
Family Organization: A Comparative Analysis," *American Anthropologist*, Vol. 67, 1965, pp. 67–79; and Nancie L. Solien Gonzalez, "The
Consanguinal Household and Matrifocality," *American Anthropologist*, Vol. 67, 1965, pp. 1541–1549. Carol Stack, in *All Our Kin* (New
York, Harper and Row, 1974), argues this point in detail for Black fam-
ilies in Chicago.

eliminated from their lives, it would be reasonable to de-emphasize the extent to which they must be culturally on the defensive. The strong images of magical power and physical aggression which survive from Micmac history reflect the harshness of their past and present position in society insofar as they are necessary psychological equipment for individual survival. Different but equally defensive self-images are common among Blacks and Spanish-Americans and other outsider groups. In the same way, these groups are in a position of expendability—as unskilled and semi-skilled labor—and are socially and politically excluded from the dominant society.

Sharing the position of outsiders hardly lightens the burden of exclusion, for every other poor person who is a stranger to one's own network is a rival for the limited goods of this world and, furthermore, represents a rival strategy. In an exploratory sense, the Micmac communicate with individuals from other minority groups and learn about their ways. But they seldom become incorporated into other groups or include other minority people among their own. The only blurring of boundaries between Indian and Black or, more frequently, Puerto Rican communities is an occasional exchange of information between groups. Similarly, the social relations which the Micmac have with Whites as a group are almost always short-lived; either the individual Indian becomes lost to his community, or the White person becomes Indianized by incorporation in the Micmac community, or the association between Micmac and White proves to be a temporary encounter.

Contacts with those who work for the municipality are equally short-lived. The assumptions on which meetings between any civil servant and any Micmac are based are usually anti-social, that is, they posit such a great social distance between the bureaucrat and the Indian that the notion of social interaction barely applies. More precisely, the idea that, when two strangers meet, the boundaries of their respective social networks somehow touch is irrelevant when a Micmac goes on welfare, is hospitalized, or gets arrested. The bureaucrat typically draws a distinction between his playful, social, private, autonomous self and his functional work self, and he makes that distinction most clear when he is face-to-face with outsiders to his institution, when he is, in fact, called upon to serve or govern. There are exceptions, but most contacts between the Micmac and people who work for institutions are superficial, since they occur between an outsider to the system whose social resources are ignored and an individual whose main resource is the bureaucracy he represents.

While social contacts with people outside the Micmac tribe seldom stabilize or lead to participation in new non-Indian networks, social contacts within the tribal community are in the constant process of accumulation. As the adolescent peer group moves to the city, each of its members is engaged in exploration of a fairly stable urban community, as well as the risky testing of personal and community boundaries. Unlike contacts with strangers, one's encounters with other Micmac Indians are often in themselves stable and long-lasting, or at least increase the sum of information one has about the community. Every fight and every affair, every journey in search of jobs brings with it a proliferation of relationships for the individuals involved and, indirectly, for their families and friends. While relationships with non-Indians come and go, the relationships within the Micmac community add up, become redundant, and, continue to bind dispersed and socially naïve peer groups together as socially knowledgeable, urbane adults in a tribal group.

In the process of becoming an active member of the urban community, a young Micmac is drawn more and more into a general network of adults whose ages range from their early twenties through their mid-fifties. The main activity of the network is a kind of continuous mutual socializing which seems so random that, to a stranger, it cannot be traced to the carrying out of important cultural tasks, such as earning money and raising children. Because the major resource of the Micmac is their human one, solutions to crucial problems are found in contacts within the group. The potential for information on work, transportation to a job center, and arrangements for child care exist in every visit between relatives and friends, in every party, in every wedding and funeral, in every barroom where Micmac congregate. The motivation to be with other people is always high, so that no other entertainment, for example, television or movies, can match the stimulation other people provide. While the process of socializing is one which we conventionally assume parents visit upon children until certain rules of behavior are learned, the socializing which goes on among the Micmac is also a continual exercise in the rules of human interaction. The etiquette of forming alliances between individuals and groups, of initiating and settling conflicts, and of meeting the responsibilities of sharing and serving, is impressed on an individual every time a segment of the social network convenes.

The following is a description from field work notes of a typically restless night of socializing in the South End in the fall of 1971. No particular crisis occurred and, in fact, it is only in the aftermath of this evening's socializing that the individuals involved acted directly to help each other. What the night's progress allowed was the possibility of responsible action.

By the time I got over to Maureen Paul's, it was already about eight o'clock. Sal and three of his friends had showed up more or less unexpectedly for dinner. Maureen complained about how he didn't kick in as much money as he should to pay for the apartment, the way a brother should. But she seemed to have given them a good dinner (stuffed chicken, Campbell's chicken noodle soup with corn bread) and one of Sal's friends, Elmer Newell, had brought a fifth of Scotch along with him. Sal declared, when I came in, that he was going out to get some beer. I took that as my cue and gave him three dollars. Maureen called out something in Micmac to him as he went out the door and there was a chuckle around the table when I asked her what she had said. "I told him just to make sure he come back with the booze." Eveline (Maureen's cousin who was living with her) came out of the bathroom, holding a towel on her head; she waved and disappeared into the bedroom. Two of the men, Elmer and Sal, were having an argument about the price of rifles. Maureen began to tell me how she and Patsy had gone to a local church bingo game and that Patsy was almost a winner about three times. Eveline came in and sat down with everyone else at the kitchen table. Butch (at her left) tugged her hair, which was still wet, and asked her what she was doing to get her hair all sweated up. "Gimundulia (go to hell)," she said to him with a smile. The phone rang and Maureen said it was Bernard Sack wanting to know if he could come over and stay the night. Maureen told him to come over but said he would be getting the floor to sleep on, not her bed. Eveline said it was crowded enough with Ted (Maureen's boyfriend). Sal came in with three six-packs of Budweiser and distributed them around. Then Elmer made the suggestion that we finish up at Maureen's and take a ride over to East Boston to visit. Eveline and I had one beer each, Maureen had one and started another, and the other fourteen went to the four men. Sal and Elmer left the apartment, each still emptying his last can of beer. We went in Sal's car (a '64 Ford convertible) with the three women and Peter (the fourth man and the most quiet) in the back seat, the other three men in front. We stopped off at Lucy Francis' place on First Street. Elmer got out and ran up to the third floor and in a few minutes he came down and told Sal to park the car. Lucy wasn't home but there were four men and two women there. I've been to Lucy's in the daytime; at night, it looked dark and it was a good bit more disorderly than I remembered: the bed was unmade and there were glasses on the table by the bed and a few beer cans on the floor. Some bourbon was available and there was beer in the refrigerator. I recognized one of the women as Mary Ginnish and went over to say hello. She told me that she wanted to send her little girl back up to relatives in Truro and asked if I was going to take a car trip "down home" in the next few weeks. I said I wasn't sure but that I would keep in contact with her. She began telling me about how she sat all day at the Emergency Clinic (at Boston City Hospital) with her uncle who has been coughing and spitting (blood) and who has to have arrangements made to go to a t.b. sanitorium. Without my knowing it, the rest of the people in the room had decided to go to the Royal Bar. Mary went with the others in another car, and I went in Sal's. Sal was driving and he made quite a show of it, considering the bar was about a block-and-a-half from Lucy's. Maureen told me she had a hunch that Ted would be at the Royal because he usually stopped by there on Tuesday nights. Eveline proclaimed, from the back seat to the front, that she understood Elmer to say he was paying for all our drinks at the Royal. Elmer had already had a lot to drink and his head was lolling around a bit. He reached in his pants' pocket and took out his wallet, which he threw over into the back seat. It landed on the floor and Maureen and Eveline reached down to pick it up. "You're crazy," Maureen said, "what makes you think you'll ever see this again?" We got to the bar before the other car. Sal ordered beer for us and paid when the order came. When the rest arrived, we took up about eight small tables along the wall. . . . By one o'clock Maureen decided she had to be going home. It was also pretty clear that Elmer would make it no farther than Maureen's place. Eveline, Maureen, Sal, Elmer, and I left the Royal and went back to Maureen's. Propped up outside her door was Bernard Sack, sound asleep with his hat on his head. Maureen gave him a few shakes to wake him up and when that didn't work she opened the door with her key and Sal pulled him inside. Elmer meanwhile was having a hard time getting up the stairs and Eveline had disappeared into the bathroom. Bernard just stayed on the rug, asleep. Sal sat down on the couch which is also his bed and closed his eyes. I said goodnight to Maureen and Sal and, as he came through the door, Elmer gave me a big smile and a clap on the shoulder.

This evening of socializing was the beginning of some interesting interaction. Bernard Sack became a more or less permanent fixture at Maureen's and his presence precipitated Eveline's leaving the apartment and traveling to New York with her boyfriend for an indefinite stay. Soon after, Bernard and Elmer, who really did not know each other very well, had a fist-fight during the course of a party. Elmer, the older and bigger man, won and the two men became rather good friends. Sal and Elmer began to include Bernard in their travels outside Boston to work in Lowell and Leominster. At about the same time, Mary Ginnish was able to have her daughter stay at Lucy's while she made arrangements for a new apartment. Maureen, who knew Mary's uncle well, drove him to the sanatorium and helped with his admission. A week later, Sal, Ted, Maureen, and Mary, with her daughter, rode together to Nova Scotia for a weekend visit. Mary and Elmer eventually became lovers and lived together until the summer of 1973.

On Public Performance

When there is a public performance quality to Micmac socializing, social relationships within the tribal group become even more charged with interest because the element of risk is introduced. Men in particular play off the fraternization of the in-group against random contacts with strangers and, more importantly, play off their own norms of behavior against conventional rules of public demeanor. Sal and Elmer and any other Micmac man would be likely on an evening in Boston to part company with the women and make their socializing a strictly male peer group enterprise. There are some bars in the South End where men of all different colors go but where very few women (except prostitutes, again of all different colors) care to be found. Heavy drinking, particularly by men, seems to be a pan-Indian trait. A man's ability to drink a lot and hold his liquor is highly praised by the Micmac. Young Simon, who had gotten "kicked in the ass" by his uncle, was chastised not because he had had a lot to drink but because his form was faulty. Ending up drunk and alone, isolated from the peer group, is a position of great vulnerability. Simon risked exposure to the police, to a gang of other South End youths, and to the elements. Optimally, Micmac men get together in a group, find a bar that is noisy and full of people, and spend as much time and money as they can drinking beer and whiskey. Each individual's spirit of adventure is maximized both by the heated social atmosphere and by alcohol until he is ready to test his physical power against that of another man in about the same feisty state of competition. If, within a man's own party, there has been antagonism between two men, a fight will easily break out between them. If a White sailor is standing at the bar, or a Puerto Rican or Black who looks equally belligerent and ready for confrontation, a brawl will start.

Age and sex are important variables in patterns of drinking. Micmac youth who are underage usually have to do their drinking in private. Elderly men and women may go to a bar, but sit and drink unobtrusively in a corner for the evening. There are women of all ages who are good drinkers, that is, who can drink without showing it, but, just as with men, the youngest among them may go beyond her capacity, and the elderly may use alcohol not for the physical effect but to underscore the kind of natural social distance which the aged, like children, have from the rest of the community. With these variations, the person who is regarded by the community as truly sick because of alcohol is the one who over and over again loses touch with his group until he or she becomes a social isolate, an alcoholic dependent on and vulnerable to White institutions.

The difference between Micmac drinking and the drinking which goes on, for example, in affluent homes in Boston suburbs is less a matter of the quantity of alcohol consumed than the style which characterizes its consumption. Alcohol has generally the same pleasurable, boundary-loosening effect on one human being as another. There are a variety of ways in which to handle this kind of pleasure and the measure of appropriate indulgence. From the dominant society's point of view, proper drinking is done in private, controlled situations. People who drink together either know each other or have been given social assurances by the host. The event is usually preplanned by personal invitation and there should be no random individuals intruding. With planned privacy, the risk of drinking too much and acting uncivilized is minimized. A suburban man may for years drink and regress to states of emotional dependency or aggression, which his culture deplores, and yet never be arrested. Only his intimates know, and if they do not approve, they simply leave him for the company of friends who behave better. Within the four walls of his home, an individual has the private right to violate public morality. True failure is marked by the breakdown between the private and the public realms, as when a respectable man lands on Skid Row because he was unable to control his need for drink. In contrast to this, the Micmac and apparently many other Indians

value the expression of aggression which alcohol facili-
tates and prefer to maximize the risk of drinking by
seeking a public arena. They cover themselves, so to
speak, only by drinking in groups. Since the police and
other keepers of the peace in urban and reservation
areas have about the same values as the rulers of American society, they perceive public inebriation as an ul-
timate degradation, a fall from civilization. They judge
Indians who drink publicly even more harshly than the
individual White, because Indians as a group would
seem to have been born uncivilized with no shame
about their categorical degradation.

The way in which the Micmac frequently engage in
physical aggression is particularly irritating to law-
enforcement agents.[5] Again, conventional values go,
being angry with another person affords no license to
strike a blow. Aggression is better abstracted to words—
one's own, or better, one's lawyer's, so that by indirection the sting of aggression is removed. If blows are

[5] See Omer Stewart's "Questions Regarding American Indian Crimi-
nality," *Human Organization*, Vol. 23, no. 1, pp. 61–66, for a statistical
rundown on Indian arrest rates in cities as compared to other minority
groups. And, for further discussion of Indian problems in the city, see
Theodore Graves' "The Personal Adjustment of Navajo Indian Migrants to Denver, Colorado," *American Anthropologist,* Vol. 72, pp.
35–54. The tendency to provoke authorities by such public performances as drinking and fighting seems to be common among many Indians in American cities. Incarceration for disturbing the public
peace, rather than for more serious crimes against person or property,
is as characteristic of the Micmac in Boston as of the variety of Indian
tribesmen who journey to other cities. The lack of data on arrest rates
for women leads to the assumption that it is men, more than women,
who take their chances in the public arena.

going to be dealt, this had best be a private matter. Ideally, the expression of aggression in the public sector is impersonal, as in a machine-implemented war where combatants never meet face-to-face and killing is accomplished without any sense of the physical experience of killing. There are no hurt feelings in war and there is nothing to take personally in the dropping of a bomb or the shelling of a village. The Micmac have a very different idea of aggression. They take conflict very personally and deal with it on the direct, human level of physical confrontation.

It is important to note that the military organizations of the ruling society have the exclusive right to use physical force in order to repress non-sanctioned aggression. An individual policeman and a Micmac may have comparable ideas about physical aggression as appropriate masculine behavior. The policeman, however, finds justification for force in legal notions of right and wrong; the Indian has only the norms of a small outsider group to support his actions. Even when Micmac men espouse larger causes, their tendency to get involved in fights supersedes organizational imperatives. So many Micmac patriotically served in the Canadian armed forces during World War II that a battleship was named in honor of the tribe. As men who are now in their forties talk about their war experiences, it becomes clear that legally-sanctioned aggression and risk-taking and an emphasis on national *esprit de corps* in the last World War temporarily gave them a place, a role they could honorably fill. The enemy outside the nation was for a time more despised than the Indians within it, so that the sting of racial prejudice seemed less hurtful in war-time. The many medals won for bravery in combat impressed even White officers. But if the Micmac made brave footsoldiers, it also seems that they could easily be provoked to fight with non-Indians. Often, in their egalitarian fashion, they ignored the rank and authority of the men they fought and had their careers terminated. Younger Indian men who fought for the United States in Korea and Vietnam felt basically the same attraction towards a military role which sanctions aggression, but they also felt a need for face-to-face conflict, which sooner or later got them into trouble and out of the military.

The distance between insiders to bureaucratic organizations and outsiders like the Micmac is otherwise so clear that misplaced aggression rarely occurs. War is an active condition of little people being consumed by political motives which require the military to open its ranks to all comers, including Indians. The lack of discrimination between insider and outsider which this promotes is missing when, for example, Indians encounter the police, welfare workers, hospital personnel, and other bureaucratic agents. In any specific encounter, the individual Micmac will more than likely shelve his or her aggression and retreat behind a stoically impassive mask as the best defense against an inevitably bad experience. This lack of emotional expressiveness, which the Micmac consider dignified, is very frustrating to organizational personnel who expect to see signs of fear or remorse or sadness. The impassive mask of the Indian is easily projected upon. The policeman finds him stupid and "thick," or sly. The welfare worker finds him arrogant and without shame. Medical professionals find him hopelessly evasive. Each bureaucrat has an ideal client in mind, a figure whose needs—moral, psychological and physical—are so blatant that the function of the bureaucracy and its managers is unambiguous. The ideal criminal is more soberly pugnacious than the Micmac; the ideal welfare recipient breaks down in guilty tears of despair; the ideal patient is grateful to consign his body to experts. It is extremely rare for the Micmac to meet any of these ideals. Their contacts with institutions always seem inadvertent, like the unfortunate chance meeting of a professional gambler with his foreign creditors. An active adult Micmac would prefer to avoid such contacts precisely because of the behavior bureaucrats expect and because of the loss of identity which capitulation entails. An Indian who becomes dependent on welfare, or has to be hospitalized, or spends a long time in jail is liable to become the good client and be lost to the tribal community. Because bureaucracies have only negative definitions of client behavior, the Micmac generally seek to avoid definition by bureaucracies. Once in a bureaucratic setting, they wear masks of emotional control and consider the best means of extricating themselves without injury, retaining as much dignity as they can for the service they can get.

The verbal reticence of the Micmac in institutional settings is frequently referred to as a language problem. There are really very few Micmac who cannot speak some English. If under duress, lost, or in pain, however, even most of those who are truly bilingual prefer their

Indian tongue to their second language. The issue goes much deeper, for having a Micmac translater available at an institution which purports to serve Indians signifies better service but does not automatically convert that social setting into Micmac turf where Indians can relax. Louis Coser, in discussing Simmel's essay, "Der Arme," made the observation that modern poverty is a public state of needing assistance.[6] The bad experiences and the negative identities lying in wait for a Micmac in every public institution which serves the poor are sufficient to keep his comments terse, whatever his knowledge of English.

The labels applied to Indian behavior are so often negative that adding another, "language problem," is all too simple to do. The labels "alcoholic" and "criminal," "illiterate" and "illegitimate," tell more about the norms of the dominant society than they do about the realities of living poor. At best they sensitize us to the kind of scripts corporations provide for the people they were instituted to serve. The self-abasing roles which outsiders are assigned (if they want to perform in a bureaucratic setting) can operate efficiently for the institution, for they usually repel precisely those poor people who feel enough self-respect to actually rewrite the corporate script.

There are more substantive issues than labeling or script-writing which explain the behavior of the Micmac and these lie in an understanding of their cultural strategies. Micmac men, for example, have more contact

[6] "The Sociology of Poverty," *Social Problems*, Vol. 13, no. 2, 1965, pp. 140–48.

with law enforcement agents than with any other bureaucratic representatives. The question which should be asked first is, "What are they learning about the law?" Basically Micmac men learn the perimeters of legal force. They know, or will push a situation to its limits to find out, just how loud and how rough a group can get in a bar. They know or will find out when policemen can be provoked to leave a patrol car for a chase on foot and when they prefer to drive by. They know or will learn by experience when a knife can be pulled or an unlocked car borrowed without legal retribution. The real crimes in Micmac terms have little to do with drinking and fighting and more to do with deceit and lack of cooperation within the group. The working out of quarrels about these latter violations is often accomplished by the very behavior on which the wider society frowns.

One young Micmac, Richie Gabriel, began to be suspicious that another man from the same settlement back home was working "on the sly" against him. He claimed the other man had taken a job away from him, although just how he managed to do this was never stated. Richie also found the behavior of the other man too proud and boastful to be tolerated and, one night, he picked a fight with him in a Boston bar. Richie first declared his discontent by refusing to drink from a round of beer his adversary had paid for, saying in a rather quiet but angry voice that the money which paid for the beer was stolen. Before the bartender could intervene, the two men came to blows. Of the eight or so other Indian men and women around, none made a noise or took it upon himself or herself to interfere. The bartender, however, gave a signal to one of his regular "heavies," who doubled as a bouncer, to separate the two men. The bartender told them both to leave or he would call the cops. The two Micmac men went and picked their coats up off the floor and headed for the door. But Richie gallantly proposed that he be the only one to leave rather than break up the party. He slipped out, with a bit more prestige to his credit for having made the gesture. His opponent had to leave anyway because the bartender did not want any troublemakers around. But, within a week, Richie instigated another fight, with the same man, again in a bar, and again with the real risk at hand that the police might be called in. This time, the manager of the bar put a phone call into the Boston station as soon as the altercation began. The police arrived in only a few minutes, but before that the two men had made their way, still jabbing at each other, out onto the sidewalk, and, having heard the approaching sirens, had disappeared into the night by the time the police arrived. Of the dozen Micmac who had witnessed the scene, about half had dispersed and were nowhere in sight and the rest were sitting quietly at tables. Two older Irish-American men had themselves gotten into an argument over the Micmac fight, just to the point of swearing and taking their jackets off, and it was these two men who were maneuvered out of the bar by the police, lectured, and sent home to their South End rooming houses. The matter between Richie and his opponent was resolved even later, at a third confrontation, once again in a public place (a penny arcade), when Richie knocked his opponent out cold in the company of four or five friends.

The procedure for resolving this conflict was much more important to Richie and his foe than conforming their behavior to mainstream American standards. Actually the risks engendered by hand-to-hand combat in a public place enhance the contest between two men because it indicates their ability to defy legal norms even as they attend to problems internal to the community. Defiance at its best, of course, escapes getting caught by the long arm of the law. Peter Wilson, in describing the *machismo* complex of values among Caribbean men, comments on how a man earns for himself a good reputation: "In fact, in its most general sense a reputation is gained according to the degree to which a man is proficient in undermining, disobeying, or circumventing the legal system of the society." [7] Wilson goes on to point out that the value system based on the notion of reputation is positive and is the only realistic one for the persons involved:

For it allows of the attainment of individual identity and social relatedness through activities and behavior accessible to these people. A young Caribbean "peasant" cannot become "respectable" in part because he cannot participate economically or politically in the total societal system within which "respectability" is the chief value. He is not literate and thus cannot enter the bureaucracy or the political or legal hierarchy. He is unskilled and hence cannot begin to climb the economic status ladder to achieve an income that will permit him to assume the signs of respectability. But at the same time he is politically, legally, and economically under the rule of the total society, and those who impress this rule on him are alien—of a different "class" and/or a different race and/or a different na-

[7] "Reputation and Respectability: A Suggestion for Caribbean Ethnology," *Man*, Vol. 4, no. 1, 1969, pp. 70–84.

tionality. From this situation arises the circumventions, the misunderstanding, and the real differences reflected in conduct and values.[8]

For the Micmac, it would seem that being "under the rule of the total society," as Wilson puts it, brings about a similar high regard for "beating the system." The kinds of behavior which contribute to a man's reputation are based on an even more general idea of risk which, independent of whatever is judged as good or bad among the ruling class, makes a man dare to approach situations of physical danger and temporarily outwit death. The human condition whereby a person is born, lives for a short space of time, and then dies, is a fact which the Micmac, both men and women, refer to frequently. The evidence of it, in frequent births and frequent deaths, is constantly before them. As adults, they seek less to avoid that fact than to confront it aggressively and test the limits of the human experience. Part of that testing is to drink and fight and make sexual conquests as basic physical and social experiences related to the life and death of the Micmac. Another part lies in knowing that outside the wider community there is, practically speaking, no power for the individual and that, in repeatedly exposing oneself to definition by ruling institutions, one risks the helplessness of isolation from one's own kind.

The subject of *machismo* as a quality of masculine reputation is usually associated with a double standard of sexual mores. The prowess of men in fighting, drink-

[8] *Ibid.*, p. 82.

ing, and fathering children is often in contrast to the modest respectability expected of women in societies influenced by Latin standards. However, the contrasts between the behavior of Micmac men and women are less dramatic than the reputation-respectability dichotomy which Wilson outlines. As mentioned before, women will verbally articulate the standards of "good" conventional behavior, but with an awareness like that of a Micmac man who knows that when he goes into a bar his own values counter the White laws which govern public behavior. Within the tribal community, Micmac women are expected to be on the defensive verbally and physically. A woman who is insulted or accused of "cheating," in a sexual triad or in the very general sense of secretively working against the good of another, must react aggressively or lose face. In the same way, a woman who suspects that she is being cheated against by another woman must call the other woman out if she is to avoid looking foolish. Rumors and third-person accounts frequently precede a direct confrontation between two women which may turn out to be more of a name-calling session than anything else. Yet among younger women, a more physical confrontation occasionally erupts, as the following description from field notes illustrates.

Clara Francis and Patsy got into a row last night at Maureen's. Clara has a younger sister who used to be a good friend of Patsy's and Patsy was, according to Maureen, often over at Clara's place during the course of last year. Clara's boyfriend, Paul, used to kid around with the two younger girls, but, as Patsy later told me, "Nothing ever was going on." In any case,

Clara walked into the kitchen last night and started giving Patsy "what for" in Micmac. Clara is tall, about 5′9″ and must weigh at least 150, so that her presence was, after all, imposing. Patsy, on the other hand, is about 5′4″ and weighs only about 120. When Clara first started talking, Patsy didn't even look at her but kept sitting in her chair. There were ten other people in the room, including Maureen and myself. The general chatter in the room continued during the incident; but I found I couldn't concentrate on what I was talking about with Simon when Clara began her tirade. When she had finished, Patsy slipped out of her chair and stood behind it to answer her. Peter and Skippy, with their backs to her, had to move a bit out of the way. When they looked over their shoulders and discovered the confrontation that was going on, they purposefully jostled Patsy a little and smiled and winked at me, as if to deemphasize the seriousness of this little dispute. I was able to catch a few words which I had first heard from Wani (*gijimic* "your ass," *makasit* "cunt") but Clara's aggressive stance and Patsy's spirited defense of herself were quite clear. Clara reached over and pulled or tried to pull Patsy's hair but Patsy gave her hand a whack with the side of her own hand and pushed the kitchen chair at her so that she almost lost her balance. A few more invectives were exchanged as Clara reached out again and caught hold of Patsy's hair and gave it a strong pull. Patsy at this point bit Clara's hand but Clara didn't let go, inspiring Patsy to bite down harder. Clara was steadying herself with her other hand on the chair-back, keeping her face averted while Patsy tried to strike at her. At this point, Peter and Terry (who had been in the living room when the fracus began) pried Clara loose from Patsy and Maureen and Skippy took Patsy to the far end of the kitchen. I thought that both the women looked more sulky than anything else as they were separated. Clara left the party and Maureen stayed with Patsy for about ten minutes until she had calmed down. Almost an hour passed before I had a chance to ask her what had happened. She seemed most intent on convincing me and herself that Clara never would have really hurt her because she was too big and slow, whereas Patsy felt that she herself was small but tough and was used to beating up bigger girls when she was in school.

Women have a particularly strong sense of revenge and a belief that injuries should be "paid off" as quickly as possible. For example, a teenage girl living in the city was attacked by several Puerto Rican girls who managed to give her a few knife cuts. Her mother, also in the city, protested that her girl was not the kind to provoke fights with others but, since she had been injured, it was her right to seek a quick retaliation. With the help of her two girlfriends, her daughter did just that by ambushing the leader of the Puerto Rican girls and beating her up. In disagreements between two Micmac women, conflicts have a way of coming quickly to a head and, after each side has represented itself, dying down just as quickly.

Because the population of the community is relatively stable, a former foe and her relatives continue to be socially present after a quarrel and must be tolerated. There is no losing an old enemy in the impersonality of urban life and therefore it becomes necessary for women who have fought to develop some responsible attitudes towards each other. In contrast to Micmac men, Micmac women seldom make of a quarrel the kind of contest which allows the protagonist and antagonist to become fast friends once the altercation is settled. For two men, the issue of a confrontation is blatantly one of control and it is usually dealt with in the simple terms of a physical match. For women, the issue is much more subtle. The good reputation of a woman relies on her ability to be strong in a social as well as physical way. She should have enough sense of herself to avoid being taken advantage of by others without becoming known as a person with a bad disposition. When men fight, men and women alike treat the incident as typical male behavior rather than a moral dilemma. When women quarrel, it is other women in particular who analyze the rightness and wrongness of the two parties involved, with a deep interest in assessing the character of each. Clara, for example, as a young woman in her twenties, had begun to accumulate the bad reputation of a trouble-maker. Patsy, still in her teens, did well to defend herself and, in fact, added to her good reputation because the blame of provocation could easily be put on Clara's shoulders.

The ideal Micmac character is phrased as *geolikwaniskic,* someone who can tolerate just about everybody and everything, who does not give other people orders or interfere with their lives. Tolerance of individual autonomy is great among the Micmac; telling another person what he should do when he or she is at the point of making a decision is frowned upon. Even a woman much more quarrelsome than Clara or a man who is reluctant to fight will be tolerated by the group, rather than excluded from it. Nonetheless, individuals have the right to personal outrage if they feel their tolerance has been taken advantage of and the right to a face-to-face confrontation to put a stop to intrusions on their own autonomy. It is women who deal with the morality of free actions and the boundaries between individual and group interest. They face issues of competition with each other in a way which is much more complex and direct than that of Micmac men. Even as the story is often told of how reservation baseball teams refuse to play against each other and insist on playing outside White teams, it is also true that a group of Micmac men would rather fight with strangers. They use physical contests among themselves as a way of shoring up their forces against the hostile outside world, for the loser in a game as well as the victor in a fight is a worthy man and worth having as a friend. Physical combat settles a quarrel with relative decisiveness. Because a Micmac man is much more likely to be suspicious about another man who is on the fringes of his own peer group, fighting becomes a way of enlarging the social network if, in the aftermath, the two individuals become buddies.

The amount and quality of information women can acquire about each other is more important to them than a proliferation of friendship ties. As a young woman becomes an active adult in the community, her sisters and the girlfriends she has had since childhood become increasingly important to her and the competitiveness she felt towards them in adolescence diminishes. Within the security of this kind of alliance, a Micmac woman can as an observer and as a performer learn about many other people in the wider network. For women, competitive conflict is a way of knowing, of gaining new information on individual character and on the notion of character itself, but it does not necessarily lead to the kind of defensive solidarity to which men are drawn. The communication which goes on among women is communication among fundamentally competitive and autonomous individuals who are sharpening their expertise on the norms and values of the community. Their conversation is often on the subject of Micmac behavior and, most specifically, on the nature of man-woman relationships—the jealousies, joys, confusions, and conflicts which surround each of them.

In the course of a lifetime a Micmac woman will have as many as five or six relationships in which she depends for a short while—or perhaps for years—on a man for some economic support. The random way in which adult Micmac Indians move around and meet each other within the community network makes the coming together and the breaking up of couples seem chaotic. In a sense, women make order out of these random meetings by demanding of each other adherence to a basic rule of fair play which governs competition for men. The rule is that information about sexual unions as social facts has to be open to the community. For example, if Patsy really had been having an affair with Clara Francis' boyfriend, Clara would have been justified in publicly accusing her, just as one could rightly accuse a person who tried to keep any information secret from the community. A man who received a lot of money and did not spend it generously on his friends and relatives, someone who found out about a good-paying job and withheld the information, someone who had a full tank of gas and drove alone to another city—each of these culprits is doing something reprehensible because it is self-serving and secretive. In somewhat the same way, a woman who becomes involved with another woman's man is liable to open accusation and community disapproval.

Prohibitions against cheating function in two ways. A woman has the responsibility to other women to share information on social relationships, that is, not to have cheating or secret relationships. Unless sexual liaisons are general knowledge, other women cannot accurately assess the social relationships of people in their group and therefore will not be able to act correctly towards them, for they will suffer not from a lack of information but from social misinformation. If Patsy and Paul are lovers, it matters to everyone who knows them, not just to Clara. Maureen, Patsy's friend, would no longer be able to treat Paul and Clara or any of their friends and relatives with indifference. Clara, if her suspicions had been justified, would have had a moral case against Patsy which would have embroiled her in a whole round of arguments and discussions, especially with women having some vested interest in the matter, e.g. Paul's mother and sisters, Patsy's allies, and Patsy herself. A secret affair would have had Patsy and Paul acting publicly in the eyes of the community as if their private relationship did not exist and, further, as if two people could strategize to put a stop on the fact of their relationship as social information, as social communication. Because a sexual union has social repercussions in the community, there is little tolerance of efforts to privatize a relationship. Instead, there exists a kind of satisfaction among women in exposing covert wishes to keep an affair secret.

Perhaps what Micmac women, always curious about relationships between men and women, are guarding themselves against is the embarrassment which falls to someone who, as Goffman sociologically grounds the metaphor, is "out of face" because of incomplete information or ignorance of social rules.[9] A Mexican-American, for example, might be out of face at a soirée in Beverly Hills because he is not familiar with the social etiquette of the wealthy. Or, to transpose the example, there is a story about Robert Kennedy's senatorial campaign taking him to an Italian section of New York. While there, he shocked the more plebian voters by eating a pizza with a knife and fork until his etiquette was corrected by an aide who instructed him to pick the pizza up in his hands like the *paisans*. Beyond etiquette, one can be out of face by ignorance of social relationships as well as social rules. In our own society, an unmarried woman who at a party spends a long and interesting time talking with a man she thinks is single, only to have his wife interrupt to tell him it's time to go home, has been deceived, perhaps by both of them, into relating with a husband as if he were a bachelor. A man at the same party whose wife has been having an affair with the host is equally out of face in his ignorance of the social relations which impinge on him; he and the hostess appear duped and pitiful to the friends who know of their deception. Deceived by whom is always the question. Micmac women hold other women most accountable for making their sexual relationships known

[9] Erving Goffman, *Interaction Ritual*, Essays in Face-to-face Behavior, Chicago, Aldine, 1967.

to the community so that the possibility of anyone's being out of face is minimized. A woman has the responsibility, too, of finding out about the social availability of others, men and women, and makes no assumption that social interaction can take place without first acquiring this basic information. When I began doing fieldwork, the initial question women addressed to me concerned my sexual availability, which was not distinguished from my social availability. They wanted to know if I were married but, more important, if my husband would be with me as I socialized, for my married status meant less and was less of a factor than my presence in their community as an individual woman without a man. Competition for men is such that Micmac women protect each other's interests by vigilantly keeping information on sexual unions up-to-date and open to the community. There may not be wide networks of friendship among women, as there are among men, but there is this ethic which generally works to keep women undeceived and responsible to each other.

On another level, the responsibility women have to each other to bring information on sexual relations to general community knowledge is a response to the fact that relationships with men, like information on jobs and transportation, have to be shared. Relative to an affluent suburban housewife, a Micmac woman goes through life more dependent on her family and women friends than on men. She also seems in her city life to be more independent of the responsibilities of child care and housework. In reality, there still exists a division of labor between men and women by which the former is recognized as the sex with the best and most continuous access to cash wages and the latter is understood as the sex most concerned with children and households. Because of this, women seek relationships and support from men in a generalized fashion that seldom secures one woman to one man for a lifetime. Men are less thought of as property which an individual woman can claim possession of than as a community resource which supports first the kin group and second potentially any adult woman at a greater kinship distance than first cousin. When women quarrel with each other over men, they quarrel more about the possibility of one or the other party secretly whisking a man away from the community and off the market, as it were, than about the issue of a man belonging to more than one woman. I came across several instances in the city of two young girlfriends sharing the same boyfriend without possessiveness or malice. This is an admittedly unusual arrangement, but that it happens at all casts light on what prohibitions against cheating are about. Because financial resources are limited and no one Micmac man can single-handedly support a woman and her children for a lifetime, the community disapproval which falls on a woman suspected of cheating is perhaps a warning that secret possession of a man is simply a bad investment and counter to the more group-oriented cultural solutions of the tribe.

When women get together in friendly groups they are emphatically possessive in talking about their men. A man's character—whether, for example, he is generous with gifts or tends to get physically violent, whether he is industrious or lazy, good or bad tempered—is elaborated upon by his current woman who gives most freely of her personal estimates. The same kind of information is likely to be withheld from another group of women which she does not entirely like or know well. In a well-integrated peer group, whatever a woman has to say about her current lover is listened to with respect and attention. That another woman in the group may have had a relationship with the same man is a fact discreetly ignored, but otherwise, talking about old boyfriends takes up about as much time as talking about present relationships. The rule is that a woman talking about a man in the here and now is accorded the authoritative and last word, indeed the only word, on his character during the time she is with him. Because relationships change, discourse on men tends to become very general. When the supplementary remarks which sisters have to make on their brothers and other male kin are included, the education with which women in a peer group provide each other on the ways of men becomes complete.

CHAPTER IV

Urban Interaction: A Closer Look

Between Men and Women

If physical contests between men serve to enlarge the social networks of both parties, sexual relationships between men and women function in an even more important way to multiply interpersonal contacts among adults and increase the store of information the community has about its membership. Ultimately, of course, they function biologically to increase the membership itself. The details of each sexual union, like the details of each altercation or feud, are mulled over by Micmac women with the same eye for moral judgment, while men, who are interested in telling their own stories of adventure and in being praised for their physical courage, almost always avoid conversations about who is sleeping with whom. Some men are openly disdainful of such women's talk and claim that the really important activity in the tribe is the aggressive hustling of Micmac men. Most men simply acknowledge sex as a subject appropriate for women to handle. Because this is generally accepted, the man whose love life goes poorly can claim to be an outsider to the rules of sexual relations; conversely, he is an innocent victim if his love life runs smoothly. In either case, he still professes disinterest in or ignorance of women's gossip.

The sad theme of having been cheated by women runs through the life histories of a good many Micmac men, as if women as experts on sexual matters frequently use their knowledge to outwit men. In sentimental retrospect, women are seen as plotters and planners who cheat in essentially two ways. First, they steal money from hard-working men. Actually women have a much more practical attitude towards money and are more calculating in expenditures than men. Adult women take on more of the responsibility of renting city apartments which many other people use and of making sure that rent, utilities, and food costs are shared. It is a woman, too, rather than a man, who takes the most direct responsibility for the raising of children, her own and others, and who closely calculates the resources of breadwinners and thus their family obligations. All these concerns make women mix their love affairs with monetary affairs and they do feel morally justified in getting as much money as they can from men. Second, while men think of themselves as more steady and true in their affections, they think of women as aggressively foraging for new partners. For Micmac men, the dilemma in cheating is to understand how one's own sex could be party to the betrayal. Thinking of themselves and their buddies as the seduced in cases of infidelity solves the problem. The women, then, seem to act as a divisive force, alienating men from each other. For example, in looking back over their lives, many men insinuate that women have tried to provoke fights between rival lovers. In reality men hardly ever fight over women; their physical contests are usually free of the complications of sexual rights. A man may feel very protective of his mother and his sisters and yet not at all protective or possessive of his girlfriend. Indifference and invulnerability to women's wiles is the typical stance of a man with a good reputation. Successful sexual relationships rank as physical conquests, with their finer emotional nuances de-emphasized. A man with pride does not broadcast the interpersonal risk he takes in involving himself with a woman. If, while he is on the road, he hears that his girl friend has taken up with another man, he may shrug his shoulders as if to say, "What can you expect of women?" The melancholy songs of a Hank Williams or a Buck Owens bemoaning the heartlessness of all females and their constant betrayal of all males give the traveling man the expressive satisfaction he does not allow himself. On every jukebox and in every car radio, the more-than-physical power of women to hurt men is reiterated in ballad after mournful ballad, like witnesses' testimony to the insoluble dilemma of the differences between men and women. The good times and other women a man has while he travels around with his buddies are a solace to his frustration with this universal dilemma and serve as a measure of his spirit.

The greater tension in sexual matters among the Micmac is between men and women as two groups rather than two individuals of the opposite sex. Western civilization's convention of romantic love is so highly individualized that the implications of group opposition can be all but lost on an observer.[1] According to our conventions, a man and a woman can choose each other as sexual partners independent of the preferences of their families and friends and, for real romance, even choose against them. The pair retreats, preferably with institutional sanction and presumably for life, to consolidate their respective social atoms into one socially regressive unit. Parents can be seen as an intrusion, and former friends as evocative of past loves which threaten the present. Given time, a couple constructs for itself a private niche in which to breed more social atoms. The individualization on which romantic love depends is related to the individualism by which corporate bureaucracies function. In the private, domestic sphere, individualism leans towards the freedom of regressive isolation; in the public arena, it is subject to corporate legality.

To understand how a community such as the Mic-

[1] See, as an example of group opposition well observed and analyzed, Gregory Bateson's classic 1935 article, "Culture Contact and Schismogenesis," *Man*, Vol. 35, pp. 178–83. My discussion of man-woman relationships is much influenced by another classic, Philip Slater's "On Social Regression," *American Sociological Review*, Vol. 28, no. 3, June, 1963.

mac handles relationships between men and women, it is necessary to jettison the notion of romantic love and consider a more diffuse participation in the drama between man and woman. Because the Micmac community provides a supportive context for individual action, the romantic regression of a couple away from it is unnecessary and even suspicious. Women, with their interest in what a couple does, are the principal witnesses to the union. A young woman's peer group has the best access to information about a couple. She comes back to it from her first dates and relates all the details of the evening: where she went on a car ride, what she had to eat, what other people were met, whether or not she had intercourse. As the relationship becomes more serious, the same kind of information is shared with girl friends and sisters. Every quarrel and every reconciliation, every minor flirtation which has its effect on the major affair is described with relish. Even if the principal actress in the drama decides to move out of the room or apartment she shares with her friends and live with her lover, she will still communicate with them often and be open with them about the relationship.

Perhaps it is this openness about sexual matters and the de-emphasis of a couple as a social unit which makes the Micmac appear naive on the subject of homosexuality. Men and women are definitively opposed to each other as sexual groups, with less tension about affection and conflict within each group than exists between the sexes. That women are allied with women and men are allied with men is an indisputable, natural fact. The real risk, the real problem, and the real excite-

ment in constructing a new relationship lies in overcom-
ing or at least quelling for a time the differences between the two distinct natural categories, man and
woman. For example, I frequently heard the terms "lesbian" and "queer" used to describe people whose behavior was unsocial in ways not related to homosexuality at all. For example, if a woman remained aloof
from the community or if she had just a bad disposition,
she might be called a lesbian or a "lezzy." If a man tried
to impress others with his education or otherwise put on
airs, he might be called a fag or a queer because he
socially failed his group. The decision to live with a
man usually comes only after a young woman has acquired social and sexual experience. Even then it is rare
to find a couple actually living alone together; relatives
and friends are omnipresent as visitors and members of
the urban household. It often happens instead that a
woman still in her teens becomes pregnant before she
has much social acumen, while she is living with girlfriends or with older relatives in the city.[2] Instead of
moving in with the father of her child, she will either

[2] In talking with women of all ages, I found that the pattern of pregnancy and the birth of the eldest child out of wedlock followed by a
marriage to a man who was not necessarily the father of that first child
has been prevalent for some time. While not every Micmac woman
follows such a pattern, relations between men and women and the
general organization of the extended family make it possible for it to
be considered relatively normal rather than unusual behavior. In par-
tial substantiation of this tendency, Philip K. Bock has noted that the
rate of illegitimacy at Restigouche Reservation was over many years
about 20 per cent ("Patterns of Illegitimacy on a Canadian Indian Reserve: 1860–1960," *Journal of Marriage and the Family*, Vol. 26, no. 2,
1964, pp. 142–48).

stay where she is and rely on her peers, aunts, and uncles for emotional support or she will make the effort to return to the reservation from which she came. There are not that many Micmac women who know how to present themselves at the prenatal clinics available in large city hospitals or who, having once presented themselves, feel comfortable having their babies in an unfamiliar, impersonal environment. The dependence on city clinics and on Aid to Dependent Children, like the dependence on welfare and housing programs, will increase if the Micmac become a stable and fixed population in Boston. At the beginning of the 1970s, when the field work for this research project was completed, there were only random cases of young women, unmarried and pregnant for the first time, having their children in Boston hospitals. As social assistance benefits have been extended to Indians in the Maritimes, rural clinics and small hospitals in townships serve their medical needs, providing care in gynecology and obstetrics.

Throughout a pregnancy, whether the first or subsequent ones, a woman has to maintain a good, cheerful, unargumentative kind of behavior, lest her unborn child be harmed by the bad wishes of antagonized people with *buoin* powers. Close friendships with other women should become even closer and it often seems that two good friends will become pregnant at the same time and share the experiences of pregnancy, childbirth, and early infant care. The idea of harboring animosity against a pregnant woman is scandalous. If she has to control her aggressions and assume a sweet demeanor, the men and women, and particularly the latter, who know her have to bury old animosities or be accused of working evil against her child. Long before a Micmac woman goes to a clinic for prenatal care, she is involved in her own private rituals for insuring the health of the baby. She is encouraged to eat for her infant as well as herself and to be very attentive to her personal food preferences, denying herself nothing, even a new and unusual craving, because in being sensitive to her body, she is doing the best by her baby. She drinks tea to calm her nerves, usually just the Red Rose brand, although sometimes an old aunt or grandmother will prepare for her a special herbal blend. In the early months of pregnancy, the fetus is believed to be particularly susceptible to being influenced by a woman's experiences and by the magic of whatever enemies she has. This susceptibility diminishes as the unborn infant develops not only physically but as a human being with its own characteristics and fate.

The same stories that researchers Wilson and Ruth Wallis heard in the 1950s about prenatal experiences producing malformed children circulate today. A young mother frightened by a cripple or a scarred or deformed person may, it is said, bear a child with a similar trait. More traditional stories are told of a woman who teased animals—rabbits, moose, bear, birds, or fish—only to have nature take its revenge by turning her unborn child into a part human, part animal monster. The Micmac children I met looked outstandingly normal, and it was a result, as was repeatedly explained to me, of diligent care during pregnancy. It is important that crises such as arguments be avoided. If an expectant mother witnesses a knife fight, a fire, or a car accident, it can make her infant permanently nervous and irritable. While she is not expected to become a recluse, the more careful she is the more she will tend to retreat to an inner circle of women friends and relatives and keep journeys to new places and meetings with new people to a minimum. Feeling as open as she does to nefarious influences, it is no wonder that a woman, especially if she is pregnant for the first time, will want to retreat to her own reservation home and be surrounded by familiar faces and a familiar environment. She will go back to the household in which she grew up or, if that is not possible, she will go to the home of a relative, usually but not always on her mother's side. All else failing, she may choose to join the household of a girlfriend who, like herself, has become pregnant and has returned home to have her baby. Sometimes it is the noise and dirt of the city that is cited as a reason for leaving the city; at other times, it is directly stated that other minority groups, Blacks and Puerto Ricans, are strange and frightening and can harm a fetus or influence the color of its skin or the texture of its hair. The people Micmac women have to sit next to in city clinics are not only strangers in a social sense but they are also physically strange to the Indians and it is sometimes speculated that these other people have a certain powerful magic of their own. In the Maritimes, the rural people using a clinic are White—of Irish, Scotch, German, Dutch, or French descent—and therefore understood to be definitely without access to great supernatural powers.

A quiet nine months on the reservation waiting for an infant to be born is a luxury which few Micmac women can afford. Perhaps it is only the sixteen- or seventeen-year-old, who has yet to become a good wage-earner and who may still play the role of a helpful daughter in a large household, who can be allowed it and who has the most to benefit by it. Older women will feel her growing belly and make sage comments on the health of the baby. They talk about their own experiences of childbirth and admonish her to avoid lingering on thresholds to houses, especially of people suspected of being *buoins*, and to avoid sitting at windows if she wishes to have an easy birth. In more remote areas, older women acting as midwives, two and sometimes three together, will take charge of delivering a baby. More typically, it is women of several generations who form an entourage to escort the expectant mother to a hospital when her labor pains begin, holding her hands and wiping her brow. At the hospital, she is on her own in an impersonal setting, but at least she knows that a supportive contingent waits out in the parking lot, smoking cigarettes and drinking cokes from a vending machine.

The woman who has her child in the city usually lacks the attendant support of old aunts and grandmothers. It is her own age-mates, three or four of her closest friends and perhaps her sister, who remind her to take care of herself and who sit in the waiting room of Boston Lying-In or St. Margaret's Hospital until the delivery of her child is announced. In the city and on the reservation, the influence of modern medicine is being felt. Older women remember giving birth without the aid of drugs to lessen the pain and remember nursing their children for as long as a year. Young women are as preoccupied with medicines as their great-grand-mothers and almost with an exploratory curiosity opt for the novelty of anesthetics during childbirth. The con-temporary Micmac woman also prefers bottle-feeding to breast-feeding her infant. These choices in no way di-minish the kind of care which is invested in a newborn child. In the very smallest and poorest of households, there is a little crib or bassinet prepared for the infant. A full stock of commercial equipment is organized around it—baby powder, oil, lotion, diapers, pins, and sponges, all articles procured at relatively great expense and with real pride in caring for the baby. This pride is shared by the women who are closest to the mother, particularly by her age-mates, who have worked while she was in the hospital to arrange the crib and all the necessary equipment.

The great interest which Micmac women show in their friends' children stems from the fact that they have been partaking of each other's experiences of pregnancy and empathizing with the experiences of childbirth and early infant care. The calm within which a woman ide-ally passes the time waiting for her baby to be born should carry over in the first several months to a year of its life. During that period, she is primarily but not solely responsible for the health and well-being of her child. Her friends will help with feeding and diaper-changing. Female relatives will, as the child passes its first few months, drop by daily and ask to handle it. If the baby has been born with a caul, as occasionally happens among the Micmac, or with a special birth mark, or if the baby has large hands or a strong kick and sturdy look, older women will predict a rosy future for it. All these women, young and old, will be persistently observant of what makes this child special, possessively interested for as long as they live in its personality and welfare. Kinship has its priorities in all this, so that if a woman has a child in the city, where kin and friendship ties all tend to merge into a single-generation, adult network, she must make a kind of social presentation of her infant to the family she has on the reservation. If she is very young, it is really her family which has gained a new member, more than the family of the child's father. If she is older her visit to the reservation should also include trips to his relatives as a reminder that their numbers and possibly their responsibilities have increased. The reservation is the place where the business of securing Indian papers for a newborn child is settled. Today, the practical advantages of being Micmac are worth more than the thirty-five dollars offered by the Canadian Bureau to the Indian willing to relinquish his rights. And a reservation baptism, although usually a minor affair, is thought to be a bit more respectable than a city ceremony.

A young woman who has had her first child may resume her role as an adult in the tribal network and, whether she continues to live with her girlfriends or decides to live with a man, she will probably become a working woman again. Part of her salary will now go in remittances back to her own family or to a large related household which functions to care for her child while she brings in a cash wage. Between jobs or sometimes on a whim she will join a car full of other Micmac Indians making the two-day drive to the Maritimes and visit her child and her family. As in the past history of the Micmac, a woman's ability to have children is a mark of her strength and value and there is really no one to shame her for having had a child out of wedlock, except an outsider to Micmac culture. The woman who cannot bear children is to be pitied.

Physical maturity is not confused with social autonomy. A seventeen-year-old mother has yet to integrate herself into the wider social network of the community and the father of her child, if equally as young, is also likely to be still circulating within the narrow confines of a small peer group. Most families and the community at large work to allow their younger members a freedom from child care which is socially functional as well as good economic strategy. The way in which one young woman, Teresa Meuse, was able to have a child and continue to be socially and economically active illustrates a very typical Micmac solution to child care. Teresa came to Boston in 1966 when she was eighteen years old. In the spring of 1967 she had her first child, a girl named Debbie, at St. Margaret's Hospital in Boston. The father of the child, Henry, was a construction worker in his mid-twenties who, with several of his buddies, traveled around New England on various jobs. After the baby was born, Teresa continued to live with her girlfriend who helped her with the baby and gave her free time on weekends when Henry was in

town. In the summertime, Teresa took the baby to Nova
Scotia and stayed at her parents' home in Eskasoni. Several times during the summer she left the baby in the
care of her mother and sisters and joined Henry in the
States for a few days. In the fall she came back to Boston
to take a waitressing job that her former roommate had
written her about; but when the tips and the salary did
not meet her expectations, she went back home to the
reservation for the winter. Before Debbie was a year
old, Teresa was in Boston again, encouraged by her family to earn what income she could and send back remittances to them that would go towards the support of the
household. Meanwhile, Henry was giving Teresa support money from his salary to defray her expenses while
she was living in the city. During this second term of
residence in Boston, both Teresa and her girlfriend
were able to stay with Teresa's aunt, to whom they each
paid about thirty dollars a month for room. When Henry
stayed over, Teresa would usually slip her aunt a few
extra dollars. From a factory wage of just under a
hundred dollars a week, Teresa was able to provide for
her own board and room and to send money in varying
amounts, depending on what changes occurred in her
own expenses, back to her parents. She occasionally
took time off to go back to Eskasoni to see Debbie.
Twice she and Henry went together and stayed with her
family, but they also visited with Henry's relatives who
were from a nearby settlement. After a layoff at the factory where she worked, Teresa heard through a relative
of hers about a similar job in Leominster and left Boston
for that. After two months, Teresa was back in Boston

again, working as a waitress in a diner and staying with a cousin who had been a foster child in her parents' household when she was growing up. Throughout all these moves, Teresa was confident that Debbie was being well taken care of and better off than if she were in the city. Teresa's girlfriend, aunt, and cousin were all helpful to her, while Henry proved to be very constant in his support for about three years, after which Teresa began seeing another man and Henry fell into the background of her life.

It should also be added that finding out what Micmac man is the partner of what Micmac woman comes less from close observation than from someone making a flat statement that "Jim and me been together for a year now" or "Caroline and me stay together." Impassive faces, a lack of physical contact or of proximity between partners, the avoidance of references by others to their relationship—this absence of signals can mask the fact of a union between a man and a woman. Micmac men and women prefer to restrain emotional expressions of affection. Moreover, as a people under rule, they have developed ways of keeping the vital matter of male-female relationships out of the sight of interfering outsiders, with their righteous recommendations for moral improvement, or their programmatic efforts (which would probably result in fewer rather than better Micmac Indians). The increase in the Micmac population has followed the general doubling of the American Indian population, regardless of whether statisticians label many births as "illegitimate" from a conventional point of view. Cross-culturally, there are a variety of ways, all

of them proper, whereby children are born and cared for
and the survival of a group is insured. The increase of
American Indians as well as other minority groups has
been due to what is right about what they have been
doing (not what is "immoral," "illegal," or "promiscu-
ous") in organizing sexual unions, families and child
care in ways which permit a great amount of personal
flexibility and security, given the context of the hard reality of poverty.

In approaching the Micmac, the unknowns about
interpersonal behavior remain until the observer allies
himself with them and, in ceasing to judge their behavior, comes to appreciate it as a different dynamic, an
ongoing system of organization that cannot be understood by assigning categories of pathological behavior.

About Legal Marriage

Historically the Micmac have had a relatively casual approach to the institution of marriage. Teresa and
Henry were typical in their avoidance of a legal con-
tract. If Henry had been younger and less of a wage-
earner, their relationship would undoubtedly have been
much more brief, for Henry took on himself responsibilities that simply cannot be demanded of most young
men. Because Micmac men work on the economic
fringes of the wider society, it is a real question whether
a man, older or younger, can as an individual support a
wife and children in a conventional fashion. The ideal
legal marriage is, after all, an alliance between an eco-

nomically viable man and a dependent wife. Their offspring legitimately inherit their property and the endurance of the marriage usually insures that the offspring
will also inherit a conglomeration of their parents' idio-
syncrasies, with very little strong input from other relatives. Since the individualism of the Micmac exists in
the context of the tribal group, a legal alliance which
emphasizes a contracted lifelong relation between just
two people is immediately going to antagonize the community or, at least, be subject to the strains that different
subgroups can exert. An individual remains close to his
or her blood relatives in an association which is natural
rather than contracted. An individual is also at ease
among his or her peers of the same sex. All through her
life a woman will share more confidences with her
mother, aunts, sisters, and girl friends than with any
man. All through his life, a man will spend most of his
time with other men and close blood relations. When a
child is born it is these associations, from both mother's
and father's sides, which are inherited, not property. A
legal marriage, if taken seriously, can pit the interests of
a couple against those of the extended family and the
peer group and actually cheat a child out of his full in-
heritance of social ties. Teresa, for example, made her
child known to a fairly large group of friends and kin.
She had no possessive pretensions to forming Debbie's
character; she noticed a natural physical resemblance
between herself and her daughter and yet considered
Debbie's personality unique and fixed, not open to in-
tervention. It was most important that this unique person have a social identity, for it is in each other that the

Micmac have their greatest resource. As Debbie grew older, Teresa only asked one thing of Henry, and that was to come and visit the child whenever he could or, even better, take his daughter down home to visit with his family.

If a young woman and a young man were to get married at an early age, they would prematurely end their own learning about the tribal community and gain a conventional intimacy at the price of knowing and being known by other Micmac. This is so not simply because a legal marriage infers a lifelong monogamy but also because of the social implications of sexual unions. Every sexual alliance an individual has in the course of a lifetime is a new social statement he makes about himself to his own group and, very often, to the social network of his partner. With every new couple on the scene, there comes the possibility that two formerly distinct networks will connect with each other and, little by little, overlap and combine. To marry young, with romantic notions about a lifetime fidelity, can actually work against the important socializing function of the community as well as against a couple's socialization and integration into the community.

Speaking generally, the idea of legal marriage which Micmac women have is different from that of men. Neither men nor women act on the premise that the marriage performed by a priest or magistrate binds two individuals together for life. For a woman, marriage is a badge of respectability which gives her a public identity. When a welfare worker comes to the house, a woman can say, "Yes, I'm Mrs. Simon." In court, in church, at a child's school, the fact that a woman is legally married indicates that she recognizes the values of the dominant society. Older Micmac women know that as long as they have the responsibility of appearing in bureaucratic settings, they will be treated with more respect as married women than as single women, whether or not they can on the spot produce a domesticated husband. Bailing a younger brother out of jail, visiting tubercular relatives in hospitals, identifying a body at the morgue—all of these performances go much more smoothly if one has an accepted, conventional, legal status.

Men are openly suspicious of marriage as a trap, and because of their particular social and economic situation their suspicions are more justified than those of affluent bachelors. Micmac men have a generalized responsibility to the tribal community which contrasts and conflicts with the family obligations implied by legal marriage. They must be geographically mobile and keep in close touch with many other adults to get important information about jobs and travel. To be tied down or settled down would mean being cut off from sources of information about work and, therefore, the means to the end of a cash income. A man has the responsibility to be economically viable and therefore mobile, but this is a lifetime responsibility to the community and, within the community, to his relatives and friends more than it is a responsibility to a specific woman. Nor does a man necessarily act as an individual economically responsible for the support of a child that is exclusively his. The way of the community is to diffuse that responsibility

among an array of adults, so that the corporate body of
the tribe, more than a parent, can lay claim to a child as
an investment which yields the profit of allegiance
when the child matures.

How, then, is a Micmac man led to the altar? Taking the role of the groom in a marriage ceremony is generally regarded by Micmac men as a gesture, a brave
and somewhat foolish risk taken to please a woman. If a
man is smart, he avoids being caught up in the legal
implications of marriage and concentrates on enjoying
his time with his woman for as long as it lasts and on
keeping in close touch, as before, with his buddies.

Whether one considers marriage a badge of respectability or a mistake, it is fairly certain that the Micmac
who do get married transform a legal union into something different from an easily quantifiable statistical category. In the city, women in their early twenties and almost all men are equally wary of getting married. A
young woman without a child to care for can be mobile,
earn a wage, and circulate within the adult community
with about the same ease as a man. As a woman ap-
proaches her mid-twenties, however, it is likely that the
pressures on her to stabilize her location and to acquire
more formal social identification will increase. If
younger siblings are old enough to look for work in the
city, she will feel the obligation to offer them a place to
live, a home. As her own child who is being cared for in
the Maritimes grows up, she begins to feel the necessity
of offering an apartment, rather than a rooming house,
for visits. A maximum amount of pressure comes to bear
when, in her second pregnancy, a woman has her atten-

tion drawn away from her peers (who once distracted her from her original family) and the idea of gathering her several children around her draws her once again to a relationship that is midway between generations. When becoming a mother for the first time, a woman turns to her own mother and older relatives for help; but the older she gets, the more her attention begins to focus on her own role as the intermediary link between generations. It is appropriate, therefore, that a woman over twenty-five be married because it is the public mark of a responsible and respectable female.

If a woman working in the city wants to have children, she has to develop a relationship with a man with or without a wedding band, a relationship that will allow her a temporary financial dependency during the latter months of pregnancy and for the first months of her infant's life. This relationship is especially important if she has been a good bread-winner and if the other adults associated with her apartment are less reliable in bringing in cash wages than she is. Micmac women claim that they know by the way their bodies feel when it is the right time to become pregnant, and it often seems that the right time has to do with a total picture of security: for example, a situation in which there is a boyfriend who is generous, a younger sister who has work, and a cousin who needs a place to stay and becomes a paying boarder. In all, not much is really asked, only an economic lull or the promise of a lull. A woman with several children has got to keep bringing in a cash income when the lull is over because she and almost everyone else she knows enjoy only the most precarious access to money.

To ease the situation for her, there will always be a greater number of adults in her city household than children. One of them may be her husband and the father of her youngest. But he may not really live with her for more than a few years, during which time he does more to help out than to take over the support of the household. While he is with her and after he goes, he is expected to be generous to his offspring, but not even the harshest Micmac wife would make legal claim to child support from a man in the same economic boat as herself. The other two or three or even four adults may have a random and what seems like a chaotic association to the household of a mature Micmac woman, yet the presence of more people insures the safety of her children while she is busy visiting other Micmac or at work. Children who live in the city are sent for visits down home or, on occasion, sleep over with relatives and family friends in Boston. It happens, too, that a city child may temporarily, because of changing circumstances, become a member of a home base household in the Maritimes and have both city and country background in his experience of growing up. The consistency and stability which families afford children is larger than a simple household unit and it lies in the community's capacity to identify each new member as the child of a particular woman and a particular man, in other words, to account for its young. Whether in Boston or in the Maritimes, a child is known as the daughter or son of socially identifiable people and is recognized by this primary kinship affiliation wherever she or he goes.

This is true whether or not the parents were married, for paternity is no mystery and there is no woman who wants it to be a debatable matter. In some ways, the openness with which women discuss their affairs acts to insure each child's knowing who his father is in a more effective way than legal marriage ever could. Women maintain close ties with their girl friends all through their lives, confiding in them the usual details about their sexual activities. Girl friends are also open about when they are menstruating and it is very common for them to reckon the approach of their periods by reference to each other's cycles. Information conveyed to girl friends also includes news of sexual relationships that one's boyfriend may be temporarily ignorant of. So it is that information on what we might consider illicit sexual activity and on the menstrual cycle is shared by a clique of friends who, if a child is born, become witnesses to a correct paternity.

Matters of sex and children are so much the province of women that when a Micmac woman marries an outsider who does not understand the implications of women's work in a society which is group-oriented, there can be great misunderstandings and conflicts. White husbands, for example, seem to assume that by legal marriage they have secured the total allegiance of their wives. The dozen or so Micmac women I met who had married White men felt that there was better economic security in doing so, but also felt strongly committed to socializing with their own families and friends. The husband would typically become concerned that his wife might gossip with her girl friends about his sexual performance, and his Indian wife would see no reason why she should not. More importantly, she would want to have her family around her, living in, if it seemed her husband could afford it, and then, with some freedom from childcare, she would want to socialize with other Micmac men and women. For a truckdriver who is trying to put every nickel towards paying off the bank loan on his truck, or the skilled blue-collar worker who believes that upward mobility means saving for a two bedroom house in Dedham, a wife who finds it difficult to isolate herself from her community could make life very difficult. Not sharing one's good fortune with kin and being isolated into a small nuclear family can make life just as difficult for the Micmac woman. In addition, the behavior of her mother-in-law, whom she would probably not have to deal with to any great extent in her own society, would come across as intrusive and hostile. Most women who are married to White men (with few exceptions, men of Irish descent) are struck by the maternal possessiveness of their respective mothers-in-law, which seems to alienate their husbands from them. They note, too, that being grouchy or unmindful of the grandchildren is typical behavior for their husbands' mothers, behavior unbecoming a grandmother and likely to cause them, if they were Micmac, to be accused of witchcraft. This interpretation of the relationship between a White grandparent and part-Indian grandchildren is undoubtedly influenced by the fact that all the women mentioned brought their children back into the Micmac community and, more specifically, brought them back to their maternal lineage—a tendency which Micmac women have anyway, even without the impetus of an intrepid Ameri-

can mother-in-law. Women who stay married to White
men are harder to find than those who do not and it is
reasonable to assume that these Micmac women must
make compromises along the lines of reducing contact
with other Indians.

Micmac men are content to leave the fundamental
issues of parenthood to women, rarely disputing paternity but not really acting on it until their children are
well past infancy. They offer occasional support to the
women who have had their children, but it is only when
a child begins to talk and walk and exhibit signs of his
unique personality that his father can begin to offer the
child the best that he has, which is not money but social
contacts. Some fathers begin by toting their pre-school
offspring around with them on visits to the reservation
area or to relatives scattered over New England. Most
are content to let the women take care of them during
childhood and wait until their children are into early adolescence before they become instrumental in their
lives. I think that Micmac men are genuinely awestruck
by the discovery that a son or daughter is physically mature, as if, on the periphery of their vision, something
had been happening which at middle age they focus on
fully. However depressed their own circumstances are,
Micmac men usually work to get their children integrated into the adult community by extending to them
the hospitality of friends and relatives in the city and
passing on to them information about jobs, without
which it is impossible to survive urban life. This is done
with equal enthusiasm for daughters and sons. While a
Micmac woman having her second and third child dur-

ing her middle to late twenties is drawn to a consideration of a coming generation and of her own role as a link between past and future Indians, a Micmac man maintains a more steady emphasis on the present concerns of his own generation. In past centuries, when more traditional Micmac Indians were undergoing the impact of Western expansion, hunters and warriors in their prime of life ate first at ritual feasts; women, the old, and children ate later. Today, the most economically viable group in the community has extended to include many women as well as men because both are potential wage-earners in industrial society. Yet the idea that the rest of the community should in a variety of ways support those in their prime of life continues unaltered. It is most clearly seen with men whose energies are heavily invested, as most are, in peer group relationships. It is also clearly seen in the return of a woman with two or three children to an active schedule of work and socializing, a return which is supported by kin and friends to the point where it becomes the rule rather than the exception. For men, the sense of the intermediary role they play between one generation and another is finally brought home when their own children appear on the fringes of the adult network.

The Wedding

In the spring of 1971, a forty-three-year-old Micmac man named Tom Hammond left Boston for Nova Scotia to go to the wedding of his daughter Grace. When Grace was born twenty-one years earlier, Tom was a young man newly arrived in the city and his Micmac girl friend, Grace's mother, returned to her mother's cabin in an Indian settlement near Truro to have their child. She used money that Tom gave her to make the journey and, when Grace was born, Tom legally acknowledged her as his child. About a year and a half later, Grace's mother came back to Boston to work, leaving Grace with her married sister and her mother in the same wooden house where she had given birth to her. When she got to the city she saw Tom every so often but went out with other men. In 1954 she was killed in a car crash in Maine. Grace Hammond stayed with her aunt and grandmother. She was pretty and bright and very much a favorite in the household, never suffering from the label "orphan" which the Micmac apply to a trouble-some child without family ties. Her father occasionally visited the reservation area and would pass some time at Truro. One year, at Christmas time, he dropped off a doll for her at the house. Tom also had two sons, one three years younger than Grace, the other five years younger, who lived with their maternal relatives in nearby Shubenacadie. Grace's grandmother had friends and relatives of her own there and took her along on visits. Once, when Grace was ten or eleven, her grand-mother pointed out Tom to her and told her that he was her father. When she was thirteen, she met Tom walk-ing down the main road in the Truro settlement. He asked her how she was doing in school and, reaching into his wallet, gave her a dollar. Four years later, Grace was in Boston living with relatives on her mother's side and, for the first time, was conscious of the fact that many people knew her as Tom Hammond's child. Tom, usually a very undemonstrative man, was openly proud of Grace, as if she were a new acquisition, which, in a social sense, she was. He made it clear to the younger men in the immediate community that anyone who mistreated his daughter would be in for trouble and he was impressed that she usually attended Sunday mass with a smaller group of older women, behavior not uncommon for young girls recently arrived in the city and yet taken by Tom as an indication of her special virtue. He did not think it right to advise Grace directly but he did make sure that information about jobs was passed along to her through the intermediary of a female cousin of his who saw Grace frequently. The longer Grace was in the city, the more she saw her father and the more he tested her in her role as a daughter by involving her in doing favors for him. Sometimes Grace would be asked to bring clothes to a friend of her father's about to be released from a hospital or to pick Tom up on the highway where his car had broken down. After three years in Boston, Grace decided to return to the Maritimes. There, at an Indian party in Sydney, she met a young man of mixed Micmac and Irish descent and they decided to marry.

The wedding was largely a local affair, without any formal written invitations being sent out. Tom was making a special trip from Boston and one of Grace's uncles on her mother's side was coming from New Brunswick; otherwise the guests at the ceremony and at the party following it were people who lived in or happened to be visiting the area of Truro at the time. Two weeks earlier the priest had announced the bans from the pulpit of the church. At the same time, Grace and her husband-to-be, George Higgins, had found an empty house on the Shubenacadie reservation not far from the paper mill where George worked and had already furnished it with a couch and a table borrowed from relatives. Grace and the aunt who had raised her went to a large shopping center department store and bought a simple, short, white wedding dress, which was on sale, and material for a veil.

Tom arrived in Nova Scotia the day before the ceremony. He went first to visit his own family, his mother and father and two sisters at Pictou Landing. There he found three old cronies he had grown up with and the four men began a prewedding celebration of their own which lasted through the late afternoon and into the night. The next day, Tom and one of these friends, a cousin to Grace's aunt who knew the family well, proceeded on to Truro. They stopped for lunch at a roadside stand that sold take-out chicken and thought about taking a detour to visit another old friend who lived in a cabin tucked away in a remote forest. They rejected the idea and arrived at Truro just in time for the three o'clock ceremony.

Close to fifty people were in the church. There were a few older Micmac couples who seemed to be putting in an appearance as testimony to the possibility of an enduring marriage. Most of the guests were single men and women who sat separated from each other by age and sex. There were guests in their teens and early twenties. There were middle-aged women with clusters of school-age children around them and very old women who made a point of never missing a wedding or a funeral. There was a small group of virginal and somewhat giggly Micmac girls in early adolescence and, lingering on the doorstep during the ceremony, a faction of young men of about the same age smoking cigarettes as they resisted being drawn into the church. The guests endured the simple ceremony more than they participated in it. Tom Hammond, Grace's aunt and grandmother, and the Indian mother of the groom left the choice of ritual performance up to the young couple and the priest who, in this case, performed a brief celebratory mass in English.

Grace and George left the church surrounded by their friends and relatives and all went to Grace's aunt's house to eat and drink. On the way, because it was warm, the groom took off the dark blue jacket and string tie he had been wearing. Other men did the same while the women kept their hats and other dress-up finery on until they reached the reception and then put decorum aside. The priest who performed the ceremony was also invited to the reception. Grace, her aunt, and her grandmother made him their special responsibility and did not really relax until, after an hour or so, he left. He was an older man with a weak heart, newly assigned to the settlement as a kind of retirement from the outside world of urban parishes. This wedding was his first major responsibility after weeks of attending to a handful of faithful women, children, and old people. Aside from quiet baptisms and funerals, he would have no other task until the fall, when he would lead a busload of his older, mostly female parishioners on a pilgrimage to the shrine of Sainte Anne de Beaupré in Quebec.

There was a white paper tablecloth over the formica-top kitchen table and a wealth of food displayed on top of it: a well-done roast beef, two roasted chickens, boiled potatoes, white bread, plates of donuts, a special chunk of fresh salmon that a guest brought, bowls of popcorn, and a platter of sliced bologna and American cheese. Another guest, one of Grace's uncles, brought a bag of clams which he cleaned and cooked during the reception. On the kitchen counter next to the sink, there were cans of beer and bottles of Scotch and bourbon. The children drank orange soda and root beer. It was the men who made the most elaborate and noisy show of eating and drinking. The grandmothers at the party made sure their plates were well-laden and retired to the corners of the living room to talk and eat with each other. Women middle-aged and younger and the oldest men seemed almost disdainful of the food and drink, taking small portions and sharing even these with the children.

More people came to the reception than to the wedding. Presents for the young couple began to pile up in the kitchen and in the back bedroom where they would spend their wedding night. There were drinking glasses, a set of plastic dishes, dish towels, bath towels, a plastic tablecloth, blankets, ashtrays, pillowcases, two coffee mugs, and a variety of other domestic items. All these would eventually outfit the couple's spare little reservation cabin.

As the celebration went on, the children fell asleep and the older folks went home. The music from the kitchen radio was turned up and extra supplies of alcohol were sent for. All the food, down to the last piece of popcorn, had been consumed. Someone circulated the rumor that the Mounties were going to put an end to the festivities but they never appeared. Two men began a combination fistfight and wrestling contest, overturning chairs and a coffee table piled high with dishes, ashtrays, and paper cups. Grace's aunt called on her brother to intervene and one of the men was flung out the back door and over a porch railing into the yard some eight feet below where, uninjured, he spent the night. The party continued cheerfully until almost four in the morning. By that time George and Grace were sleeping soundly in the back room, and the guests had either passed out or gone home, or, like Tom Hammond, had curled up in the back seat of a car.

The next day, a Sunday, the young couple set off to pick up a bed from an elderly woman in Sydney who was a distant relative of George. Their new home had plumbing which brought cold water into the kitchen but no indoor bathroom. There was a small gas stove and a refrigerator. Once their bed was installed in one of the two bedrooms, George and Grace were officially a new household but neither invested much time or energy in their home. Grace had several close friends within walking distance and spent most of her time with them or on trips back to her aunt's house in Truro. George worked and often visited with his relatives, particularly a married sister who lived in Sydney. Together George and Grace would take an evening's ride to visit people who had not been able to come to the wedding or simply to visit friends they shared. The wedding presents were casually delivered from the house in which Grace grew up to the house in which she was the woman in charge and many of them remained for weeks unpacked in their cartons. There was no conventional domestic enterprise being set up with material goods. Micmac children from down the road would sit on the living room floor reading comic books and movie magazines while Grace had coffee with her friends in another house. George could come home in the evening anywhere from six to midnight and find his wife somewhere within calling distance. She would always make sure there was some food for him to eat in the refrigerator but he was just as likely to want to go out for a bucket of fried chicken. There will not be a typically Micmac household until well after Grace, who was ten weeks pregnant at the time of the wedding, has had her baby and begins to gather around herself extra children and extra adults, perhaps even her father, to create the additional supportive social ties needed to maintain a home base household. There is also the possibility that Grace will eventually return to the mobile life of an urban Indian if the economic tide should turn on her and George.

The South Enders

The Micmac Indians most in public view are those who, usually for reasons of illness or old age, participate less actively in the social network of the tribe. Less mobile and less able to earn money, they become more stable residents of Maritime Indian settlements or of urban areas. In Canada, the old and the sick frequently rely on relatives for social support, living in or very close to a large household. In Boston, the same people are more on their own, although not entirely cut off from the tribal community. They meet with the more mobile Indian wage-earners as they pass through the South End, sometimes getting money from them or a ride to visit Micmac relatives outside the city or, occasionally, a room to sleep in. Getting along in the South End is difficult even for those who can move around and find jobs. It is more trying for those Indians who, as familiar as they might be with city life, do not have the energy to strategize. Circulating very slowly within the social network and dependent on the support of a segment of the adult community which operates principally on the reciprocity of favors, elderly men and women and people with tuberculosis or heart disease or drinking problems are vulnerable to the institutional organization of the city. Their lives are more affected by the welfare system and by medical and rehabilitation programs than any others in the tribal community. Their consciousness of the values and attitudes of the personnel they meet in the public settings of municipal offices is surpassed only by their sense of subjugation to those same standards. There are no Indians a researcher can meet who are quicker to estimate the range of his conventional values and expectations than those who have become permanent residents of the city. The more down-and-out they become, the more the Indians' experience of urban institutions is intensified. Sometimes the police, as much out of kindness as out of their responsibility to keep the peace, will pick up a vagrant Micmac who is wandering the streets either sick or drunk or just homeless, and bring him to a flop house or a public agency. There is the Pine Street Inn, which offers beds to destitute men. There are alcoholic rehabilitation centers in Boston which flourish and die and then spring up again according to fluctuations in municipal funds. There are always jails and hospitals where vagrants can be stashed for a night. The most isolated Micmac Indians find places to sleep in vacated warehouses or in abandoned cars. In the winter, they cover themselves with rags and newspapers to keep warm. If they have truly become cut off from the rest of the Micmac community, their vagrancy will seldom be softened by respites in the apartments of friends and relatives, and they will become, as lonely individuals, socially dead before they are biologically dead. Relative to the several thousands of Indians who pass through the Boston area, the number of Micmac who drift into a *lumpenproletariat* state is only incidental and not really representative of the community's adaptation to urban living. Because they are visible even to the most casual visitor to the South End and because they often present a striking visual image of poverty and physical debilitation, these urban Indians are mistaken for the typical Micmac Indians in Boston, while the real community continues in its patterns of social interaction and geographic mobility. The Indians who exist for longer or shorter periods of time at the edge of the interpersonal network seem to function passively as intermediates to the dominant society in much the same way that men, when they violate public conventions, actively keep the rest of the community in touch with an exterior legal reality. Instead of earning reputations for strength and courage, of course, those who are physically weak and who tend to become socially exposed to dominant institutions earn the watchful pity and sometimes the disdain of the rest of the tribe.

The few older people who choose to stay in the city instead of returning to the Maritimes are the most pitied. They poise themselves between an inevitable reliance on some sort of municipal institution and the benefits of closer contact with younger Micmac Indians whose earnings are often spent right in Boston. For the older Micmac who live in Boston, its police and welfare and medical facilities are part of a scene which has become familiar to them after many years of association with the city. As their mobility decreases, urban institutions become increasingly important to their survival.

While not old by White standards, Indians in their late forties and older bear physical testimony to the rigors of working hard and living poor. In their own lives they have participated in the tribal network and the industrial economy in the same way as their children do now. One Micmac Indian, Paul Sack, is fifty-three years old and lives in a small room in the South End. As a young man he served in the Canadian army for about three years and then spent the next twenty-five years working at some forty-eight different jobs in and around New England and eastern Canada. He gradually retired as jobs went to younger and stronger men than himself. His four children, three by one woman and one by another, have all become involved in the adult community and, on and off, they stay in Boston. Sometimes Paul meets them on the street or at a friend's house and sometimes they visit him at the rooming house where he lives. Most of Paul's family lives in Canada. His mother is still alive and lives with his older sister in Truro. Another sister and brother live in Shubenacadie. They keep up a good correspondence with Paul and often encourage him to leave the city. Paul reminds them that he sold his Indian papers many years ago and they persist in reminding him that he could live with one of his nieces in an off-reservation settlement and apply for social assistance as a Canadian citizen. Paul, however, has a kind of social life in the city. Three friends, men he once worked and traveled with, are his companions. He goes to bars with them and to occasional meetings for Indian alcoholics. A cousin, a woman of sixty-three, also lives in the city and comes every once in a while with her girl friends to visit and drink with Paul. Their socializing is limited without a car and their drinking, when they do get together, is the quiet drinking of people used to solitude. Paul sees his welfare worker about as much as he sees his cousin, every three or four weeks. Sometimes, when his three buddies are not available, he will walk around the South End by himself on the chance that he will find someone, a Micmac or a younger White person, with whom to chat. Often he meets older White men he has seen at the alcoholic center, men who, like Paul, have become well-known as characters who walk the streets.

If the weather is not too cold, they stop and talk to each other.

Until the winter of 1972, Paul was also likely to meet Ross Pictou, a Micmac almost twenty years his junior but just as much a fixture in the South End. Ross came to Boston in 1956 when he was nineteen. He traveled the job circuit around New England until tuberculosis, the disease by which both his mother and father died, forced him at the beginning of the 1960s to become less and less mobile. Rather than going back to Nova Scotia, he continued living in Boston, picking up odd jobs when he felt well enough. Over the years, he became a permanent resident of the South End, living first on handouts from friends and then on welfare. He also began drinking with his friends and then drinking alone when his friends left for work. When his social worker came looking for him, Ross would genially agree with him that he should kick the habit and stop drinking. But Ross really knew his way around the bars of the South End and knew how to keep himself in friendly contact with his fellow Micmac. The first time he passed out at a curbside, a small group of Micmac Indians found him and brought him to a roominghouse. By then, in 1971, due to the combination of illness and drinking, Ross looked more like sixty than thirty-four. A year later he was dead and his body was shipped back to Canada for the kind of simple Catholic burial accorded most Micmac Indians.

The old and the sick, like children, need care and, while it can be obtained from the community, the community puts a higher priority on the needs of the young than on those of the ill or elderly. There can be heard among old people on reservations and in cities the universal complaint that young Micmac Indians do not give their elders due respect. It is true that children on reservations sometimes make fun of the speech and behavior of the old but they are also taught to serve bedridden, elderly relatives and run errands for the aged. When young people are on their own, involved in peer interaction, they seldom have the opportunity, or the interest in creating the opportunity, to serve the sick or the elderly. Paul Sack's children were much too involved in traveling and socializing with friends to take the time and effort to insure his well-being. In this way, they were lacking in respect and regard for their father and, like his other relatives, they were continually encouraging him to go back to Canada where they believed it was easier to be old or sick. In addition, Paul's children were involved in supporting their own offspring. Each of them was sending remittances back to the Maritimes for the care of one or more children. These payments varied with changes in wages and would diminish severely when big expenses, such as a security deposit on an apartment or a weekend party, were incurred. Paul's wants could never be as important as the main business of socializing and child support or the expenses of urban living and travel.

In Ross's case, as in the case of most Micmac Indians who suffer from serious illness while they are still young, the predisposition to sickness is noticed and remarked upon from early childhood. The child who tires easily is described as having thin blood and has to submit both to the potions of modern medicine and those of the old women who are concerned about him. The child who lacks an appetite, the child who tends to get colds and earaches gets the same double treatment. The closer a sickly child gets to adolescence, the more fatalistic the attitude of his caretakers becomes. If their ministrations have not made him or her a robust energetic member of the family by the age of ten or eleven, the possibility of a transformation is usually abandoned. Sickliness becomes an endemic aspect of his personality, as if it were an inevitable component of the individual's personal makeup. Most of the Micmac are less than enthusiastic in accepting germ theory as an explanation of disease and, like many other American Indian groups, have alternative explanations for sicknesses which, to our minds, are spread by contamination. Each Micmac Indian is a unique composite of physical and spiritual resources and, past the point of childhood, cannot be dissuaded from his fate. Ross Pictou, because he was Ross Pictou and not because his parents were tubercular, had a place at the edge of the tribal community which suited who he was, a specific man who was liked and even loved, though not respected.

For an individual to turn his or her back on the past and make a great effort at self-reform is a very difficult thing to do. As a personal history accrues and as a young person becomes known to a wider and wider social network of Indians, the limits of his personality become generally defined and the potential for an about-face in behavior is severely reduced. Mary Ginnish, the same young woman who was terrified by unfamiliar noises and sights in Boston, also fell into a period of heavy drinking which marked her as a woman capable of totally isolating herself from her Indian family and friends. After losing her job in the mattress factory, Mary went on drinking binges which lasted two or three days. She began by drinking with other young Micmac Indians, then moved on to drinking with White men in bars in the South End, East Boston, and Charlestown. Her drinking sprees became longer and more frequent until she had almost completely cut herself off from the rest of the community. Eventually she became a prostitute. In the beginning of close to three years of this kind of living, Mary would be able to make her way to her own home or the home of a friend and sleep off the effects of alcohol. Soon she lost her room in the South End when her girl friends moved out and she could not pay the rent herself. After that she began waking up in strange apartments or hotels, not remembering how she came to be where she was. One day she woke up in Boston City Hospital, bruised and beaten and very sick. As Mary described her own fear and resolution to reform:

Death was staring me right in the face. I was so scared that I promised myself then and there I wouldn't drink again. That was seven years ago and I can say I've kept my word. I go to parties and I do have a few beers but nothing like it was before.

Interestingly enough, the fact of Mary's drinking problem, which lasted about three years, was general knowledge in the Micmac community. Because she was among the first Indians I met, I often mentioned her name, particularly when I was with a new group interested in my social connections. Mary's relatives as well as non-relatives, old people and children in Canada, and some people in her own age group who had never met her personally readily identified her as an alcoholic or heavy drinker. The fact of her reformation into a sober, fairly industrious woman raising her child in a tidy home in Boston impressed no one. It would probably take years for the tribal community to relinquish Mary as a case of deviant behavior and accord her a good reputation. Her potential for turning away from the community and facing Death at Boston City had been duly observed and noted by other Micmac Indians with less faith in will power than in the inevitable rigidity of the human personality. One man, after I had spent some time assuring him that what I had seen in two years of contact with Mary Ginnish confirmed her complete reformation, archly replied that he had suspicions she was a lesbian. It was only later that I understood how succinctly he had rejected my observations for his own sense of Mary's inborn deviance. It was still later when I realized that, in his eyes, Mary's friendship with me, a White woman, must have reinforced his feeling that she had tendencies to turn away from her own kind.

Families in Greater Boston

If there is a significant change coming about in the urban organization of the Micmac it consists of the recent ability of small families to establish themselves in residential areas outside the city as a more stable part of the Indian community. Adjacent to downtown Boston, there are low-rent residential districts such as Dorchester, Chelsea, Revere, Charlestown, Somerville, and Quincy, where a scattering of Micmac families have settled down. Twenty years ago, a child born and raised in the city had his every character flaw attributed to the misfortune of an urban background. But today, the possibility of raising a family in Boston is being explored by a small number of Micmac Indians, none of whom, it must be remembered, have ruled out returning to the Maritimes. In neighborhoods of two- and three-story frame houses, where there are more White people than Blacks or Puerto Ricans, a respectable married couple or a married woman with children will take the risk of trying to coexist with strangers, hopefully avoiding interpersonal conflict. The people who are likely to opt for living outside the city are already different from the more mobile adults in the Micmac community in their awareness of and acceptance of more conventional norms of behavior. Not only do they seek a better place than the South End to raise their children but they often have doubts about reservation life, extended family organization, and the very socializing which is the heart of the community. A stable income of some kind allows the establishment of a household in a residential area and allows, too, certain class pretensions which limit general circulation in the tribal network. White neighbors will put pressures on some Indian families to curtail the comings and goings of Micmac men and women because the intimation that the home is not a private sphere is too disconcerting. Other Indian families have already assumed the same values as their neighbors and do not want the riff-raff of the tribe hanging around. One couple, Frank and Marie Bassett, for the five years they have lived in Dorchester, have kept the foldout couch in their living room available only to their parents and a few close siblings who are invited for brief visits each year. The Bassetts' three children go the local grammar school. Every once in a while they are teased for being Indian, but generally they fit in with their urban schoolmates and have relatively few chances to meet or know other Micmac children. Frank has been able to afford this relative isolation because he has worked steadily at the same paint factory for most of the time he and Marie have lived in Dorchester. Reliance on an exchange of room, board, and travel opportunities has not been essential to his work and in this he has had an unusual experience of the city. Other men who live with their wives outside the South End often have to be away from home, leaving their spouses in charge of domestic organization and relations with neighbors. For one married woman, Ida Campbell, the problem of living in a section of Somerville among apparently quarrelsome strangers made peaceful domestic organization impossible. As she put it:

I won't say that I'm not prejudiced against White people myself sometimes. There are Indians who act worse, though, I know that. But this woman who lived downstairs from us was a real devil. She had a daughter, a big girl about Ellie's age [14]. That girl would pick on Freddie every time she saw him coming home from school. He'd just be coming home from school and he'd be in his good clothes and all. He does very well at school, don't make no trouble. But this girl would see him coming and she'd tell him, "My mother says that Indians is no good." She [the daughter] was saying the same thing to Ellie and Susan [Ida's two daughters] and saying that her mother wouldn't let none of their family come near them. Freddie and Susan were right in the apartment playing with some kids when she comes running in and grabs one of the kids and starts hitting Freddie. She had no business doing that. She went on and on about "dirty Indians." I didn't know that one of the kids playing was her sister. Anyway, Ellie was just coming up the stairs and when she saw her shouting and hitting Freddie, she lit right into her and gave her a couple of good punches. About an hour later her mother came up and said she was taking me to court. She said her daughter had to go to the doctor. I told her that she was lying and that her daughter had no business busting into my house. Besides Ellie don't even weigh any more than a hundred pounds and she couldn't send anyone to the doctor. Ellie had her own bruises, too. I told her I was going down to the courthouse, too. When I went down next morning, I saw her coming out of the courthouse just as I was going in. She got there before me. When I made my complaint, it was too late, you know, she had already made hers.

As it turned out, Ida and her neighbor did go to court only to have the judge dismiss the charges and countercharges with an admonition that the two women had better avoid such incidents in the future or they would both be penalized. Within a matter of days, Ida and her husband Frank and their family, rather than risk another confrontation, left the Somerville apartment for an older and smaller flat in Dorchester.

It was no good trying to live in the same house with that woman. I don't want no trouble. I got enough to do taking care of the kids, with Frank away so much. I can't say it's more friendly here [in Dorchester] but at least no one's come breaking the doors in on us.

In a way that is typical of the Micmac Indians who live in residential areas outside the city, Ida presumed the existence of a tight-knit community in the neighborhood in Somerville based on the fact that many of the people there had Italian last names. Having noted that the woman with whom she quarreled and the judge who dismissed their cases both had Italian surnames, she concluded that, in the event of further conflict, she would not have the chance of a favorable hearing. Neither was bringing a dispute to court Ida's style of handling a quarrel. She preferred more informal measures for making peace and was, I believe, intimidated by her neighbor's quick resort to legal action. The Micmac notion of respectability permits association with the least controversial legal institutions, such as the religious and educational institutions, through which some group action of a civil rights nature is possible. But appearance in court as an individual with the legality of one's actions in question is avoided unless, as with Ida, one is provoked. It took really great courage on her part to make her countercharge, and it was a defense of herself and her children she did not want to have to make again.

For women without men to support them and their children, the establishment of a household outside the South End has let them combine work and childcare without the usual tension about the kind of urban environment in which their families are growing up. Marie

Doucette was married to a Boston man and had three children by him before they separated in 1965. Receiving no child support allowance from him, she lives alternately on welfare payments and by working as a waitress in a diner near her Dorchester apartment. In the past four years she has given over one of the two bedrooms in her home first to one younger brother and then to another as they made their first trips to the city and found their first factory jobs. Her three children walk to the local school and the eldest, Elaine, age nine, has a key to the apartment in case Marie is away at work when school lets out. As Marie puts it:

The school has some rough kids in it. But I lived in the South End before I was married and I know that kids can't even walk around there. The lady upstairs here is old but she's nice. She lets me know when there's too much noise, you know, and she's always peeking out the window, like everyone else, wondering who's coming to visit here. But Elaine and the boys [Michael and Richard] got friends here to play with. Mike looks real Indian. He hears about that from the brats at school. But Ellie and Richie take after their father and they don't get no trouble.

During the summer vacation months, Marie brings her children to her sister's home in New Brunswick and returns to Dorchester to work full time and to mix more with other adults in the community than during the school year.

I kinda hate to leave Canada. It's beautiful there in the summer, just like I remember it. It's good for the kids, they're still young. I get to do a lot of traveling and seeing people just on the way there and back. I got relatives at St. John and Amherst and all over. Last summer [1969] I made more than three dollars an hour at Sal's, with tips. I always have a good time working there. Weekends I'd go over to the Kansas City [a country-and-western bar on Washington Street] with my cousin, Lou Ann, to hear the music. There are more people from home there in the winter but I always see folks I know there. I get a chance to catch up on things.

Claude Wilson, his wife Lorraine, and their children represent another type of Indian household, one which more resembles the extended family establishments that can be found in the Maritimes. The Wilsons' acceptance of relatives and friends in their home has been selective. But since they settled in Chelsea in the early 1960s, they have each year accepted other Micmac adults and children into their home on a fairly regular basis and relied on cash recompense for this service to continue as a household. Claude, now forty, has worked on a variety of construction jobs over the last two decades but travels less now than before he and Lorraine established themselves in Boston. In addition to their four children, Lorraine's younger sister Sarah has been a more or less permanent member of the household since 1967, along with her own child, a boy named Patrick, now eight years old. Another sister, Annette, lived with the Wilsons from 1963 to 1965 until she married and settled with her husband in Dorchester.

When Lorraine's sister-in-law became ill in 1968, the Wilsons took care of one of her sons, installing the boy with their own school-age children in a small bedroom furnished with a double set of bunk beds and a fold-out cot. Nephews of Claude and one of his younger brothers have also found a place to stay with them between trips around New England and to Canada, almost always as paying guests. The single category of Micmac most explicitly excluded from this hospitality have been Claude's friends and fellow workers who have reputations for drinking and/or playing around with women. In their early years of living in Chelsea, when Claude was away on a job, Lorraine was awakened in the small hours of the morning by a trio of Micmac men banging at the door. She knew all of them by name but, angry and embarrassed at the scene they were making, she told them they were not welcome in her house. When Claude came back, she laid down the law, that their apartment would be available only to respectable people, and while he did not see her point of view at first, Claude now defends his wife's efforts to keep their place "nice":

I've done my own bit of back-fence howling, so I know how them fellas felt. One of them was really hot for [Claude's niece] Anne who was here at the time. But Lorraine was right. The neighbors here notice things like that and they'll come right up to her and the kids and speak right out. Lorraine and them got to be able to get along. I can go off to the South End and pretty much do what I want. The rest of them stay here. Anyway, she knows what's what, she's got a house to keep. She don't want nothing to do with wild kinds, men or women.

On Micmac Politics

As households take on an aura of respectability, the men and women associated with them tend to assume a sense of political responsibility which unites their interests with those of their urban neighbors. For example, the Bassetts, the Wilsons, and other Micmac Indians like them have demonstrated with tenants' rights and welfare rights organizations. They have taken their places at meetings beside other Bostonians—White, Black, and Puerto Rican—and spoken their minds on the moral responsibilities of landlords and municipal agencies. The relationship of these Indians to the law is based on the belief that as respectable people, they deserve its protection.

To the extent that some Micmac Indians are political in ways easily recognized by a wider society, they also conform to the blue-collar image of hard-working, law-abiding, family oriented citizens. Their counterparts are found in the reservation area and often form the backbone of church groups and tribal councils. They are moderate in their demands, yet liberal in the extent to which women, especially as they reach middle age, play a political role as important as their husbands'. The Micmac currently have an elected woman "chief" and compared to national Indian organizations, permit women a greater participation in political decision-making.

Most of the organization of the recently formed Boston Indian Council, another example of political action which involves the Micmac, was done by just such respectable Indians, not all of them from Canada, and by Whites who identified with the Indian cause. They frequently presented their own work ethic as an example for the rest of the Indian population to follow. The goal of the Council, to give a political voice to Indians in the city, has been achieved through hours of committee meetings, typing, stuffing envelopes, and making telephone calls. Yet the rank-and-file Micmac membership and, outside it, the great number of adult Micmac Indians who might gain some obvious social service benefits from its success have resisted performing according to bureaucratic standards of efficiency. In the early days of the Council the leaders who thought of themselves as more politically sophisticated than most of the Micmac contributed to this resistance. At one Boston Indian Council meeting, the Micmac were told by a White woman serving on the Council to put aside their "drunken laziness" and take on the responsibility of doing volunteer office work, which was their "only hope." During this harangue, small groups of Indian men sitting at the back of the meeting hall made their way over to the exit, muttering such comments as "Who does the bitch think she is," and "Only hope, my ass." When a break was called in the meeting, almost all the remaining Micmac, about forty, left in silence. On another occasion, several weeks later, a Penobscot man rose to give essentially the same speech, but there were at that point very few "irresponsible" Micmac around to hear it. The Council has since come a great distance from conventional ways of handling its organization toward the development of what is a uniquely Indian union.

Given a political forum, the Micmac act in a way which subjects procedure and language to the egalitarian norms of the community. Indians who take up too much floor time in expressing their opinions have to end their speeches by shouting above the noise of the smaller groups into which the disinterested audience has broken down. Indians who claim to speak for the group as a whole will quickly be contested by ten or fifteen other Indians voicing dissent, not particularly about the issue in question, but about the right of anyone to speak for the others. Individuals who suggest plans for action are apt to get themselves in trouble if there is any hint of coercion or manipulation in their presentation or if they show themselves impatient with prolonged debate. In a meeting, the interaction of the moment is more important than future goals because it is the morality of interpersonal behavior which is being tested. The Micmac know when vaulted ambition is threatening the rights of the community membership and when abstract goals are impinging on the democratic ethos of a small group. For a White person educated to perceive the impersonal nature of work and to take on the personal responsibility for getting things done, sitting through a meeting of Indians deciding such a minor issue as the best title for a subcommittee can be torture, because the task may take hours to accomplish and involve what appear to be many needless diversions and expressions of alternative points of view. The unhurried calm of the Micmac in political situations, whether a meeting of tribal representatives in the Maritimes or a Boston Indian Council meeting, reflects the attitude of a people who find pleasure in subjugating the decision-making process to human priorities, thwarting a machine-like efficiency by allowing time for social interaction.

Such necessary procedures as the nomination and election of officers can be completed relatively quickly, but in the eyes of the Micmac community, the capacity of even the most virtuous man or woman to resist the corruptive influence of power is quite limited, and only a frequent turnover in elected leaders counteracts its effects. For example, in what is still a brief history, the Boston Indian Council has undergone numerous changes in its administration, without ever really changing its purposes or potential to help the people it represents. Officers are always being toppled from their public posts with others elected to take their places. The turnover has little to do with individual incompetence. It has a great deal to do with rumors which, after a short time, begin to circulate about the fancied sense of superiority a certain council leader or committee head is displaying. The suspicion that an Indian might forget the representational nature of his office and mistake his title for an increased measure of his personal worth is always lurking in the minds of other Micmac. Sometimes, as one of the duties of a council officer, an elected Indian may have to spend time with administrators from municipal or national bureaucracies. The more he has to do this, the greater is the fear of the group that its interests might be betrayed as personal ambition succumbs to the goals of a truly powerful organization. If too successful at interacting with Whites, for example, he may find himself without a constituency or simply removed from office. There is for the Micmac no uncontested leader because potentially everyone has the chance for some kind of leadership statement. While a political meeting puts contest on a more abstract level than generally occurs in the community, the issue of power is nonetheless recognized and dealt with by a process which converts it to a totally social issue grounded in immediate social concerns. For a single member of the community to assume a spokesman-like role for a long period of time would mean that other voices might not be heard or that, secure in an official position, he or she might be at too great a distance from the changing mood and feelings of the group, for an election occurs at one point in time and represents only a specific period in the group's history. To keep its administration *au courant*, an Indian organization is more likely to rotate its representatives than to allow a single person to become a permanent spokesman.

Hundreds of years ago the first Europeans to come to America felt it necessary to label tribes as nations and to appoint "kings" and "chiefs" among the Indians. While these early intruders into the New World were attempting to set up relationships with political units which paralleled their own understanding of monarch and state, they cared little for the indigenous order and dismissed as chaotic native systems within which political power was decentralized. Even today, those men with the authority to change our contemporary legal climate refuse to admit the legitimacy of minority grievances unless the oppressed organize themselves on a bureaucratic model. Crucial to this recognition is the appearance of a minority leader of presidential proportions. As an example, Dr. Martin Luther King, Jr., until his assassination, was able to win a nod of legal acknowledgement for Blacks because he was seen as the charismatic leader of an undissenting mass of people. Power lends to power, yet there are many legitimate groups, too small, too local, and too democratic in organization ever to produce leaders on a national scale. If one takes a moment to reflect on what it means for a man or woman to represent many people over a long period of time, the question arises, "Is that kind of leadership valid or good?" A statesmanlike leader is himself the most tenuous abstraction of many wills, of many individual fates, and of the many subgroups he is supposed to represent. As one person, he cannot humanly interact with more than a fraction of his constituency, so that their social reality is as lost to him in abstract images and projections as he is to them. The more overreaching his power, the more his conduct is expected to conform to lofty standards of moral perfection, as if to insure the masses of his immunity to the corruptive forces of power. In American movies, it is only God and American presidents who are represented by stentorian, off-camera voices. The possibility of a politically active minority well-versed in the fundamentals of representational democracy producing such a strangely dissociated type of leader is slim. But it is also true that anything that resembles dissension in the ranks, any indication of less than unanimous support, and any of the rumblings of factionalism within a movement has repeatedly served as an excuse for inaction on the part of the dominant society. What is most respected is the power of a united front, with all the militarism that that implies. A political unit touched by the vicissitudes of human interaction is seen as weak. Again and again, American governments have thrown up their hands in mock despair at what has been perceived as the inability of Indians to speak with a single voice within and across tribal boundaries. Indians like the Micmac have, in turn, obstinately clung to tribal and community alliances which allow them maximum control of representation, even if, as it often seems, few practical things get done.

Generally speaking, the Micmac who think and talk about national and city politics are undeceived about the human foibles and weaknesses of government leaders. A premier, a president, a commissioner, a mayor—these are all ordinary men thought to be involved like the Micmac in their respective social groups. That governmental departments are hierarchically organized is not as important to the Micmac as the fact that, to their way of seeing, the people who work for the Bureau of Indian Affairs, for example, are in collusion with one another, as are the people who work for the city of Boston, the people who control the Canadian government, and the people who control the United States. Each, it is assumed, is a narrow group with its vested interests identified by a bureaucratic label.

The Indians' experience of corporate bureaucracies has impressed them with the difference in behavior and appearance between government people and themselves. But the abstract forms of organizations which rule them are about as invisible to the Micmac as their kind of community is to the politicians, clerks, accountants, and office workers who run government institutions. Politics is an activity which they understand only in the context of the present moment. The Micmac are most politically responsible to each other, to people known and near at hand. They rule no other group and, in their internal social organization, they govern themselves quite well.

CHAPTER V

Urban Indians in Industrial Society

"You might not like them," Nick said to the boy. "But I think you would."

"And my grandfather lived with them too when he was a boy, didn't he?"

"Yes. When I asked him what they were like he said he had many friends among them.

"Will I ever live with them?"

"I don't know," Nick said. "That's up to you."

Ernest Hemingway, *Winner Take Nothing,* p. 242.

American Colonization and the Behavior of "Savages"

The reservation system which arose in nineteenth-century America was essentially a means of legally categorizing and containing a people whose ways were fundamentally antagonistic to those of most colonizers, both on the level of local interaction and on the level of the pragmatic and progressive aims of the federal government. The communal ownership of land and the tribal "nomadism" of many Indian groups contrasted sharply with the emphasis on individual title to property and the agricultural background of most settlers, from the Puritans of New England to the farmers of the far West, who found it difficult to believe that land unfarmed was really owned by anyone. While the federal government of the United States, and to a lesser extent that of Canada, saw the Indians as hostile obstacles to the final settlement of the continent, at the end of four-hundred-year era of American colonization the federal bureaucracies on both sides of the border took on the role of civil "guardian" to diverse groups of Indian people who were apparently defeated by the expansion of Western civilization and doomed to extinction because a progressive industrial society could not support the existence of tribal communities.

The prediction of extinction is something which Indians have had to live with for several centuries, and it has been inextricably bound to the judgment of their failure to conform to civilized society. The same Jesuits who pitied the Micmac for their material poverty saw in their resistance to agriculture the forecast of their inevitable doom in a spiritual sense, which included a social demise brought about by failing to adopt a superior mode of existence which would make them independent of the fur trade. New England colonizers, unconcerned with the spiritual fate of "savages," justified the destruction of Indians and the take-over of Indian land on moral grounds: "By a right of just occupation from the grand charter in Genesis 1st and 9th Chapters, whereby God gave the earth to the sons of Adam and Noah, to be subdued and replenished." [1] The noted eighteenth-century champion of American colonization, Hugh Brackenridge, subscribed to the same kind of principle, that of the inherent superiority of agriculture over other kinds of human endeavors, and contrasted it to the livelihood of "the animals, vulgarly called Indians": "To live by tilling is *more humano,* by hunting is *more bestiarum.*" [2] While Catholic missionaries worked for changes in Indian character and Protestants dwelt on their immutable savagery, colonizers in general explained the misfortunes of Indians as a result of their being nonagricultural and thus uncivilized. The assumption behind this explanation is, of course, that if only Indians had changed their behavior, the great impersonal force of colonial expansion would have halted, sparing them their lands and tolerating their presence as civilized people. Yet the small-scale farming of many tribes on a variety of colonial frontiers—the Iroquois, the Creek, the more settled Apache groups—was no deterrent to colonial settlement and did not forestall the

[1] From John Cotton's sermon, "God's Promise to his Plantations," printed in London in 1630 and reprinted by the Old South Association, Boston, Leaflet no. 53, p. 6; reprinted in part in *The Indian and the White Man,* ed. Wilcomb E. Washburn, New York, Doubleday, 1964, pp. 102–5.

[2] From a letter by Brackenridge, published in *Indian Atrocities: Narratives of the Perils and Sufferings of Dr. Knight and John Slover Among the Indians During the Revolutionary War,* Cincinnati, 1867, pp. 62–72; reproduced in part in *The Indian and the White Man.*

removal of Indians from their traditional lands. In the early part of the nineteenth century, the rise of the Cherokee Nation as a confederation of literate, politically organized, agricultural, and otherwise "civilized" tribes proved the ability of Indian groups to make creative compromises with White civilization, to do what seemed to be necessary in order to survive. The response of local Georgians and of the federal government, which was to remove the Cherokee to the West and pass ownership of their lands over to White colonizers, dramatically refuted the belief that changes in the behavior of the colonized could solve the problem of their survival as integrated and equal members of American society. Instead, the dispersal of the Cherokee and the increase in military campaigns on Southeastern Indians were justified by a new depiction of the American native as inherently and irredeemably savage. The inevitability of Indian doom and the fixed nature of the Indian as barbarian were never so emphatically expressed as during the nineteenth-century era of colonialization, when White incursions, whether they provoked the gentlest reactions or the most fierce hostilities, were justified by the immutably inferior nature of the "savage." Even while a more impartial observer, de Tocqueville, could see that the primary misfortune of American Indians was "to have been brought in contact with a civilized people, who are also (it must be owned) the most grasping nation on the globe," his contemporary, Gobineau, was voicing a more common explanation of the coming demise of Indians:

They will die out, as they know well; but they are kept by a mysterious feeling of horror, under the yoke of their unconquerable repulsion from the white race, and although they admire its strength and general superiority, their conscience and their whole nature, in a word, their blood, revolts from the mere thought of having anything in common with it.[3]

Within the basic history of culture conflict between Indians and Whites, the Indians usually at first allowed the presence of White neighbors and expected to relate to them as equals, while the majority of White settlers had no use for non-whites, except as servants, and little tolerance for a democracy shared by such outsiders. In most cases, the removal of egalitarian Indians was imperative. The *Herrenvolk* democracy of this era was the political expression of the belief that the only real people were White and that only White people were potentially equals.[4] Its reflection in the sciences came with the hierarchical classification of human races into types more or less different from the superior White race of men. Negroes and Indians were invariably described as "inferior" on such scales, being categorized, for example, as respectively "night" and "dusk" races in contrast to the White "day" race, as "passive" and "small-brained" in contrast to the "active," "large-brained" White man.

---

[3] Alexis de Gobineau, *The Moral and Intellectual Diversity of Races* (first edition, *Essai sur l'inégalite des races humaines*, Paris, Charles Gosselin, 1853–55), trans. H. Holt, Philadelphia, Lippincott, 1856.

[4] The description of the *Herrenvolk* democracy is presented by Pierre van den Berghe in his book, *South Africa, A Study in Conflict*, Middletown, Connecticut, Wesleyan University Press, 1965.

Such stereotypes of Negro and Indian character appear in the light of history as obvious justifications for their actual economic exploitation, the slave for labor and the native for land. The rhetoric which defended slavery depicted the Negro as biologically suited for slavery and dependent on it for his otherwise unlikely survival, while the American Indian was portrayed as a stubborn, intractable remnant from barbarous times whose elimination was first a military imperative and then a foregone conclusion. Nott and Glidden, in their well-known defense of slavery, sounded the following note of despair on native Americans:

To one who has lived among American Indians, it is in vain to talk of civilizing them. You might as well attempt to change the nature of the buffalo.[5]

The preliminaries to the containment of native Americans, so that White civilization would have room to expand, came about in a variety of ways. But whether it was the decimation and gradual isolation of Northeast Indians, the forced removal of the Cherokee, or the military defeat of Western tribes, race relations between Whites and Indians finally took the form of a federal guardianship of Indian land and lives and a spatial segregation of Indian communities from White ones. The peoples who eluded servility, who were supposedly doomed because of their barbarity, were, by the end of

[5] J. C. Nott and G. R. Gliddon, *Indigenous Races of the Earth*, Philadelphia, 1857; quoted in Franz Boas, *The Mind of Primitive Man* (first edition London, Macmillan, 1911), New York, The Free Press, 1963, p. 35.

the nineteenth century, relegated to small homogeneous communities and anchored by federal jurisdiction to fixed land bases that were to be both their prisons and their property. Efforts to force the solution of agriculture on Indians reached a new and final phase of legal impetus backed by the urgings of sympathetic Whites. So it was that John Wesley Powell, founder of the Bureau of American Ethnology, reported back from his 1874 expedition to the defeated and scattered Indian groups in the Rocky Mountain area that, with a view of ultimately civilizing Indians, incentives be offered to deter their straying away from the reservations and to make each an agricultural community run by industrious Indian peasants. In what was an enlightened recommendation for the time, Powell also advised that a civil as opposed to a military administration of Western reservations be set up to complete what seemed like an ideal program. Thus he wrote,

The only course left by which the Indians can be saved is to gather them on reservations, which shall be a school of industry and civilization, and the superintendents of which shall be the proper offices to secure justice between the two races, and between individuals of the Indian race. For this purpose on each reservation there should be a number of wise firm men, who, as judges and police officers, would be able in all ordinary cases to secure substantial justice.[6]

[6] *Report of the Special Commissioners J. W. Powell and G. W. Ingals on the condition of the Ute Indians of Utah; the Pai-Utes of Utah, Northern Arizona, Southern Nevada, and Southeastern California; the Go-si Utes of Utah and Nevada; the Northwestern Shoshones of Idaho and Utah; and the Western Shoshones of Nevada*, Washington, Government Printing Office, 1874, p. 26.

Despite competition with the military for control of American Indians, the United States Bureau of Indian Affairs became the recognized arbitrator of native needs and federal policies. Within twenty-five years of Powell's proposals, a civil restructuring of Indian-White relationships had come about in both the United States and Canada and, matters of justice and wisdom aside, American Indians and their land became the responsibility of the federal governments and their agents. They were theoretically to be protected, perhaps improved, but more generally they were the "finished business" of the dominant society.

Reservation Indians and Freed Slaves

The larger economic context in which Indians were supposedly confined to reservations and Black slaves were supposedly freed was formed by the development of this continent as a major locus of industrialism. Pierre van den Berghe, in addition to his description of the *Herrenvolk* democracy, has also made an interesting analysis of race relations and colonial systems which allows an overview of the continuing relations between a dominant White American society and two of its principal minorities, Indians and Blacks, during the transitional period of the nineteenth century up to the present.[7] The two models of race relations which he

[7] Pierre L. van den Berghe, *Race and Racism*, New York, John Wiley & Sons, 1967.

proposes are the "paternalistic" and the "competitive."
The first is characterized by a master-servant relationship in a basically agricultural economy with a generally rigid caste system based on color. The dominant
group is numerically small relative to the colonized
group and the value system of both is of one accord, "integrated" or without conflict. This system is maintained
in an atmosphere of "distant intimacy," permissible because the status difference of master and servant or
slave is uncontested, because the servant "knows his
place." In contrast, the competitive system is characterized by an industrial economy with complex stratification of general castes into classes, and the dominant
group is a majority of the population. The rule of the
dominant group is ideologically open to question and
the status difference between oppressors and oppressed
is vulnerable to the potentially insurgent minority. This
necessitates the spatial distance of segregation between
majority and minority groups. Stereotypes of minority
people in the competitive system are aggressive and
negative, as opposed to the paternalistic portrayal of
people of color as indolent and lazy.

The paternalistic system describes contacts between most Whites and Negroes in ante-bellum America
on Southern plantations. After the Civil War, however,
the shift to a competitive and industrial system was dramatically apparent, so that slaves freed from one kind of
subordination passed into another, partly as a result of
the disruption which followed the defeat of the Confederacy and partly as a consequence of wider and more
profound transformations which affected the entire

country. The old agrarian, feudal world of the slave plantation was destroyed, and with it the traditional master-servant model of race relations. Freed Negroes migrated in great numbers to the cities of the South, and to a lesser extent to cities outside the South. They entered for the first time in the labor market in direct competition with the poor White farmers of the South and the urban White working class of both the North and the South.[8]

If we follow this comparison of systems, American Indians were consistently involved in a competitive form of race relations, starting at the time when informal and piecemeal segregation from White communities began and continuing through the final stages of segregation in the nineteenth century. The dominant economic mode, whether agriculture or a beginning industrialism, seems of less importance in this segregation than the fact of conflict between a basically tribal, egalitarian people and the individualistically-oriented, "civilized" colonizers whose values allowed and encouraged colonial expansion just as later they effected industrial expansion. The believer in protestant "industry" in a sixteenth-century agrarian context had spiritual descendents in those nineteenth-century believers in the virtue of "efficiency" in an industrial context. The values of a tribal community were as much an irritant to one as to the other, and the necessity on the part of a dominant White society to segregate itself from such a native people was probably as great in the time of Powhatan as in

[8] *Ibid.*, pp. 85–86.

that of Sitting Bull. The important difference over time was the change in method and scale of the machinery which forced separation—from local skirmishes by which New Englanders dispersed Indians, to the larger military campaigns of the Creek Wars in the early nineteenth century, to the all-out, popularly supported and federally-directed war against the Plains Indians, and finally, in our own times, the more abstract bureaucratic handling of the "Indian problem."

Before the Civil War, the American writer Samuel G. Morton could offer stereotypes of Indians and Negroes which conformed to their respective positions as excluded and incorporated "non-people": "In their mental characteristics the Americans are averse to cultivation, slow, cruel, boisterous, revengeful, and fond of war." Negroes were depicted as "joyful, flexible, and indolent, while the many groups that constitute this race possess a singular diversity of character of which the far extreme is the lowest strain of humanity." [9] In the latter part of the nineteenth century, however, the structuring of Indian-White relations and of Negro-White relations were aspects of a single reality in which industrial society was in ascendance and agriculture, plantation or otherwise, was beginning its long and gradual decline. The reordering of race relations for both minority groups presented important contrasts and similarities as they became a particular part of the new "urban" society in an era characterized by "a syndrome of *laissez-faire* cap-

[9] From *Crania Americana*, Philadelphia, 1834. Quoted in Franz Boas' *The Mind of Primitive Man*, p. 34–35.

italism in the economic sphere, of jingoism and imperialism in foreign relations, and of racial and ethnic intolerance in the domestic social sphere." [10]

For the many freedmen who stayed in the rural South after the Civil War, the local level of interaction, now without the support of institutionalized slavery, became structured by a more rigid spatial separation between White and Black communities and, to the extent that agriculture was still viable, the landlord-sharecropper roles replaced those of master and slave. Keeping the Negro "in his place" in a social sense as well as a spatial one entailed the organization of White vigilante groups to terrorize and, paradoxically, to increase the solidarity of Black communities. In addition, local formal and informal restraints on contact between the two groups were established, so that segregation in the South was enforced through a multitude of laws and customs providing for separate and unequal (or for Negroes nonexistent) facilities in virtually every sphere of life. It became a punishable offense for Whites and Negroes to travel, eat, defecate, wait, be buried, make love, play, relax, and even speak together, except in the stereotyped context of master-and-servant interaction. [11]

The segregation of Blacks and Indians alike to a separate, non-White space within a rural setting was a deceptive confinement. With the rise of industrialism, the Negro population of the United States changed from predominantly Southern and rural in 1910 to predomi-

[10] Pierre van den Berghe, *Race and Racism*, pp. 86–87.

[11] *Ibid.*, p. 87.

nantly Northern and urban by the 1960s. Their segregation and poverty continued in the cities of the North, with the important difference that their subordination could, by the latter half of this century, be recognized as a national rather than regional situation, one which involved the social, economic, and political condition of most Blacks vis-à-vis most Whites. The basic restraint on remediary action for this situation was and still is the difficulty in assigning responsibility for oppression, in finding the "masters" in a dominant population which professes to be democratic and has left the rule of urban industrial centers to the indirection of its economic, political, religious, and social welfare organizations.

For American Indians, the spectacle of a final military defeat on the Plains and the assignment of their rule to an abstraction called the federal government also obscured the fact of their subordination. For local White communities located near reservations and for the many other members of the dominant society who never even saw Indians, they became a people who were fixed in the past as noble warriors or as comic figures wrapped in blankets and communicating in grunts. Nonetheless, Indians were probably being drawn to cities in similar proportions, if not in the same numbers, as Blacks during the early part of the twentieth century. The appearance of many Indians in Western cities in the United States during the 1920s as a "problem" population prompted the investigations of the Meriam Committee and its recommendations to the Bureau of Indian Affairs that urban Indians be attended to. More up-to-date and very conservative statistics on United States Indians have revealed large communities in western and northern industrial centers and the appearance of the urban Indian alongside other minority peoples in cities (Table 1).[12] Still invisible as far as census measures are con-

Table 1. *Estimates of Urban Indian Populations—United States Bureau of Indian Affairs, Community Development Office, September, 1969*

Urban Area	Indian Population
Los Angeles County	47,000
San Francisco Bay Area	18,000
Tulsa	15,000
Minneapolis-St. Paul	13,000
Oklahoma City	12,000
Chicago	12,000
Phoenix	10,000

Sizable Indian populations were also reported in the following cities: Seattle, Gallup, Albuquerque, Rapid City, Sioux City, Milwaukee, Tacoma, Spokane, Portland, Crescent City-Eureka (California), Sacramento, Fresno, San Diego, Duluth, Great Falls, and Buffalo. As is the case with other minority groups in North America, American Indians have increased in "urban" visibility even as they have increased in general numbers. The present estimated population of United States and Canadian Indians (600,000 and 300,000) represents a doubling of their estimated population in 1900.

[12] United States Bureau of Indian Affairs, "Urban Indian Distribution and Population," a paper prepared by the Community Development Office, Washington, September, 1969. James E. Officer, in his article "The American Indian and Federal Policy," in *The American Indian in Society*, ed. Jack O. Waddell and O. Michael Watson, Boston, Little, Brown and Company, 1971, pp. 58–63, gives a concise rundown on American Indian populations in cities. See also Murray Wax, *Indian American*, Englewood Cliffs, N.J., Prentice-Hall, 1971, pp. 157–73, for another general summation on the subject of Indians in cities.

cerned are those Indians, such as the Oklahoma Cherokee, the Klamath, and until recently the Menomini,
who have had no land base held in trust for them by the
federal government, whose viable communities were
struck from the list of officially "Indian," and whose
migrants to cities rarely appear in the official census. In
addition, members of Canadian tribes, including the
Micmac people who come to New England, often cross
the international boundary to the United States. The
"high steel" Caughnawaga Mohawk who travel between their reservation near Montreal and the cities of
Detroit, Buffalo, and New York City are popularly
known, thanks to Edmund Wilson. Yet within the Canadian cities of Vancouver, Toronto, Ottawa, and Montreal, to name a few, there are visible (if unrecorded and
less specialized in their skills) diverse groups of North
American Indians who are surviving industrial life even
as they survived "civilization." The tribal nature of their
lives has changed and is, without question, as affected
by the facts of this age as it was by the fact of colonial
expansion, particularly as their experience of subordination has been a formal bureaucratic arrangement.

In migrating to cities, American Indians have followed the same route as many other peoples—Southern
Blacks, Spanish-Americans, African tribesmen, Pacific
Islanders, Australian Bushmen, and West Indian
villagers—who have gone through the stages from traditional autonomy to a post-colonial state of race relations.
To use Nancie Gonzalez's term, these "neoteric" societies have been "placed in a position of having to adapt
to an economy dependent upon industrialization

through the mechanism of migrant wage labor, while being denied full admission to the industrial society as a whole, both as a class and as individuals." [13] The urbanization of such people has had less to do with their stable residence in an urban industrial center than with how they have adapted to a more general bureaucracy, to a segregation often shared with others, and to the extension of tribal organization over the distance from rural homeland to the industrial center. For most American Indians, the experience of the reservation system is a miniature of what awaits them in the city and their basically tribal, that is, loosely-organized and mobile, social organization has been accommodating to the one locale for about as long as to the other.

What the Urban Indian Knows

Indians in this industrial age often have as their initial experience of legal society interaction with the authority figures of national White institution such as government, school, and church. In being legally relegated to reservations, many American Indians know "The Man" in a way which is different from but which parallels that of Blacks.

The successive phases of White settlement and in particular the final settlement of the West were marked by atrocities no less severe than the lynchings, beatings, and intimidations visited by Ku Klux Klanners on Ne-

[13] *Black Carib Household Structure*, Monograph 48, American Ethnological Society, University of Washington Press, 1969, pp. 9–10.

groes. In addition, the early administration of reservations was a mixed bag of corruption and neglect of responsibilities that no amount of good intentions on the
part of missionaries and no tonnage of used clothes from
concerned benevolent societies could ever have ame-
liorated. As wards of the federal government, however,
most Indians were segregated from Whites in a way that
was structured to reduce the necessity for terroristic dis-
tance-making. In a reservation outpost, a small number
of White people acting as representatives of political,
economic, and religious institutions exterior to the tribal
community dominated its official center. Indians existed
as a kind of faceless body over which they presided.
While the paternalism of the reservation system has
been much commented upon and deplored, it was re-
markably different from the atmosphere of "distant intimacy" which characterized the plantation system, for
the function of the Indians was not to serve as labor, but
only to exist as poor Indians who would give a *raison
d'être* to White bureaucrats. The Indians learned to
cope either with bureaucratic careerists, who might be
moved to another post, or with less successful, less mobile agents, missionaries and traders who were stuck
with a remote outpost of reservation Indians.

Even with the reforming spirit of the 1930s and the
liberal wave of the 1960s, the relationships of Whites
and Indians have remained part and parcel of bureaucratic structure, with the missionizing "will to serve"
being as much an obstacle to understanding and parity
between the two groups as the intention to exploit. Murray Wax made the following observation of the roles of

those Whites recently involved in programs to "improve the Indian situation":

Dropped into an atmosphere of crisis, the new member of a professional team such as VISTA has no time to become acquainted with the local Indian folk and, indeed, the more sincere and dedicated he is to serving the Indians, the less time and opportunity he will have to associate naturally with them. So by a paradoxical involution, the only staff members who learn to know individual Indians well are those who are less than conscientious—the cynical and the time-servers and those who covertly regard the program as a federal boondoggle; as they loiter in taverns, chase Indian women, or poach game on Indian lands, they learn much about some aspects of Indian life, but not in any fashion that is publicly mentionable.[14]

In general, most American Indian communities, whatever the amount of interbreeding with local Whites, have been historically without power. They have been ruled by a small number of bureaucrats who, if bent on change, lacked understanding, and, if bent on maintaining their own positions, understood how Indians must remain in need in order to have an administrator take care of them.

Far from being spoiled by the generosity of federal guardianship, most Indians learned to evade the more arbitrary agents and the more avid missionaries. Their own social organization continues, not unaffected by subordination but unknown to the subordinators, out-

[14] Murray L. Wax and Rosalie K. Wax, "The Enemies of the People," in *Institutions and the Person: Papers Presented to Everett C. Hughes*, ed. Howard S. Becker, Blanche Geer, David Riesman, and Robert S. Weiss, Chicago, Aldine, 1968, pp. 101–18.

side the comprehension of White representatives. The obvious material changes, such as the use of the automobile and television, have usually been taken as indications of culture loss while social adaptations go unnoticed.

The sincere belief that native Americans were doomed to extinction by industrial society motivated many scholars in the early days of anthropology to do retrieval studies on Indians before they and their cultures disappeared. Although an ethnographer like Frank Speck might pursue such exotica as the last Beothuk woman living as a gypsy somewhere in Maine,[15] most recorders of Indian tradition in the late nineteenth and early twentieth century went to reservations or remote Indian villages the way one might go to the bedside of a dying old man and ask for an account of the good old days. While the most beautifully detailed accounts of Indian customs emerged—from Morgan on the Iroquois, to Boas on the Kwakiutl, to Lowie on the Plains Indians [16]—Indian culture became a collection of customs

[15] Frank G. Speck, *Beothuk and Micmac,* Indian Notes and Monographs, Museum of the American Indian, Heye Foundation, No. 22, 1922.

[16] Lewis H. Morgan, *The League of the Ho-De-No-Sau-Nee or Iroquois,* New Haven, Yale University Press, 1954 (Reprint from 1901); Franz Boas, "Social Organization and the Secret Societies of the Kwakiutl Indians," *Reports of the United States Nation Museum,* Washington, D.C., 1895, pp. 311–738, and "Ethnology of the Kwakiutl," *Annual Reports of the Bureau of American Ethnology,* Vol. 35, Washington, D.C., 1921, pp. 43–81; R. H. Lowie, *The Crow Indians,* New York, Holt, Rinehart, and Winston, 1935, and *Indians of the Plains,* New York, McGraw-Hill, 1954.

for the wonderment of academics. The more American Indians were considered culturally in their last sunset, the more the study of their social organization regressed to dry antiquarianism and their anthropologists came to resemble the sixteenth-century collectors of curios described by Margaret T. Hodgen in her work on the early history of the discipline:

As long as the owners of such collections remained content with the simple joys of accumulation, as long as they remained content merely to look at their treasures, as long as they refrained from asking difficult questions of their *cabinets de curiosités,* there was no need for classification, conceptualization, or an appeal to the verbal devices of description. The steady addition of new rarities to their hoards, their neat placement in appropriate trays or compartments, was enough. If an overly inquisitive visitor raised questions, the items in the collection could again be displayed; they could be handled and rehandled, turned this way and that, or even placed elsewhere, until the difficulty seemed to be removed.[17]

The details surrounding the bureaucratic rule of reservations, and its parallel, the increasing participation of Indians as "cheap labor" in industrializing society, went unobserved. When studies of contemporary American Indians did finally begin to be published, predominantly in the 1950s, many Indians, like many Blacks, had already done military service in one or another of the two World wars and had already taken their place as a lower-class minority faction. Still, research emphasis continued to be on the reservation as a place where eth-

---

[17] *Early Anthropology in the Sixteenth and Seventeenth Centuries,* University of Pennsylvania Press, 1964, p. 164.

nographers would locate Indians but would ignore the full implications of the reservation's bureaucratic order, as a place where Indian problems would be causally linked to disorganized personalities rather than social structure.[18] In "acculturation" studies, there were generally but two perceived realities, that of a dysfunctional Indian tradition and that of an opaque, successful "American way." As in the four hundred previous years, the Indian "problem" was defined by Indian misbehavior. Between the polarities of "traditional" and "middle-class", there could be placed an array of individually "disorganized," poor natives who were supposedly hanging between two cultures and not functioning well in either. The specialists who took upon themselves the task of recording Indian culture usually saw individual personalities rather than the White institutions ruling Indian communities. Secondly, they often had a view of American society as an infinitely expanding system which would solve the problem of Indian poverty if only the Indians would "behave." The view

[18] Among the acculturation studies which appeared after the Second World War are George D. Spindler's *Sociocultural and Psychocultural Processes in Menomenee Acculturation,* Berkeley, University of California Press, 1955; Fred Voget's "Acculturation at Caughnawaga: A Note on the Native-Modified Group," *American Anthropologist,* Vol. 53, 1951, pp. 220–31; and Evon Vogt's more imaginative effort, *Navajo Veterans: A Study of Changing Values,* Papers of the Peabody Museum of Archaeology and Ethnology, Vol. 41, no. 1, 1951. The comparative approach to the study of value orientations which began in the late 1940's at Harvard represents a more objective and more fruitful comparison of American Indians with White settlers. See *People of Rimrock: A Study in the Values of Five Cultures,* ed. Evon Vogt and Ethel M. Albert, New York, Atheneum, 1970.

of the human personality as mutable was a far cry from the rigid racial categorization of people of color which dominated the nineteenth century and the first part of the twentieth; but implicit in the new view was the belief that modern Indians were culturally bankrupt, that there persisted only a single correct way of living, embodied in respectable middle-class norms. The price of Indian survival seemed to be the forfeiture of what appeared to researchers as a very meager community life.

This is not to say that anthropologists of twenty years ago failed to describe what they saw. The problem lay and, to a great degree, still lies in not being able to see beyond the apparent facts to the more total reality of which they are only a part. The material poverty of a reservation and the Indian "problem" in cities are important parts of Native American social organization, but they are not by themselves descriptive of the viable urban culture by which American Indians survive. Between the two geographically locatable points of reservation and city circulates the mobile adult population of Indians whose social activity is the very heartbeat of the community. They feel no responsibility to academic observers who would prefer they be more stable and more available to analytic description. Their individual energies, while at the height of their powers, are invested in the tribal community—in defensively maintaining its boundaries and in successfully securing its cultural and biological continuity. If the organization of urban Indians were ever to be captured by the metaphor of a "network of social relations," there would have to be added to it the dimensions of human energy to properly describe the action and shape of the community through time. Imagine, for example, that there existed a special film sensitive to the health and age of every Micmac Indian, by which an aerial view of the greater Northeast could visually render the spatial distribution of high and low energy areas in the tribal group. Small groups of mobile adults socializing with each other and hustling for jobs would read as "hot" concentrations of human energy in and around the city of Boston. The old and the ill in the South End would register as the coolest part of the community, while in the Maritimes, the presence of many children and their caretakers would alleviate the concentration of low energy associated with the resident elderly and the sick. More than advanced technology, it takes a sociological imagination to grasp the simultaneous occurrence of mobility and cohesion which characterizes urban tribalism. To be on a constant journey and yet never really leave familiar faces behind is the essence of urban Indian culture. A tribe like the Micmac is indeed a network which has expanded its perimeters, but it has also maintained communication among its members and the sense of tribal affiliation born of a common, successful cultural strategy.

At this point in the research of urban cultures, it is impossible to do more than guess at the diversity of social forms which exist within an urban Indian tribe. The Micmac Indians are a small group and the scale of their social organization is a factor which sets them apart from larger tribes. Boston does not offer a truly pan-Indian scene where the boundaries between Native

American groups are tested and sometimes dissolved. The Navaho in Denver, the Sioux, Cree, and other tribes in Chicago, and the variety of Indian groups which have migrated to California's cities undoubtedly have a different experience of the urban passage. The people who share the poorer parts of town with them and the people who man municipal institutions in other cities in many ways look, speak, and act differently than the same groups in Boston and have, as ethnic groups and individuals, different histories of association with the metropolis. The distance an Indian has to travel to get to the city must also affect the nature of the tribal network. When circulation between the reservation and the urban area is difficult, Indian people really do become immigrants at home, taking on the burden of cultural adaptation without the assitance of a more stable, relatively rural population. Geographic mobility, the size of the tribal group, and the nature of the urban area which supports minority laborers are perhaps the most important variables in the study of how American Indians have responded and continue to respond to the industrial economy.

What is most striking about the information available on urban Indians—information which can distract us from an appreciation of cultural diversity—is the revelation that certain behavior patterns are common to many minority groups that are, like Indians, outsiders to legal institutions. What has been described of Micmac behavior is essentially from the same "Culture of Poverty" matrix as the behavior of many Blacks, Chicanos, Puerto Ricans, and a whole retinue of the urban poor as they are found around the world. Loosely organized extended families, serial monogamy, the prevalence of unemployment, criminal records, high birth rates, the lack of educational credentials, high rates of infant mortality, and a briefer life span than that enjoyed by the dominant population—these are the familiar and apparently universal characteristics of living in urban poverty. What is unique about the situation of American Indians as a subculture relative to the wider society is the legal recognition accorded each group as a tribe. This concession to the internal organization of native peoples was perhaps only an historical fluke, a tidy means of categorizing a defeated people. Yet, as Vine DeLoria has pointed out, a tribe is sufficiently corporate a form to be used as a kind of technical weapon in dealing with White institutions.[19] Ideally, serious acceptance of a tribe as a representative political unit would leave the internal machinations of self-government to the Indians while the ruling government provided a supportive context. A multiplicity of self-ruling units like tribes would, in their political dealings with large bureaucratic corporations, radically change those organizations, leveling out what are now pyramids of power to the point at which the service function of each would be adequately balanced against its efficiency goals. The scale of legal institutions, however, continues to prove resistant to tribal representation, just as recognition of minority groups without tribal status waxes and wanes according to corporate priorities rather than human priorities. Even the

[19] *Custer Died for Your Sins*, p. 239.

planned decentralization of Indian Affairs in Canada can be seen as a rejection of Native American tribal organization unless the national government gives budgetary and political control directly to Indian groups without depriving them of national status. In the United States, the administrative indirection which characterizes the relationship between American tribes and the government beclouds the issue of Indian autonomy. A single mammoth organization imposed by fixed jurisdictional departments, a hierarchical distribution of individual offices, and an overload of red tape militate against other forms of organization simply by the often unwitting complicity of managers whose energies are fuel for the bureaucratic machine.

On Social Responsibility

Over the years American Indians have had but four categories of "friends": churchmen, reformers, anthropologists, and romantics. With the exception of the latter, a role which can feed on abstractions, none of these positions is morally tenable today. Indians have become their own religious leaders, their own social reformers, and, if not their own anthropologists, at least conscious of having had enough of academic scrutiny. There is hardly an Indian community still existing which welcomes the kind of friendship from Whites which is based on the assumption that Native Americans need civilizing. What then is our social responsibility to Indians now that the social roles once available to the sympathetic are gone? Will we ever live with them? The answer is yes; because of the national level of our politics we have never ceased to live without them, to have had them and the great numbers of people governed by our legal institutions sharing our existence and touched by our decisions. The indirection which cloaks our domination obscures the very notion of social responsibility but it cannot, particularly in the case of American Indians, diminish the fact that something is owed the many people who are from birth required to live at the margins of society. Canadian and American Indians have already had instituted for them the bureaucratic means for the payment of the debt owed them; they have only lacked support from the dominant population which would do better to stop sending old clothes to reservations and start writing letters to congressmen and representatives.

Indian culture, like the experience of living in a traditional community, is available to most of us only in abstract forms, like this book, like film, which offer small testimony to Indian reality. Abstractions are, however, almost all that we have to go on and they give us visions of other systems, other cultures whose integrity has been too long repressed from our private and public consciousnesses. There is no Plains chief riding off into the sunset, there are Indians who live and work in cities. There is no alluring Indian princess, there are women who are raising their children to a precarious existence in which the only solace lies in sharing and the only triumph is outwitting convention. Knowing these things, it is our responsibility to acknowledge them, by allowing autonomy, by relinquishing power.

Beginning with the Civil Rights movement of the

early 1960s and continuing up to the present, extending the concepts of "real" and "equal" to non-Whites has constituted a political dilemma. The problem which the ideology of democracy presents to a dominant society, such as it exists in North America, is that it asks us to give up our hold on cultural superiority, and, even as political supremacy is relinquished, cease to look at the behavior of minority peoples as inadequate or patholog-ical. Instead of conjuring up faceless masses of inferiors, we are being asked to look around at other groups of human beings, and to let go of a perspective which has been able to understand non-Whites and the poor only by superimposing our own values, moral judgments, and laws on their reality. In essence, the consideration of the autonomy of other people, with an understanding of the political facts which have historically determined our rule and their subordination, is the new and frankly painful task of this society and the bureaucrats who are its executors.

In academic literature, the last decade or so has wit-nessed serious grappling with this new perspective and a coming to terms with the social organization rather than the social disorganization of minority groups. In In-dian studies, the questions being posed are those deal-ing with what American Indians are doing to survive and how, as outsiders, they are acting strategically to maintain viable cultures. This new look requires giving up the study of isolated categories of Indian behavior, which is easily susceptible to negative interpretation (e.g., unemployment, participation in welfare, drinking, having children outside legal marriage) and reaching instead for an understanding of the cultural whole, the urban community which organizes and gives coherence to those "facts." The contemporary social organization of the Micmac, for example, can be described by the social interaction which goes on within extended families, between men and women, within the peer groups of each sex, within the community at large. It can also be described, in some instances, in terms of the evasion and defiance of an oppressive system and, in others, in terms of creative accommodation to the fact of being a minority group. In neither case does good description have to be a defense of the overriding political status quo. On the contrary, the ideal of a moral social science should be to demonstrate that the "status" of a group relative to the dominant society has nothing at all to do with varying human worth, for the worth of every human group is great. An accepted diversity of cultural strategies would detract from the tyranny of a single order and add to a balance of shared power, refurbishing our sadly depleted store of optimism about urban culture and the world's future. Like old Mercator, in some innovative "portraiture of the universall earth," we hope for an urban ethnography of "lively descriptions, clad in new robes" [20] and based on flourishing cultural diversity.

[20] Gerardus Mercator, *Atlas, or a geographicke description of the regions . . . of the world . . .*, trans. Henry Hexham, Amsterdam, Henry Hordius and John Johnson, 1636,***i, v.

CHAPTER VI

Fieldwork in the City

Fieldwork and Definitions of the Self

To do responsible fieldwork today, it has become an intellectual duty to extend one's awareness not simply to the people who are ostensibly the objects of inquiry but to one's self as well—one's self as a limited instrument, a culture-bound personality consciously bent on interacting with a group of strangers. The fact that former researchers were fully social and occasionally fallible beings in the field can only be occasionally glimpsed in traditional reports, although wise students always strongly suspect what all professionals know, that the private personality in fieldwork is as much a reality as the more edited public monograph. For myself, the discovery that Franz Boas was nicknamed the Kwakiutl appellative for "fart" or that Malinowski was bothered by the noise of the "damn niggers" or that Raymond Firth had difficulty in compromising his Western idea of material possession with the Tikopian demands to share in his store of supplies was genuinely pleasurable.[1] It was an assurance that the stuff of fieldwork, whatever the objective stance assumed later, was unavoidably a human experience.

The nature of that experience is now an object of interest in itself, in a way which seems to me an analogue in the social sciences to Freudian proddings of the Victorian unconscious. The popularity of Laura Bohannan's *Return to Laughter*, the interest in Malinowski's diary, and the release of such books as *Women in the Field*, and *Being an Anthropologist: Fieldwork in Eleven Cultures* are specific indications of such interest.[2] Intellectual awareness of knowledge itself has meant in our tradition a certain kind of advantage, usually phrased in terms of control: having a *grasp* on reality or "knowledge as power." If one thinks of the history of sociology and anthropology, it is apparent that an investigator, either by class status or colonial affiliation, was in a position of "knowing" another human group by virtue of his controlled association with its members and his acumen

---

[1] Franz Boas, *Kwakiutl Ethnography*, ed. Helen Codere, University of Chicago Press, 1966; Bronislaw Malinowski, *A Diary in the Strict Sense of the Term*, trans. Norman Guterman, New York, Harcourt Brace and World, 1967; *Elements of Social Organization*, Boston, Beacon Press, 1963, pp. 190–92.

[2] *Return to Laughter*: New York, Harper, 1954; *Women in the Field*: ed. Peggy Golde, Chicago, Aldine, 1970; *Being An Anthropologist*: eds. George D. Spindler and Louise Spindler, New York, Holt, Rinehart and Winston, 1970.

in phrasing the nature of their social reality. In its innocent lack of awareness and self-consciousness, the group being objectified by study was somehow vulnerable, certainly vulnerable to researchers. But as the exploration of our awareness comes full swing and focuses on the investigator we find it is we ourselves who are our own objects of investigation, potentially as open to being exposed by analysis as any Victorian, including Freud. True objectivity, I was told in my early years of graduate school, lay in knowing one's biases, a happy maxim which reduced the whole notion of subjectivity to a few correctable character flaws. Now it occurs to me that the notion of subjectivity is and will be central to our notion of the researcher and, in ways we have yet to perceive, will be destructive of our former goals of overview, abstraction, and theory, and, inevitably, of the role of fieldworker unless he is also the journalist or novelist who lays himself open to a new vulnerability, being nonscientific.

The academic value placed on self-awareness is so great and so fundamental to Western notions of learning that a process like participant-observation is insured a future in education. There is perhaps no better way to discover one's own psychological boundaries than to take on the role of stranger in a community. Is good fieldwork, though a more mutual process which disallows self-revelation, without an attendant complex revelation of the group studied? For many years it has been assumed that, for academic purposes, the community or unit of research is an object or thing. The social scientist would work to gain an abstract control of this thing by formulating its reality. Human social organization, being at once too pliant and too intricate, has more often than not eluded theory that would contain it. If a community can be reduced to abstractions at all, it must be given the breadth and dimension of time, so that the researcher, instead of producing a photographic still life, can acknowledge the system and process of its organization. Rather than supporting an imperialistic image of the researcher as capable of abstractly incorporating the community, such an acknowledgement makes fieldwork a coincidence of histories, the investigator's and the group's. The individual fieldworker engages in and even surrenders, to use Kurt Wolff's sensitive phrasing,[3] to the ongoing process of the community until, having artificially intruded, he must artificially withdraw to assess what has been learned.

In my own work among Micmac Indians in Boston and the Maritime Provinces, the fact that I was with people who were "urbanized" or "acculturated," who had a material culture which was not foreign, who lived in physical settings which fit into familiar city and country categories, and who spoke English as well as Micmac, made it unavoidable that I consider a common social structure in which both the Indians and I exist together. Some researchers simply go native and make the community a miniature world. Elliot Liebow in *Tally's Corner* came to terms with the social division,

[3] Kurt H. Wolff, "Surrender and Community Study: The Study of Loma," in Arthur J. Vidich, Joseph Bensman, and Maurice Stein, eds., *Reflections on Community Studies*, New York, John Wiley and Sons, 1964, pp. 233–63.

expressed in the metaphor of the chain-link fence, which finally separated him as a White from the total experience of being Black. Yet with the issue of self-involvement in fieldwork, urban research also must deal with the issue of the wider society's political and economic reality, which invariably casts the researcher as the bureaucrat and the community as lower-class "ethnics." In fieldwork interaction, the line between bureaucrats and outsiders is mutually recognized as a border by which two kinds of people maintain their separateness and also a way in which they acknowledge each other's existence.

In using the term "mutually recognized" in conjunction with an idea of interaction, I am speaking as a specialist, like the social worker, the policeman, the housing expert, the volunteer doctor or lawyer, for whom association with people of other than the dominant majority is not necessarily a novelty. For most people, the recognition of what is lower-class behavior (street fighting, wiping one's face on one's sleeve, using ungrammatical English) is distinct from the notion of interaction. To the extent that the middle-class people are "above" lower-class people, they find such behavior painful in a moral sense, the "bad" which defines their "good" manners but which also threatens to contaminate them. To avoid contamination by the poor, the majority seeks, not always successfully, the protection of the exclusively middle-class neighborhood with its "good" schools which serve to protect the children from exposure. The specialist, like a priest in a plague, has a certain immunity born of professionalization which lets him or her handle the poor. Within a well designated and bureaucratically supported role, he or she can approach a considerable number of lower-class people as a superior individual to a mass of inferiors. The asymmetrical relationship of specialist to the poor is based on the assumption that the beneficence and goodness of the former will absorb the inadequacies and problems of the latter by consciously taking account of them.

The urban fieldworker, a curious person (in both senses of the word), is perhaps the only specialist who can resist the existing asymmetrical role relations. The university or funding organization which supports such academic ventures as urban fieldwork usually allows enough independence to let the researcher settle on his own method of approach to the community. In addition, the institution supporting the fieldwork, even if it is a city university, usually has its ties to the urban poor well camouflaged and its physical plant, whether offices or a campus, set up to service a different population recruited by bureaucratic standards. But the urban fieldworker is financed, after all, to be innovative, to explore, to bring new information back to an institution in quest of knowledge which it assumes it can incorporate. His role is based on the very antiestablishment idea that, in often unstipulated ways, the inadequacies of the present system require more knowledge and perhaps a new vision of urban people, and he is actually funded to sensitize the dominant society alternative social organizations, a sensitivity which strains its own organizational values.

Unhindered by more traditional bureaucratic structures, the fieldworker often has a vested interest in gaining some kind of morally superior image of himself and in proving his beneficence through interaction with the poor. For example, the obvious "bad" people who define one's "goodness" are the bureaucratic employees who run the repressive machinery which refuses to give the poor full credit as equal human beings. While reveling in his moral superiority, the researcher will also find occasion to champion individuals in the community against the malfeasance of city bureaucrats and become a leader of the oppressed before returning to his own bureaucratic milieu. He is oblivious to his need to be ultimately correct and right, along with his need for efficiency and direct action, which make academic researchers and city bureaucratic personalities cut from the same cloth.

To be open about a moral stance in a way which is nonimperialistic, one must ask where a morality at a level higher than that of individual gratification exists, where is the new, right way to approach "different others," to discover other-than-bureaucratic ways of relating to urban minorities? The answer perhaps lies in knowing what the personal limits to interclass contact are.

In my own work in Boston, I have found that there are, as formal specialists, two kinds of welfare workers. One is the "old guard" type who has been able to handle literally thousands of cases because of the distance which rigidly asymmetrical roles maintain between social worker and the poor. The other is the young worker who comes into the system with a kindly, egalitarian ethic, wanting to "help," but who leaves after a short while when the limits of human caring, spread out over hundreds of cases, are realized. The endurance of the older bureaucrats and of the old bureaucracies is not a chance occurrence: the poor are defined as inadequate, their inadequacies are classified and dealt with so as to perpetuate the bureaucracy which, of course, relies not only on the existence of the poor but on that of the ruling population which supports its stewardship of the poor.

Whether welfare workers or researchers, the younger we are and the more we are suburban children, the more it seems we have been protected from knowing about social class differences or even where our managerial group is located vis-à-vis the poor in a national society. We seem to have great confidence in ourselves as capable of absorbing the reality of other groups without much interactional experience across social boundaries or much idea of where it is that our world is institutionally connected to theirs. It is the real, down-to-earth differences in values and behavior of which we are ignorant, and it is these differences which are the greatest threat to our particularly arrogant morality: goodness is the capacity to accept all differences and be threatened by none. The morality behind our belief in human equality is more severe than we know, for, if followed to its logical conclusion, it demands that we relinquish notions of ourselves as more fortunate, better prepared to cope with life, and less limited in our pursuit of "happiness" than any other people. It demands that our openness become vulnerability if, in

fact, we do admit the existence of other people and
other systems than our own. The specific lesson of fieldwork, as I see it, is to give up a liberal (and moral)
image of oneself as capable of tolerating a complete cultural organization different from one's own and to learn
to deal with areas that are mutually defined between
oneself and the unknown community.

In retrospect, I can see my resistance to dealing
with social boundaries existing on several levels. I carried into the field a certain intellectual preference for
"cultural relativity," and was prepared to take on the
perspective of the Indian community and defend it
against my own corporate system. I also had very am-
bivalent feelings about being a member of the managerial elite. How had I found myself in the company of
oppressors when I had no will to oppress? In the field,
the subject of my status embarrassed me: I was equally
fearful of being catered to as a "superior" and of being
"put down" for my association with tyrants. During the
summer of 1970, when I was living with a family on a
reservation in Nova Scotia, a young Micmac who had
just come up from the city asked me, "Don't you find
this place just wild?" I thought he was referring to a
party held several nights before which I had found, in
my own terms, "wild." He said, "No, I mean all this,"
and he gestured to the abandoned cars and the rows of
houses in disrepair that we could see outside the window and then to the small, sparsely furnished cabin in
which we sat. I nervously replied that I didn't mind
(also knowing very well that I did not have to live on a
reservation) and I got a knowing smile in return.

In still another way, I would have preferred to have avoided any issue which would mark me as different from the community I was intent on entering. Early in my fieldwork, references to my light hair and skin were a source of frustration to me because they indicated that people were regarding me as a separate object when what I wanted was inclusion in the group. Ironically, I wanted a lack of racism from the Indians which my part of society is incapable of allowing them. The first time I ever went to a Boston country-western bar with a group of Indians, a White stranger came over to the group and asked me to dance. I did not want to ally myself with another White and thought that if I stayed with the Micmac at their table, they would understand my decided preference for their group against my own. Except for the din of the music, there was a dead silence at the table as I refused and I was, once again, conscious of being an object of some interest rather than an insider. I wished sincerely that the incident had never happened; yet, at a later time, several women who were there told me that the whole group wanted to get an idea of whether or not I, as a married woman out alone, would consent to dance with a stranger, as any one of them would have done. In my refusal, I proclaimed myself a more respectable woman than I knew.

Previous field work in a rural village in the Caribbean had not diminished my estimate of my own personal flexibility. I tolerated native food, folding bed, heat, and mosquitoes as neutral rather than unpleasant factors. Perhaps geographical remoteness made me tolerant of almost everything. I had a sense of having parachuted into another world for a temporary stay, which was not so much a result of the distance between my home, the city of Boston, and the Island of Antigua as the fact that the people in the village were hard put to place me. I was American but not a tourist or Peace Corps volunteer. I could not be cast into the role of a proper Englishwoman because I did too many unusual, unrespectable things. For example, in deciding to learn about fishing, I went out at 2:30 one morning in a row-boat with several fishermen and re-entered the village at 9:00 in less-than-triumphant style, walking its length in wet salty clothes with a broken bag of fresh fish in my arms. I was not concerned with making myself intelligible to the villagers; my goal was to gather information, and to do that successfully I had to be a directive force, demanding responses and explanations about a reality separate from my own.

It seems quite comprehensible to me now that I was operating as the traditional, aggressive researcher-as-scientist, in an exclusively male, action-oriented role model, without any emphasis on the more reciprocal aspects of investigation. It is doubtful that the community would have allowed me to maintain this kind of rape mentality for longer than the summer's duration. Even before we left the field, the four of us—myself, my husband, and our two small children—were getting indications that our neighbors had tolerated enough of our strange behavior and would be more comfortable if they could assign us to one faction or another. The more respectable civil servants who first greeted us as equals were increasingly distant and unavailable, having found that we sought the company of "low" villagers. Among the villagers, one group of kin and friends swore eternal friendship and trust, while other groups with whom they had feuds became as distant as the respectable people. Just before we left, we found the witchcraft sign of a dead toad on our doorstep, a sure bid for our involvement in factionalism and a certain sign that my relatively unfettered investigation could not endure, that the community would analyze me even as I would try to analyze it.

In a field situation closer to home, the community was more socially distant and yet generally quicker to assess my role. The Micmac knew my type and the distance between my group and theirs. They knew the contrasts between our values and behavior in some detail. They knew what my customs were as a bureaucrat and of course they knew their own. It was I who knew only one system of values and behavior, which I sought to de-emphasize. The experience of fieldwork was one of almost continuous communication of tribal social reality, which put pressures on me to define myself as a social being and at the same time define the limits of my flexibility as an investigator. The following descriptions, some of them probably familiar to other researchers as well, tell of various issues around which the community educated me to self-awareness.

Being Categorized

Having informants take guesses about who you are is the first feedback about the self a researcher gets. It was common both on the reservation and in the city for

both men and women to size me up as a social worker or
a teacher or as someone connected with a government
bureaucracy. I never found this flattering and would
take care to explain that I had no affiliation with agencies, that I came from an educational institution. For
some people, this meant I was not very helpful or worth
cultivating. As time went on, I became reconciled to the
fact that for them to take me as a middle-class bureaucrat was a very reasonable guess at my identity and that
the distinction between a young social worker and
woman fieldworker was not as telling as that between
them and the Indians.[4]

Another category into which I fitted, although I was
very reluctant to see anything but error when this was
told to me, was that of the available female. From my
point of view, I was on a cerebral mission and preferred
to discount my sex as a factor in research. If I had better
rapport with women than men in the field, I thought it
was due to rigidities in the mens' sex-role typing which
placed limits on my otherwise unlimited ability to move

[4] Rosalie Wax and Robert K. Thomas, in an article entitled "American
Indians and White People" (*Phylon*, Vol. 22, 1961, pp. 305–17) have
described general characteristics of Sioux behavior in interaction with
Whites—for example, a seeming passivity which is really a "sizing
up" of the contact situation, anger handled by leaving the situation,
children not encouraged to interrupt adults in conversation, etc. Despite the fact that the Micmac are usually considered more acculturated than western tribes, these same personality traits might also be
attributed to the Micmac in interaction with Whites, although the subject of this essay focuses on what I believe are more important contrasts between Micmac and bureaucratic values, namely those having
to do with perceptions of social divisions and with norms of social interaction.

as easily among men as among women. It was my duty,
or so I thought initially, to overcome *their* limited social
categories. In actuality, I was always on the scene as a
woman without a man and yet a woman who was resist-
ing the more common bureaucratically-defined category
of teacher or social worker. I was moving freely in
avoidance of any social responsibilities, institutional or
informal.

Occasionally another kind of White person seeks
Indian company for "back-to-nature" purposes. There
are, for example, businessmen who hire Indian men as
hunting guides for a week of shooting and drinking, the
hippies who want to get back to basics and camp for a
summer on the reservation, the concerned female radi-
cals who begin by wanting to help the poor Indians and
wind up living with one for a few months. The informal-
ity of my association with the Micmac lent itself to an
interpretation of me as this kind of White. I would drink
beer and hard liquor, I would joke and appreciate the
sexual banter that often went on between men and
women, and I was apparently enjoying being with Indians. My behavior, insofar as I was oblivious to my
own sex role, could have been perceived as a sign of my
availability in a more than spiritual sense. It happened
several times that I would take my place among a small
group of Micmac without much regard for which people
were nearest to me; I just wanted to join in and then not
be noticed. On one occasion, in an apartment in Boston,
I came into the kitchen where there were about a dozen
Micmac, most of them sitting around a formica table. My
primary concern was to be part of the group, so I took an

empty chair at the table, greeting people and returning greetings as I went. I settled into place, yet after a few minutes I noticed that two women directly across from me were giggling and putting their hands over their mouths to hide their smiles. I was trying to observe the social interaction in the kitchen, but I was also becoming increasingly uncomfortable. It finally dawned on me that the two men sitting on either side of me were facing straight ahead, both sipping at their cans of beer, without either of them saying a word to me or to anyone else. Both of them were single, available men. I had, of course, made a rather aggressive social movement by putting myself between them, especially when, as I realized after sitting down, there were other places to sit. The same move towards men of my own class could have been interpreted as a sexual strategy. But, not unlike the stereotype of the American girl who cannot understand why a Mideastern man would be "upset" by her miniskirt, I thought I could separate intention from presentation and be easily understood. Realizing my predicament, I removed myself to a socially more appropriate place in the room, hoping that my *faux pas* would be forgiven.

The most clarification I could give to my role was to call myself a student, a vague designation that carries little meaning at all. The Micmac in recent years have not had much attention from anthropologists or other social scientists. A crew of linguists from a Canadian university had reportedly visited the reservation area in 1970, but for the single purpose of recording language. And there were Indians in both the city and the Maritimes who had met Wilson Wallis during his 1950s research. But for them, and I think for other Micmac, my status as student and as woman contrasted with their general idea of the authoritative academic male studying Indian life.

In retrospect, it seems that my presence was handled by the Indian community with greater acumen than Whites would handle it if, for instance, one of them had declared his or her intention of moving into White suburbia. I was an atypical outsider. Even so, a community of widely extended kin networks, of relatively loose family organization, and of considerable geographic mobility could tolerate a stranger; this is a tolerance most anthropologists have relied on to a considerable degree. In addition, my chief informants were also my protectors and, whether in a bar or within a family group, assumed the responsibility of getting me through situations where my ineptitude was most obvious. On at least one occasion, burly Boston policemen stomping into a South End bar to stop a fight involving an Indian elicited more panic from me than the scuffle itself. Was there a rear exit? Should I be authoritative and interpret the situation to the officers? Could we just ignore the incident? The reaction of the Micmac with whom I was sitting was complete silence and a quiet appraisal of the policemen's behavior, which in this case was a rather matter-of-fact "Okay, let's break it up" combined with some arm-bending. After the police left with two men—one White, one Micmac—the group, with no verbal reference to the incident, decided to move on and, with a friend on either side of me, I found myself ushered quickly out of the bar. The Indians' exit was defensively calculated and unobtrusive.

At another time, on the reservation, I had enjoyed talking to a relative of the family I stayed with, a young man in his thirties whose life experiences I was interested in and wanted to record. Andrew and Kathy, the parents of the family, had both assumed responsibility for structuring my role as visiting bureaucrat. They understood the intellectual nature of my goals and also sought to protect their kin from complicated sexual involvement with a White stranger. I would accept a ride from Sam, the relative, down to the general store, only to find that one or two of the older children were sent along to help as I bought a roll of film. On other, longer rides around the countryside, with five or six or more people in the car, I would invariably end up in the front seat between Andrew and Kathy, or, if in the back seat, between two women and away from Sam or any other man outside the immediate family. It might have been my status as guest which merited such careful handling; but, on the other hand, when the group in the car was just women and children, I could just as easily land in the back seat with an assortment of children on my lap or take some other woman relative's place in the front seat holding an infant.

At one point, when he had been drinking, Sam began to insist that we go out "for a good time." I wanted to get through the situation with easy good nature and yet still communicate that I was not really available. I said things such as "I have a husband in Boston." Sam replied, "And I have a wife in Montreal, so what the hell. You don't live with your husband either." Sam appeared and reappeared throughout the day, like a recurring and ever more insistent theme. I happened to be returning to the house from a visit next door when I saw Andrew talking to Sam behind some cars in the side yard. I went into the house and a few minutes later Andrew came in. He addressed Kathy with a brief "That's settled," and walked past us both to his armchair in the living room. I had a sense that I had caused trouble, even more than Sam, who doggedly avoided me for the rest of his stay on the reservation. His behavior was not atypical or unusual; the Micmac presume the individual social autonomy of every adult and the natural tendency for men and women who appear single is to have physical relations. In their context, it was my behavior which was strange. I would make my social availability obvious and then qualify it by declaring only cerebral intentions.

In the city, I was less dependent on any one household. There were several families who welcomed my overnight visits and I had my own car to move around in. Nonetheless, there were at least five or six people who felt the obligation to make my presence as an outsider to their group less problematical. All of these were adults who at one time or another had hosted me for two or three days in their apartments and felt consequently that they could do a good job of interpreting my existence to the rest of the community. This responsibility was not always an easy one, for there were several Micmac who were quite hostile and would not even talk to me, even though we might spend hours in the same group together. One man, a construction worker, would glare furiously at me every time we met. I made a point of knowing his nickname and greeting him directly, but to no avail. Finally I asked one of my protective friends if she knew why this man was so unfriendly to me. I was told that he was not like most of the Micmac Indians, who would let people do what they wanted and who did not mind my being around, whatever my reasons. I was not quite satisfied with this answer so I asked one of the teen-age boys I knew for a better assessment. The reply was, "Jeannie, he doesn't know what the hell business you have with Indians and neither do I."

By my persistence in simply hanging around, I found that I was eventually able to talk to people who were initially mistrustful, including the construction worker, and to discover the nature of the way in which I could fail or succeed. I think it is fair to say that all agreed that my presence had to be for personal reasons, either negative or positive. I could not like or dislike a tribe which I did not know, so I must be in the group for reasons of liking or disliking specific persons. If I announced to my first contacts, as I did, that I was writing a paper on the Micmac and wanted to meet many of them, it could be taken, and it usually was, that I was saying: "I like you. I think you know a lot of people and could help me. I intend to be around for a while and I want you to be one of my friends." There were only a limited number of people I had to make that statement to in order to know where and how the Micmac were living and to include myself in their activities. For those to whom I had to be explained second-hand, there was less assurance that I was a friend and there was this mysterious abstraction called a research project which could easily be interpreted as a pretext for doing them harm. If, in explaining me to other people, my initial contacts emphasized my project (as opposed to our friendship), it was to demonstrate that they had a weapon, so to speak, in my persona and wanted others to know it. The notion of a project, as an explanation of me, was only a tie-up to expertise and authority, to a hostile objectivity which could be used against other individual Micmac.

If I had good friends in the group, it also meant that there were people with whom I was likely to be at odds. In one instance, I was visiting the apartment of a woman, Anne, with whom I had spent the whole previous day running various errands in her car. The phone rang and it was another woman I knew who had several grievances against this woman and who, in voicing them, also criticized her as an "apple Indian" (red on the outside, white on the inside), for driving that "White bitch" around all day. Anne hung up and then reported the conversation to me and several other women who were in the kitchen. My first reaction was: "I feel really bad about that. I wish I could talk to her." The subject was changed and I did not have a chance to say any more. Still, I was upset and later in the day I brought the subject up again. I said that I felt I should do something, but I did not know what. When I received no response from my friends, I tried a more retaliatory tack by pointing out that the woman who had called has probably had as many White friends as any Micmac. Immediately Anne and the other women gave their enthusiastic agreement and recounted a list of reasons why the woman had no cause to be so nasty. Anne ended the list by saying, "If she wants to fight, she should get a kick or two in the ass." My initial reaction, to be conciliatory, was in line with my conventional notion of how one handles interpersonal aggression and with my goal in fieldwork to keep as many interactional doors open as possible. To my mind, if I were hostile in return, it would be "war," a total and irrevocable commitment to hostility. For the Indian women, hostility was on a human scale, something which was more or less stirred up, argued back and forth, and then dropped. In this case, I witnessed several more telephone calls in subsequent days between Anne and the woman who had criticized her and two arguments between them which took place at social gatherings. I also saw, in the following weeks, that the woman had not been dismissed as an enemy or treated as a social cipher. Anne and the other women in the apartment had little difficulty after the quarrel subsided in including her and her family in their social life as was done before. That is, they concluded that ever since boarding school days, she had been troublesome and would probably start more quarrels in the future. Some people were like that; it was humanly tolerable to have them around. In contrast, I found it very difficult even to greet this woman, not because she had called me a name but because I had spoken out against her by defending Anne from her attack. Despite her friendliness to me in other, later situations, I could not help but feel that I had committed myself by retaliating rather than maintaining a conciliatory spirit. This is not to say that the Indian women were less principled than I, but that they were more flexible, more adept at contending with variations in human moods and at seeing others as ongoing personalities within the community. Whether a relationship was defined predominantly by contention or by friendship, the goal was, it seemed, to have a relationship. For me, the choice was between a positive relationship, a reflection of my good self, or none at all. Many of the Micmac recognized this and other cultural limits of mine. In small ways, when it was explained to me that "this is the way we eat here" or that there was a "shitpot" in the shed instead of a bathroom or that "Indian boys fight more than they should," I felt the Micmac were trying to bridge the distance between our values by verbal comparisons. The more fundamental differences in habits of interpersonal relationships could not be so easily and adequately accounted for in words, although one of the women had this comment, "You're not so used to nastiness. You shouldn't be hurt."

Being and Acting Alone

Despite my concerted efforts throughout the research to be as convivial as possible, there were real obstacles to my easy inclusion in the community. I did want to be liked and I acted the way I would act with people in my own society. I tried to be accommodating,

I tried not to lose my temper, I tried to be supportive. This was my public behavior, the way in which I could act for brief social sorties out and away from my family. What I found myself involved in, both in the city and in the reservation area, were situations of continuous public socializing within which it was almost impossible to sustain the exclusively pleasant stance reserved for parties, dinners, classes, etc. One whole day of being with adults and children meant one whole day of continuous bombardment by voices, faces, ideas and projects picked up and dropped, physical tuggings at my hands, claims being laid to my attention, and, in the background, the constant noise of television or jukebox.

In the midst of all this, I was also trying to gather information like a research instrument, that is, selectively to direct my attention and powers of observation. I could no more help this tendency to be purposeful than I could help my limited idea of sociability, i.e., that one was pleasant only to a few people at a time. It was only about halfway through my fieldwork that I began to see, beyond the genuine irritation which days of constant stimulation could provoke and beyond the pleasure I would get when affection or approval was expressed toward me, that there was a whole and valid organization of human experience among the Micmac. It was based on the understanding that being in the company of other people, as a mixture of pleasure and pain, was a constant assurance of being alive. Visitors came and stayed, relatives moved in and out, children were adopted and grew up, everyone traveled and wrote and telephoned. Within a specific situation, it was the jostling and bumping up against one another which was important, more important than an individual directive or a group's getting a task accomplished. One had to be something that could be bumped up against and to the extent that I was consistently affable and resisted getting into quarrels (as, for example, with Anne's adversary), I was less a part of that reassuring world.

In retrospect, it seems to me that I could have participated more or been more of a social person in Indian terms by making my purposes less explicit or being less action-oriented than I was. If I could have made my project subordinate to battling it out as a social equal among equals, I would have been truly a participant in that community. As it was, my tendency to seek out information, rather than to be at one with the group, set me apart. During my stay in Nova Scotia, Andrew frequently had occasion to tease me, saying: "Relax, relax. You people always ask too many questions. Why don't you listen? The Micmac have been here for thousands of years; we'll be here for many more."

My kind of individuality, I began to think, knew no middle range of sociability. I could dictate any number of bureaucratically-phrased letters, I could handle such abstractions as nation and government and American people. I had even abstracted a notion of a tribe of Indians and resolved to study them. At the other extreme I existed within the intimacy of my small family. The easy tolerance of a community which continually demands that one be a part of it, giving and receiving human vibrations, is outside my ken. It goes against my ideals of privacy and order and quietude. I began to realize also how much those ideals are based on the assumption that other people are irritants, contact with whom has to be controlled, and how much my family is an extension of myself and therefore a fairly safe bundle of relationships. In theory, I can order human events on an enormous scale, forgetting how illusory the connection is between understanding life and being able to control or direct it. Interpersonally, with my husband and children, for example, I operate on the empathic model, using understanding as a way of possessing their experiences and demanding that they understand mine as well, although it is also understood that I am the feminine expert in this kind of knowing, this kind of domestic imperialism.

The fact that I was alone in the field, a lone individual "traveling the fastest," caused comment. This was partly because I was without my husband, but also because I was without anyone. Weren't there people I saw when I wasn't with Indians; didn't I have a large family of sisters and brothers, aunts and uncles, nephews and nieces; didn't I have girlfriends I saw every day; and where were my children? From a Micmac point of view, my other life seemed peculiar. When I was not in the city, I was usually alone or with my immediate family. If I saw other adults it was by invitation or appointment.

Finally, I was prevailed upon to bring my twin boys, then age seven, into Boston for visits with me. Again, this was at a point when the totality of Micmac social organization was becoming evident to me and I felt less interested in detailed fragments of information than in a more complete understanding of their world view. I felt I had to see their world from the perspective of a social being, rather than of an efficient recorder. My children were the most chaotic and warmest part of my life and I had visions of all three of us relaxedly mixing in with whatever small group of Indian people might be together. I had not realized what faithful products of corporation culture we had raised them to be. They are trained to understand everything and quickly verbalize their reactions to new experiences. In fact, they like a new experience because it gives them the opportunity to offer a plethora of those ingenious observations which delight suburban parents and teachers. For example, both children at that time would sit at the same table with me and several other adults and include themselves as serious participants in conversation. But the Indians did not do what White teachers and parents would do. Among the Micmac, the children were either ignored or frowned at, and I bore the burden of attending to their precocious observations. The result of such attention was that I could not continue as an adult talking with the other adults. The Indian men and women in the same situation were handling their children in a very different way. Shouts would frequently be sent out from the kitchen to the next room where the children were playing. These would be messages on the order of, "Dougie, you brat, don't leave your bike on the stairs," or "Mary, goddammit, stop that noise." They had very little to do with tasks and everything to do with both assuring and warning the children that the adults were near. A child walking through the room would be hugged, or pinched, or slapped, or kissed, and then go on its way. Conversation never got so intense, so purposeful, that it could not tolerate this simultaneous flow of physical communication between adults and their children. At last, finding no audience, my children would leave the adults, including me, and I would find myself able to give full attention to grown-up concerns. What I found myself paying close attention to, of course, was a mixture of stories, and jokes, and phone calls, and shouts, and exits, and entrances which defied my intense focus and linear task of information-gathering.

In one instance, near the end of my fieldwork, I brought the boys along to a church meeting house where I had volunteered to sort clothes for a rummage sale. They behaved in what I thought was a good way by exploring the hall, searching through some boxes, and generally assuming that this situation was grist for the mill of their curiosity. There were about seven Indian women there at the time and some ten minutes after we arrived I heard one older lady ask in a perturbed voice, "Whose children are these?" The question seemed rhetorical, as I had greeted her holding both the boys' hands. Perhaps there should be some restraints on their behavior, I thought, and I left my work to speak to them. Then I returned to the job of sorting clothes, more mechanically intent on getting the work done than any of the Indian women. They combined coffee-drinking, cigarette-smoking, trying on some of the donated clothes, and supervising their children with the business of preparing for the sale. I tried to take my cue from them and stopped for a "coffee-break," my understanding of how to handle the polar distinction between work and socializing. As I drank my coffee, I began to get the feeling that the independence I had given my children disconcerted the other women who were keeping closer watch on theirs. The Indian children in turn were a subdued and even helpful presence. My own were rambunctiously playing hide-and-seek among a pile of empty cardboard cartons. I did not mind their noise or their independence as long as I was left free to work, but I wanted to know if others were annoyed. So I asked one of my Micmac friends what, if anything, she would say to my children if they were hers. From where we were sitting, across the room from the twins, she yelled without the slightest hesitation, "Cut it out, you Guillemin kids!" The other Indian women broke into laughter. One, with six children, said, "That sounds just like me, just like a broken record, my kids say." The women all agreed they sounded just the same and I think that they were genuinely relieved that a gesture had been made to account for these children as they did their own.

It was inevitable during fieldwork in a small community, where I felt the power of the group to absorb an individual, that I would have second thoughts about having been educated to value objective verbal assessments of social events more than a relaxed immersion in them. I regretted at times that I could not just for once cease to reflect. In a room full of people and noise or at a bar with Tammy Wynette's "Stand By Your Man" blotting out all talk, I would get a feeling of how good that could be and then I would conscientiously return home and write up the experience as data. The final image in Kubrick's *2001*, that of a fetus with its eyes open, began to seem to me the appropriate symbol of conventional self-awareness devoid of the means to act, for I gradually lost belief in any link between an intellectual understanding of life and the larger goal of our culture: to bring experience so under our control that pain and even death are avoided. I was taught that knowledge is power, but I have come to conclude that, as a society, we have arrogantly tried, with science, to engineer ourselves out of the realities of the human condition into immortality. We began by hoping that machines would release us from drudgery, we systematically eliminated physical hardship by allocating it to the poor, and ended up with a technology which threatens literally to disembody us. Our abstract and depersonalized way of ordering life has allowed us to repress the fact of our human mortality even as it requires that we live with the possibility of global destruction. Nor do we have the power, once we realize the limits of our culture, to easily adapt other ways. There are few of us members of the ruling society who could tolerate permanent membership in a true community, who would not prefer a private combination of psychic pain and physical comfort to a more basic communal mixture.

To use Herodotus' quote, the tendency of all people to "end by preferring their own, so convinced are they that their own usages surpass those of all others," is difficult to criticize. It seems, however, that the implementation of that preference to the social domination of other cultures is a prerogative we must question more seriously each day of our lives. The burden of understanding the limits of our own ways is to observe more than we can act upon, to witness more than we can experience and, ultimately, to acknowledge the validity of other cultures, finishing with the realization that as a society we have really done nothing better, just differently.

Index